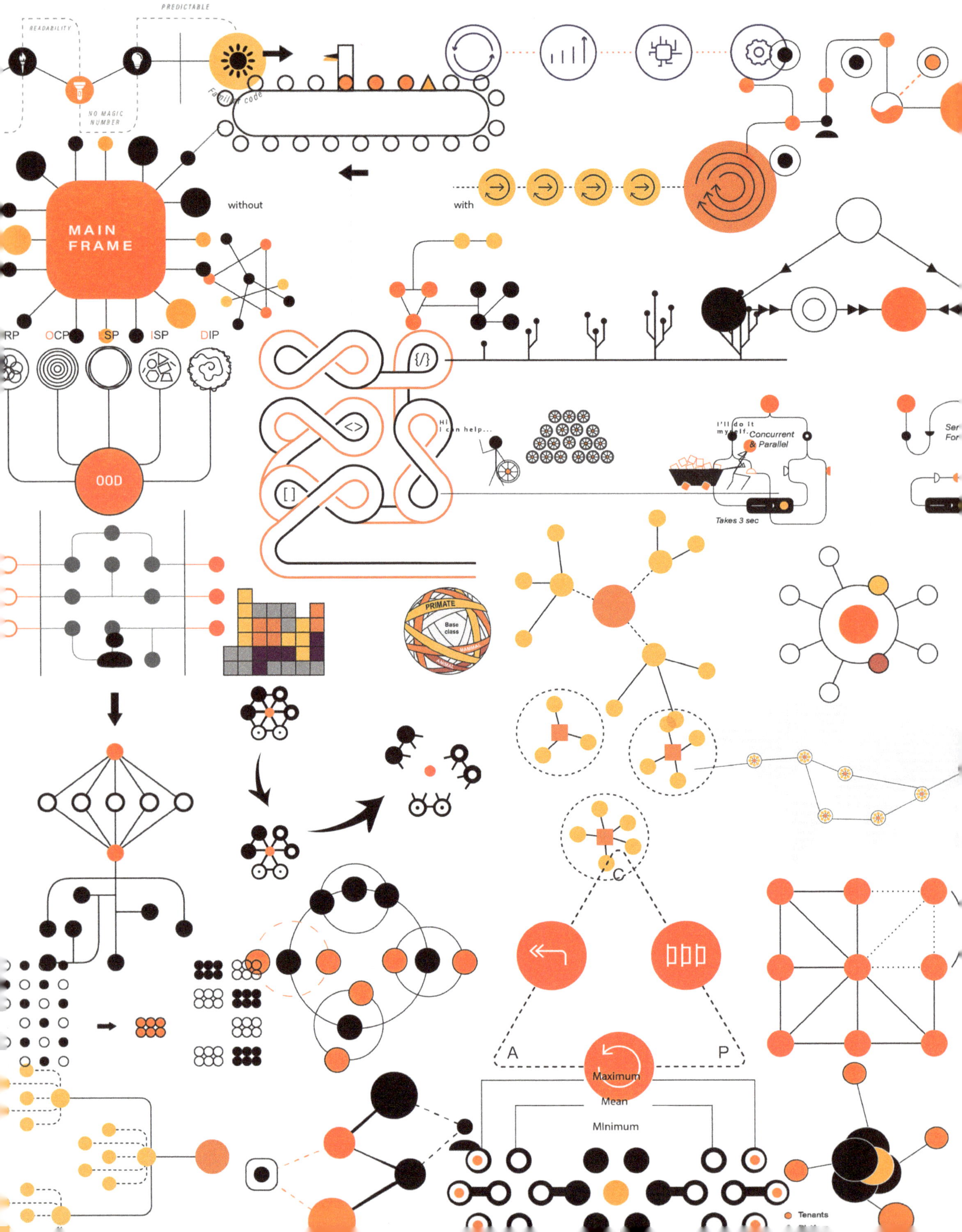

PREDICTABLE
READABILITY
NO MAGIC NUMBER
Familiar code
MAIN FRAME
without
with
RP
OCP
SP
ISP
DIP
OOD
{/}
<>
[]
PRIMATE
Base class
Hi
I can help...
I'll do it myself.
Concurrent & Parallel
Takes 3 sec
C
A
P
Maximum
Mean
MInimum
Tenants

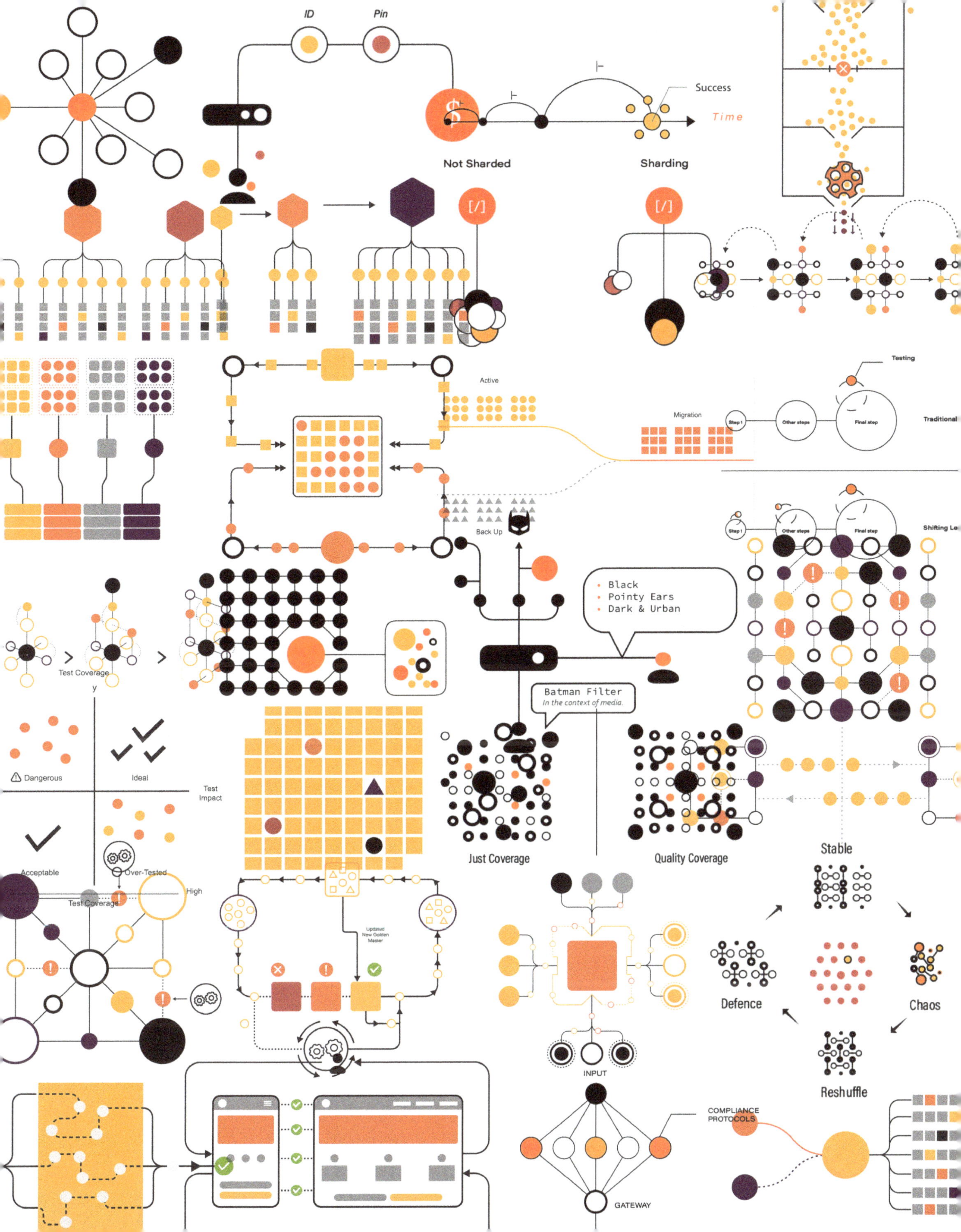
ID
Pin
Success
Time
Not Sharded
Sharding
[/]
[/]
Testing
Active
Migration
Step 1
Other steps
Final step
Traditional
Back Up
Shifting Le
Black
Pointy Ears
Dark & Urban
Batman Filter
In the context of media.
Test Coverage
y
Dangerous
Ideal
Test
Impact
Acceptable
Over-Tested
High
Test Coverage
Just Coverage
Quality Coverage
Stable
Defence
Chaos
Reshuffle
Updated
New Golden
Master
INPUT
COMPLIANCE
PROTOCOLS
GATEWAY

FROM CODE TO SCALE

Timeless Principles for Building and Scaling Great Software

A Field-Tested Guide for Engineers, Product Leaders & System Thinkers

DHAVAL PARMAR

From Code to Scale: Timeless Principles for Building and Scaling Great Software

All views expressed are my own and do not reflect the opinions, policies or positions of Amazon.

Paperback ISBN 978-1-970973-09-9

Hardcover ISBN 978-1-970973-06-8

Ebook ISBN 978-1-970973-07-5

Design and Production by Credible.Ink

Greensboro, NC

Printed in the United States of America

First Edition

DEDICATION

To our teachers in every form, from colleagues and managers to coaches and books, expected and unlikely, who suffered our lessons so we could learn.

CONTENTS

Introduction

The world is moving at an unprecedented pace, and technology is accelerating even faster. Every week, a new framework, tool, or paradigm promises to redefine how we build software. Amidst this whirlwind, it's easy to get caught up in fads (we will 10x, 100x!), doom-and-gloom narratives (all the jobs are gone!), or the pressure to keep up (run fast to stay where you are). While things change, humanity's fundamental truths and expressions remain the same. Even in software, while tech evolves, certain core principles endure. They have staying power regardless of the latest trends.

While the tech industry offers competitive compensation, as you know, every job demands that you hit the ground running, making high-impact contributions while somehow managing expectations that only seem to grow. If anything, the performance bar and expectations are rising even faster than the overall tech. So, how do you guide and prep yourself in a world that seems to move at a breakneck pace? There's no onboarding manual that prepares you for the transition from college to your first tech job, from engineer to senior engineer, and from individual contributor to someone responsible for systems and your company's technology stack.

That's where this book comes in. It's an antidote to the constant change. It distills timeless principles to help you filter noise from signals, avoid common pitfalls, and accelerate your growth as a technical leader. The timeless part here is important because these principles have staying power, and as the technology around you keeps changing, they will continue to add value. So, if you're looking for actionable insights, hard-earned lessons, and frameworks that work in the real world, you're in the right place. These principles will accelerate your career and your team's success. In some ways, this book is the conversation I wish I'd had with my younger self, now distilled into a guide that works across technologies and career stages.

WHY I'M WRITING THIS

Like many engineers, I have earned an engineering degree, then another, and then some more (see the "Who Am I" section below), only to discover that what school teaches and what the real-world demands are worlds apart. This meant that I had to start over when it came to software development. The first few years were spent in the dark, wandering without a clear sense of direction, unsure what a good engineer looked like. I didn't know what "doing a good job" meant and had no framework to guide me.

That began to change when I started paying attention. I have sat through and actively participated in more than a thousand code and design reviews. I have read hundreds, maybe thousands of books. I have asked for peer feedback and did my best to look at everything I learned objectively. I found myself writing things down to make sense of them. Over time, patterns emerged across these. The noise started to separate from the signal. Eventually, I noticed I was writing for me and someone who used to be me.

That's who this book is for. My younger self. The version of me who didn't yet know how things worked, who made the same mistakes repeatedly, and who would've benefited from hearing this early. If you're trying to make sense of the tech world, build your skills with a bit more of a straight line, and avoid the traps that slow people down, this book is for you, too. It's a set of principles filtered through experience. They are field-tested and handed to you with care. These are the things I wish someone had given me when I was starting out. Now, I'm handing them to you.

WHO AM I

I am a Director at Amazon, and for over a decade, I've led global teams in product, engineering, and program management for Amazon Prime. I, with my teams, shape how the more than 200 million paid Prime members worldwide and as well as other Amazon customers around the world experience e-commerce, membership, subscriptions, and all that powers it. This includes everything from member engagement, major sales events, payments, and retention to the core membership experience. I have done it at a scale where even small changes carry billion-dollar consequences, and the stakes are high with system designs. Imagine leading and operating systems that need to hold up when the internet breaks a sweat, things like major shopping events like Prime Day.

I've launched zero-to-one products that crossed multi-billion-dollar impact, scaled engineering hubs across continents, and led machine learning efforts that personalize the customer experience in real time. I've helped build the experimentation platforms, automation tools, and AI infrastructure behind one of the most complex membership systems in the world. Before Amazon, I worked in finance and healthcare, building actuarial and cloud-based platforms that handled sensitive data and critical decisions. This required systems thinking and cryptography before they were buzzwords as they are now. I attended schools in the USA (the University of Texas) and in India.

Still, like most engineers, my real education started after school, as I dealt with production issues, code reviews, system design debates, and the occasional 2 a.m. fire drill.

Through all that, what matters most to me is building things that work and serve millions of people (is there anything more satisfying for any engineer?), growing leaders who move fast with purpose (this book is part of that) and enjoying the ride along the way (something I'm still learning to do).

WHY SHOULD YOU LISTEN TO ME?

Call me a skeptic, but whenever I am about to commit to learning (and let's be real, learning takes energy and time), I want to know that it is a worthwhile investment. You know now why I wrote the book, and there are two main reasons beyond what I mentioned in the bio above for why you should listen to me.

First is intention. For me, this book isn't a business; it's also not a personal brand strategy or a stepping stone to content creation. Writing a book like this is a terrible investment. It takes time, solitude, and effort that rarely pays off. But that's okay with me. In a nutshell, I'm not trying to sell you anything. In fact, I'd encourage you to be skeptical of people who make their living packaging advice they've never had to test in the field. I, on the other hand, have lived it.

Second, whether it is Prime, Prime Day, or the financial apps I worked on before joining Amazon, you have likely used multiple products I have built and led. These products serve hundreds of millions of customers and handle billions of transactions every day. I have been blessed to work with some amazing engineers and leaders. I also have had the pleasure of leading teams that were (and are) solving challenges you only encounter when pushing the edges of complexity and scale. This book is built on those hard-earned lessons. It doesn't pretend to offer original ideas. These are timeless principles, and that's the point. What makes this book different is how rigorously it's been tested and how much fluff has been stripped away. Each topic represents a domain deep enough to fill shelves of books. What I've done is distill those fields into the principles that actually get used, the ones that hold up when things go sideways.

I'm not claiming to have mastered everything. No one has. However, I've spent years trying, and this book reflects what I've learned along the way. If it helps you navigate your path more clearly or make fewer avoidable mistakes, then it's done its job. I believe it will help you; I have also made a sincere attempt to make it easy to follow and retain.

WHO IS THIS BOOK FOR?

As you know, most learning curves have inflection points, and this book is shaped around those transitions with the intent to serve three primary audiences.

Early-career engineers, tech leads: If you're early in your career and want a strong jump-start, it will give you a structured approach to mastering the principles that matter most, helping you accelerate your growth and stand out. Mid-career professionals: If you're already in the middle of your journey, many of these principles will feel familiar. That said, simply knowing something doesn't mean you've entirely distilled it or applied it effectively. For you, this book serves as a refresher and reference guide, reinforcing what works and helping you sharpen your approach. Senior leaders, product and non-tech professionals, system thinkers: If you're in management, senior leadership, or have a product or adjacent technical background, this book will give you a strong foundation in key technical concepts. It will help you understand the critical elements of software engineering, provide the proper vocabulary for discussions, and ultimately support you in making better decisions and tech investments.

The structure is layered for a reason. The early material establishes a foundation that can accelerate learning and has proven to be durable over time. The latter material focuses on the kinds of decisions that reach beyond individual tasks or teams, and this material makes more sense once you have a foundation in place. In between, the goal is to strengthen what connects those two points.

WHAT THIS BOOK DOESN'T COVER

As the name suggests, this book is structured around the tech development lifecycle, covering coding, system design, and quality assurance that allows you, your teams, and systems to scale. However, principles around Release, DevOps (software development and IT operations), and overall resilience are not covered here. They will be covered in a separate book. As for the roles the advice applies to, this book covers principles that will apply to professionals up to the director and senior director level (say, organization or functional heads) who make decisions that are rooted in tech.

It does not go deep into full-on product-tech strategy, profit and loss considerations, or product-market fit. The main reason is that I only want to write about what I have done and verified with a long enough track record to see what works. I also do not cover product management or leading teams (although I do have a track record here). Roles like product lead, cross-functional leader, or

SDM (software development manager) are very important, especially if you are leading an entire business or product or managing stakeholders across different areas. This book won't cover that whole skill (soft skills like effective communication, leading, change management, influence) that applies to those fields. They're important enough to cover in depth separately.

THE BOOK'S STRUCTURE

This book's structure follows a waterfall model, with the process broken down into linear sequential stages. However, you don't have to read them in the order they're presented in. Instead, the principles here can be iterative and nonlinear, just as modern software development cycles operate. I chose this structure because it allows you to jump straight to the area most relevant to you. After an introductory part covering how to apply the principles, *Principle of Principles for Tech and Beyond,* the 61 principles in the book are divided into six parts. If you're an early-career individual contributor, start with *The Code Creed* and *The Artist's Way.* If you're a senior engineer, tech lead, or software development manager, start with *The Invisible Architecture* and *Symphony of Systems*. If you are a cross-functional lead in data engineering or quality assurance, start with *Data, the Lifeblood of Systems* and *The Covenant of Confidence.*

BOOK WRITING TENETS

Before we dive in, I also want to share a few tenets that guided how this book was written. You don't need to agree with them, but I think you deserve to know where I'm coming from and why the content is structured the way it is.

First, I've prioritized (at least attempted) signal over noise. I have tried to avoid fluff here; there are no fillers designed to entertain or impress. My test for every principle was simple: would I find this helpful if I were reading it? If the answer was no, it didn't make the cut.

Second, everything here is grounded in real-world experience. I haven't built this book on theory or secondhand summaries. The ideas inside come from building, scaling, reviewing, debugging, and, yes, occasionally breaking real systems. Where needed, I offer brief intros and key takeaways. Where it helps, I've included personal observations or lessons learned the hard way (directly embedded in narratives; there's no separate section for personal observations).

Third, I've optimized for quality over quantity. While I've used multiple tools (including AI) to cross-check facts, avoid blind spots, or strengthen narratives, you won't find AI-generated slop here. If any of the writing is sloppy, it is me.

Fourth, I've deliberately avoided focusing on the entertainment or humor. You won't find punchlines or cute analogies for the sake of keeping things "light." I'd rather you remember a concept clearly than remember me trying to sound clever.

Fifth, I believe visuals matter. Software principles could get dry or get so much into the details that they lose the key points, so for every principle, I've added a custom visual. They are sometimes metaphorical, sometimes structural, to help you retain what you've just read. I enjoyed doing this part, and I made a deliberate choice to create abstract images because the process of designing them forced me to get to the heart of each principle. It will also allow you, the reader, to fill in your own color/interpretation. They're also good functional memory aids. My hunch is that you'll remember the abstract visuals longer than you'll remember the text, and that's by design.

If these values resonate with you, you'll probably find this book useful. If they don't, you'll at least know what you're getting into. Either way, my goal is to be clear from the start so you can decide whether this is a good fit for you.

HOW TO USE THIS BOOK

These days, videos and podcasts seem to get all the clicks, and as technology advances, we will invent new ways to access information, be it social media, AI, or whatever's next. All that said, honestly, I still think reading (and books specifically) is one of the fastest ways to absorb someone else's knowledge, experiences, and deep thinking. No wonder the Gutenberg printing press is often ranked as one of the most significant inventions in human history.

While books are still one of the best ways to truly see the world through someone else's eyes, they do have drawbacks. I've read hundreds, even thousands, of books, some even multiple times. I take notes obsessively, summarize key ideas, and constantly look for ways to optimize how I learn and retain information. The goal is to learn once, apply forever. You know, like Neo downloading kung fu in The Matrix. Here's the problem: retaining information is hard. Studies show that people forget 50% to 80% of what they read within twenty-four hours, a phenomenon psychologists call Ebbinghaus's[1] forgetting curve. A week later, that number jumps to 90% if no effort is made to retain the information. You might remember the broad strokes of a book, a key phrase, or a central theme. But what about recalling the nuanced details, the actionable insights that can improve your life or career? That part is hard.

---

1 Hermann Ebbinghaus, *Memory: A Contribution to Experimental Psychology,* trans. H. Ruger & C. Bussenius. (Teachers College, Columbia University, 1913; original work published in German in1885.)

So, what's the solution? First, you must look at the way you take in information. Long, drawn-out resources (any type of content) that belabor the points being made and are not clear themselves are not a good recipe for success. One of the reasons that I have approached this book as a set of principles is to force the distillation of knowledge. Second, through trial and error and backed by research, here's what I've found works for me and people in general. The good news is that you don't have to remember an entire book.

A Simple, Effective Plan

You need an action plan, and even if you already have a system, chances are you can make it better. My recommendation is to read this book once, from start to finish. Let the ideas settle. If there are ideas that you really liked or you know you want to get better at, I would recommend that you take some time to write down your learning and understanding. As you know, writing is a multipurpose tool that helps you to communicate what you know, to learn new things, and also to clarify your own thinking. Across a variety of academic disciplines[2], writing can deepen understanding, sharpen thinking, and clarify complex subjects, and you don't truly know something until you can explain it clearly in writing. In parallel, look for ways to put this into practice. You use this book as a reference guide. When you hit a challenge at work, flip to the relevant section and apply the principles immediately. Then, jot down your notes on an index card or sticky note to integrate the idea. Retention is about reinforcement and application, so take actionable ideas on a principle, apply them, and you'll be miles ahead of most people.

Three-at-a-Time Rule

A bonus input, from any given principle, is to pick no more than three ideas that you want to apply at a time. Why three? Research[3] on cognitive load suggests that humans struggle to juggle too many changes at once. Studies show that focusing on just 2–3 key ideas at a time leads to much better adoption than trying to overhaul everything at once. More than three, instead of reinforcing positive progress, you risk feeling overwhelmed or overly critical of yourself for not getting all the points right away.

---

2 William Zinsser, *Writing to Learn* (Harper & Row, 1988).

3 John Sweller, "Cognitive Load During Problem Solving: Effects on Learning," *Cognitive Science,* 12, no.2 (1988): 257–285. https://doi.org/10.1207/s15516709cog1202_4

A FINAL THOUGHT

With that, good luck on your journey. Remember that you possess the most critical skill of all, your personal drive. By picking up and reading this book, you're already ahead of 99% of the competition because you are action oriented. Taking these steps and completing this book will put you on a better path.

Now, let's get started.

PRINCIPLE OF PRINCIPLES FOR TECH AND BEYOND

"Strategy without tactics is the slowest route to victory.
Tactics without strategy is the noise before defeat."

— Sun Tzu

LEVERAGING PRINCIPLES TOGETHER

Learning and internalizing the principles that follow will take some time. Once you learn them, you will realize that some principles reinforce each other, while others are in conflict with each other, and will require judgment on when to push or pull. This chapter focuses on meta-principles, guidelines that will help you integrate and apply principles in real-world scenarios, hopefully with meaningful success.

PRINCIPLES ARE NOT ENOUGH

Knowing a principle isn't the same as using it well. If you want to cook a world-class meal, you need more than a list of ingredients. Beyond knowledge, you need timing and intuition. Otherwise, you're just tossing things into a pot and hoping for the best.

Judgment is the secret sauce that makes principles useful. As you know, judgment comes from deeply understanding a principle and seeing the bigger picture (the context). You will need to know what problem you're actually solving before you can test these principles in the real world. The following principles will give you a strong starting point, but they aren't foolproof. Apply them with awareness, adapt as needed, and always stay sharp to what's working and what isn't. Also, don't be too careful; we all improve by making mistakes, learning what works, and adjusting for good or bad. There is no way around it.

STATIC VS. DYNAMIC COMPLEXITY

In tech, business, and life, some challenges are structured (static complexity) while others evolve as you engage with them (dynamic complexity). If you try to handle dynamic problems with a static mindset, you're toast. The static complexity is like assembling IKEA furniture. It's frustrating, sure, but at least there's an instruction manual. Dynamic complexity is like trying to play chess, but halfway through, someone turns the board into a Rubik's Cube. What worked five minutes ago is now completely useless. Either way, when faced with complexity, your first move should always be to simplify. Break problems into smaller pieces, identify what matters (to you and the end users), and cut the rest. When possible, put some constraints on the problem regarding what you will and will not solve. You might have noticed that I used that approach in the Introduction, where I called out what this book will cover and what it won't. This is important because constraints will make dynamic complexity move toward static complexity. Once you have simplified enough, then, and only then, apply the principles.

MENTAL MODELS AS SHORTCUTS

Mental models are cheat codes (blueprints?) for thinking that let you navigate complexity and make decisions efficiently. Although they're a lot more popular now, mental models are not new. Philosophers like Kant and Locke explored them centuries ago. This makes sense; great decision-makers don't reinvent the wheel every time they face a problem. They pull from tried-and-true frameworks. Think of it as borrowing someone else's brainpower. When applied correctly, the right mental model can turn an impossible problem into a manageable one. The following principles are mental models, but applied specifically to software development. Within the context of this book, I want you to consider each of them as one of many mental models and be open to mixing those models to solve new problems. In this book, I borrow from diverse disciplines beyond software development, like psychology, philosophy, and economics (see below), to show you how to solve problems.

THE LEONARDO EFFECT

If you stay in a narrow field too long, you start seeing the same patterns, thinking the same way, and ultimately, that limits your ability to innovate. That's the danger of specialization without breadth. While deep expertise is valuable, true breakthroughs often come from those who can bridge multiple domains and apply cross-disciplinary thinking.

This is the essence of the Leonardo Effect, inspired by none other than Leonardo da Vinci. He wasn't just a painter or an engineer; he was both, along with being a scientist and anatomist. His genius didn't come from mastering a single field but from synthesizing knowledge across many. Leaders, engineers, and product builders who embrace this mindset unlock new levels of creativity and problem-solving. Cross-disciplinary knowledge is about strategically blending insights from different fields to solve problems and innovate. Here is how to make this work: cognitive arbitrage. The best ideas in one field often seem less obvious in another. The trick is applying insights from an area where they're well-established to a domain where they're novel. Think of how Agile software methodologies are borrowed from lean manufacturing, or how behavioral economics reshaped business and investment strategy.

THE LOLLAPALOOZA EFFECT

Warren Buffett's right-hand man, Charlie Munger, loved discussing the Lollapalooza effect. The term started as American slang in the late 1800s / early 1900s. It meant "something or someone" outstanding or remarkable. The Lollapalooza effect points out that when multiple psychological, economic, and scientific forces align, they don't just add up; they multiply. You get wild, outsized success when incentives, social proof, feedback loops, and market demand all come together. If you want exponential results, stack multiple principles at the same time. Another term to keep in mind is boundary spanning. As you go through these principles, see if you can combine them with business strategy, engineering, and user experience. The more disciplines you can bridge, the more your force multiplies, and you become more indispensable. A systems engineer who understands psychology will design better user experiences. A programmer who studies history might spot technological cycles and trends before others do. Learning outside your field sharpens the way you approach problems within it.

THE POWER OF COMPOUNDING

In tech, the pressure to chase the next big thing is relentless. Jumping on trends can yield quick returns, but deep expertise, whether in knowledge, skills, or product development, often compounds exponentially over time. The problem is that most people quit before they see the compounding effects take hold. They expect immediate returns; when those don't materialize, they move on to the next shiny opportunity. As you apply these principles, give them time to compound. Play the long game. Just as consistently investing small amounts outperforms trying to time the stock market, steady, incremental progress will always outshine sporadic bursts of effort, so trust the process. It's working even if you don't see it right away.

EXAPTATION: THE POWER OF REPURPOSING

Exaptation is a fancy biology term. It refers to when something evolves for one function, but that same component becomes useful for another. Feathers are originally thought to have come into existence for warmth; however, later they were used for flight (a far more interesting application). Similarly, social networks were originally meant for college students; later, they ended up becoming the backbone of global marketing (or... political dysfunction?). As you look to leverage the principles, keep your mind open. In tech, many breakthroughs come from unexpected applications. Look at existing tools and knowledge from different angles; they might solve problems in ways you haven't considered.

THE HEDGEHOG AND THE FOX

In the book *On Grand Strategy,*4 the analogy of the Hedgehog vs. the Fox describes different ways of thinking and solving problems. Hedgehogs focus on one big idea: mastering a single domain with deep expertise. On the other hand, Foxes rely on broad adaptability, knowing a little about many things, and leveraging multiple approaches.

In technology, both mindsets have merit, but neither is sufficient on its own. The best minds hold two modes. They commit to a core area of expertise like a Hedgehog but stay curious and responsive like a Fox. Rigid experts often struggle to adapt when the world moves beyond their specialty. Shallow generalists may lack the precision to drive high-stakes execution. Those who honor both depth and range develop the ability to build enduring systems, lead through ambiguity, and make good decisions under pressure. As you look to adapt the principles that follow, see the big picture. Understand overarching trends, industry shifts, and strategic priorities, and go deep when needed. Master key technologies and principles critical to your domain and stay agile in execution. This way, you can adapt your approach, explore multiple solutions, and pivot when required.

YOUR MINDSET

After absorbing all these ideas, there's one more step. You must decide on your mindset: how will you approach your work? Will it be with a fun and curious mindset, or will it be a grudging, "must do this to pay the bills" mindset? How will you show up when things get hard, when you're backed into a corner and the path isn't obvious? This isn't theoretical. When you're under pressure, tired, or doubting everything, you need something clear to return to.

It is also deeply personal; what matters to me will not be the same thing that will resonate with you. However, just the act of defining what you believe, in your own words, is essential. Otherwise, you'll default to reacting to stress and someone else's expectations. That's a dangerous way to navigate designing anything worth building.

In case it is helpful, I provide some of mine (no way near fully exhaustive) below that have served me well. As you read the rest of the book, use them if they are use-

4 John Lewis Gaddis, *On Grand Strategy* (Penguin Press, 2018).

ful, or build your own. Either way, developing your own set will help you stay clear on what you stand for.

1. **Life Is Lived in the Arena.**
   Effort Requires No Skill, So Give 100%.
   - It's the effort and doing that matters. Regret comes from not trying.
   - A work ethic is free. No excuses.
2. **Play the Infinite Game.**
   Abundance Beats Scarcity.
   - Opportunities aren't zero-sum.
   - Focus on creating value, not hoarding resources.
3. **Self-Reliance Is the Only Guarantee**
   - No one is coming to save you. Own your outcomes.
   - Extreme ownership leads to extreme progress.
4. **You Deserve What You Earn, Nothing More**
   - Hard work compounds. Stop worrying about fairness.
   - Ignore comparisons; focus on execution.
5. **Give Without Keeping Score**
   - Generosity builds allies who want you to win.
   - Help others without expecting immediate returns.

ON TIMELESSNESS

A word of caution. It is foolish for me to think that I can see through time and predict that all the principles that follow will stand the test of time. Only time will tell. What I can do, though, is look back and see what has endured. We can attempt to see the patterns. We are pattern-matching machines, after all.

There are also some tailwinds for this specific subject matter of software development. Timescales work a little bit differently in tech. If you have worked in tech, you know that if you have built something that survives 5, 7, or 10 years without major rewrites, you consider it a good success. In other words, time moves faster in software development. If you pair that fact with the notion that we have had the last 30–50 years of history (maybe more) in software development, you can see things. You can notice tech oscillating between trends (like mainframe to personal computers to cloud, monolithic to distributed to centralized AI) but things like organizing your code so it is easy to understand, distributing your work to make it easy to change, having clear lines of ownership, and testing what really matters are common across all.

To illustrate what I mean, consider a moment from 1940. Pablo Picasso (a famous artist) visited the Altamira caves in northern Spain. It is a prehistoric site famed for its Paleolithic cave paintings of bison, deer, boars, and horses, dated to over 15,000 years ago. The walls are alive with pigment, shadow, and motion, drawn by early humans using charcoal and ochre, their art blending with the natural contours of the cave to create something startlingly lifelike. These are masterful paintings, and despite being created millennia before modern civilization, these paintings pulsed with raw artistic intelligence and force. In awe, Pablo Picasso called out, "After Altamira, all is decadence."

I feel the same about many of the principles in this book. These are not my inventions. I've simply placed them in the context of software. I don't expect every principle here to remain equally relevant forever, but I do believe their core spirit will. That's where I'm placing my bets. The rest is up to you. Also, since the principles are timeless, I can't claim ownership of them. That is why I included references directly with each principle; credit is due to them and others. If I've missed something or credited it incorrectly, I hope you'll let me know.

A FINAL THOUGHT

"These are my principles, and if you don't like them... well, I have others."

—Groucho Marx

The principles that follow are a strong starting point. However, they aren't sacred, know that ordinary people, like you and me, shaped these principles. You don't have to accept them as is. Test and then challenge them to find what works for you. The real value is in adapting and refining them until the principles feel like your own.

I THE CODE CREED

"You play for yourself, but you perform for others." — jazz proverb

The word "creed" comes from the Latin credo, meaning "I believe." You might be wondering why something like a coding creed is even necessary anymore. We live in a time when machines can write code, clean it up, and even simulate decision-making. When that's the reality, it's fair to ask: Why still care about how the code is written?

Here's why. It is about your work, and it's your personal statement to show that you care about your work and anyone who is going to see that work. Automation can handle the mechanical parts, but it doesn't replace thoughtfulness. It doesn't replace the decisions you make when you tell it to name something well, organize your code so others can follow it, or build something that's easy to extend a year from now. That's still your job.

In any case, the more the tech progresses, the more the rote stuff will be handled by tools. What's left is the work that requires your thinking, and it is your opportunity to show how you think. Your thinking will set the structure that helps someone else understand what's going on without needing to ask you directly. Those parts matter more now, not less.

When you write code, you usually do it alone. It's just you, the problem, and a blinking cursor. But you also know that it doesn't stay yours for long. As soon as it's committed and pushed, it becomes part of something shared. Other engineers will read it, modify it, build on top of it, and if you didn't make things clear, they will struggle with it. That's the real audience. Not the machine. The people who come next.

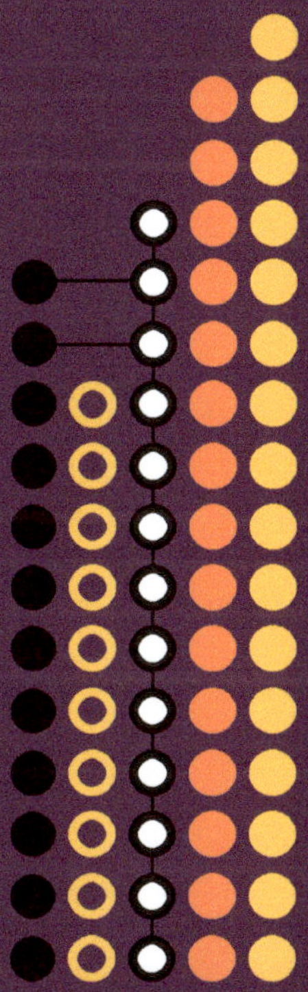

That's why this section exists. This is to remind you that the code you write isn't just a technical artifact. It's a trail you're leaving for others. A signal that says, "I took care with this," or "I was in a rush and hoped for the best." Either way, it communicates something. And you get to choose what that is. This set of principles will not make you a better coder overnight, but I hope that it helps you write with intention. When you are naming a variable, splitting a module, or leaving a helpful comment, I hope that it reminds you to make life easier for someone else. That mindset will shape everything: your code, your impact, and the kind of teammate you become.

So, as you get going, I want you to remember this: how you write code still matters. The decisions you make still matter. The way you show up, even in the smallest details, has a lasting effect. Let's write code like that's true, because that mindset is where good artisans are born.

01 • Code Should Be Familiar

"If you can't explain it simply, you don't understand it well enough." — Albert Einstein

INTRODUCTION

The best code isn't just correct; it's readable, understandable, and easy to work with. You should never have to guess what a variable means, decode a clever one-liner, or wonder why a particular value is hardcoded. Writing for clarity and predictability makes your code a reliable communication tool. This principle brings together five deeply connected ideas: choose meaningful names, prioritize readability, keep code familiar, avoid magic numbers, and treat your code as its own best documentation. Together, these habits ease onboarding and make debugging less painful.

KEY CONCEPT

Clarity starts with a strong intent to write code that speaks for itself. Every variable should carry intent. Every function should do what it says. Formatting should feel predictable. The structure should be easy to follow. You're not writing code for machines because they'll understand anything, no matter awkward or clunky. You're writing it for other developers (and future you) who deserve clarity, not cleverness. Reviewing, testing, and improving are easier when the code is predictable and clear. It builds shared understanding, and it ensures your software scales in the real world, with real people.

WHY IT MATTERS

You can't scale cleanly or sustainably if your team has to waste time deciphering code. That's why clarity and predictability matter. Clear code speeds up onboarding. New developers can get productive without constant handholding. It also reduces bugs since ambiguous names and obscure logic can hide unpleasant surprises. When the code is easy to understand, feedback loops become shorter, and reviewers focus on design and behavior, not on what the code is trying to do. This clarity also lowers maintenance costs, because there's no need to explain what's already obvious. People work faster and ask fewer questions when they trust what they're reading. In the end, predictable code is what separates quick and dirty code from a production-ready product.

IN PRACTICE

Putting this principle into action means treating every line of code as something another human will eventually need to understand and extend. That starts with naming everything with intention. For example, totalRevenue is far more helpful than tRev, and a function named deleteCustomerAccount() should do exactly that, with nothing hidden and no side effects. Clarity always takes precedence over cleverness; a concise one-liner might save a few lines of code, but cost someone else 30 minutes trying to understand it. Avoid magic numbers by using named constants: SECONDS_PER_MINUTE is clearer than just writing 60, and USER_ROLE_ADMIN is more robust than hardcoding "admin."

Familiarity also matters. Stick to your project's conventions so the code feels predictable and seamless. The best code is the kind that feels familiar because it aligns with expectations. Aim for self-documenting code that explains both what it does and why. Save comments for context, not for restating logic that the code should make clear. Organize your code by grouping it logically: files, folders, and functions should mirror how people mentally model the system, so do not surprise them with misplaced logic. Finally, choose to refactor over commenting. If a block of logic needs a paragraph to explain, the better move is to rewrite it until it doesn't. Comments should express intent, not serve as translations for confusing code.

COMMON PITFALLS

One common pitfall is over-commenting instead of rewriting. If it takes five lines of comment to explain a single line of code, the problem usually lies with the code itself, not the lack of documentation. Inconsistent naming slows readers down and invites mistakes. Switching between camelCase, snake_case, and abbreviated_names within the same codebase adds friction for readers and maintainers. Developers also forget to update names after refactoring. If a function called getUser() starts returning user preferences, its name becomes misleading and can introduce subtle bugs. Finally, avoid letting style rules become a form of control. Formatting should support readability and not enforce rigidity for its own sake.

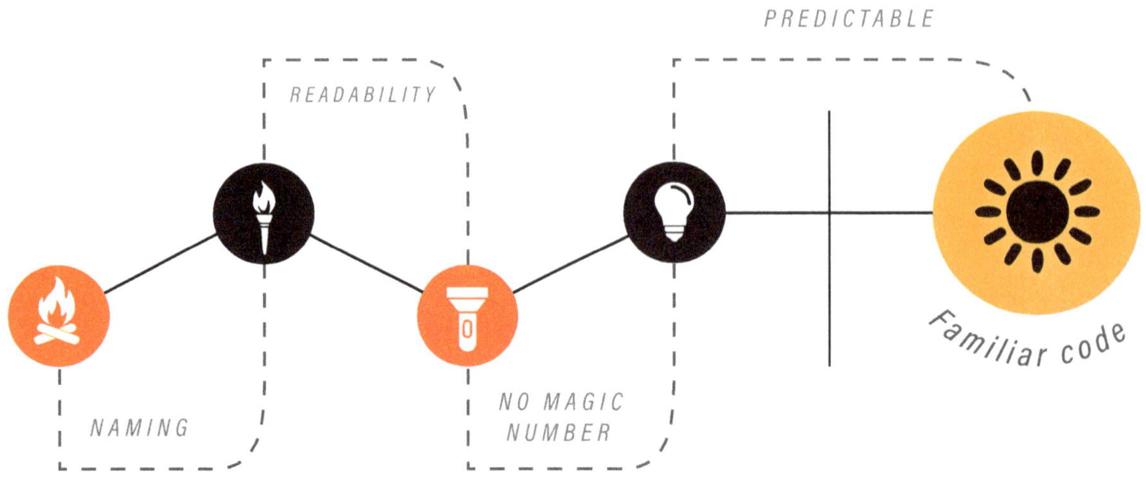

Figure 01 – Code Should Be Familiar

CASE STUDY

Google maintains one of the world's largest codebases, yet its code remains readable and consistent across teams. This is driven by a deliberate engineering culture that prioritizes clarity over stylistic freedom. At the center of this effort is Google's "readability" program, a certification process requiring engineers to master internal style guides before they can approve code in a given language. Every code change must be reviewed by a readability-certified engineer. Style guides are strictly followed, and consistency with existing code is expected. Google's review tool, Critique, integrates static analysis and linting to catch deviations early. This process ensures that code written by different teams looks and feels the same.

The results are measurable. Code written by readability-certified developers is reviewed and integrated faster. Internal studies show improved onboarding speed, higher self-reported maintainability, and greater cross-team mobility. Uniform style also enables Google to apply automated refactoring across millions of lines of code, a task only possible in a consistent environment.

Google's experience shows that code familiarity scales. By investing in clarity, the company improves review speed, lowers defect risk, and supports a large engineering organization without creating silos or drift.

SUCCESS INDICATORS

You'll know you have nailed familiarity when your codebase feels inviting, not intimidating. A new teammate will open a file and know what's going on without asking. You'll notice that your code review conversations are about what the code does, not what it means; when debugging is about solving problems, not deciphering names; when everyone follows the same structure; and merge conflicts are easier to resolve. When new features plug into the existing system with ease, not friction, clarity turns code into a shared asset.

SUMMARY

Design for clarity and predictability is about writing code that's easy to understand, easy to extend, and hard to misuse. Use clear names. Avoid surprises. Keep things familiar. Explain your logic through the code itself. If your code is readable and predictable, everything else becomes easier.

REFERENCES

R. C. Martin, *Clean Code: A Handbook of Agile Software Craftsmanship*, Prentice Hall, 2009.

R. P. Buse and W. Weimer, "Learning a Metric for Code Readability," *IEEE Transactions on Software Engineering*, vol. 36, no. 4, pp. 546–558, 2010.

Google Engineering Practices. (n.d.). Google engineering practices documentation. Retrieved July 6, 2025, from https://google.github.io/eng-practices google.github.io+6google.github.io.

Winters, T., Manshreck, T., & Wright, H. (2020). Software engineering at Google: Lessons learned from programming over time (Kindle ed.). O'Reilly Media.

02 · Explicit over Implicit

"If it's not obvious, it's wrong."— Anonymous

INTRODUCTION

This principle combines two foundational ideas: explicit over implicit, and pure functions. These concepts help you communicate intent clearly and isolate logic that behaves the same way every time it runs. If code feels surprising or unreadable, one or both principles have likely been compromised. By making behavior explicit and logic pure, you build a code corpus that is understandable and far less prone to bugs.

KEY CONCEPT

This principle rests on two complementary foundations that promote clarity and predictability. First, favor the explicit over the implicit. Code should reveal its intent without requiring guesswork. That means using clear names, predictable control flow, and direct declarations. Second, prefer pure functions. Pure functions are self-contained units of logic that always produce the same result for the same input and avoid modifying shared state or triggering side effects. When you structure your code this way, it becomes easier to test, reuse, and understand in isolation. Together, these foundations make code behavior self-evident and ensure that side effects don't lurk in unexpected places. As a result, your systems become more verifiable, easier to modify, and more resilient to change at scale.

WHY IT MATTERS

When you make code explicit and logic pure, you stop making developers dig for answers. Developers no longer wonder, "What's this doing?" or "What else might this affect?" They can focus on solving problems and delivering value. Conversely, when code relies on hidden behavior or side effects, even minor changes can feel risky. Bugs creep in unnoticed. Refactoring becomes dangerous. Testing becomes harder because it's unclear what needs to be verified. Over time, code gets hard to change and productivity drops.

By coding for clarity and purity, you make your code easier to read and safer to change. Teams move faster, debug less, and build trust in the system and each other.

IN PRACTICE

Implementing this principle in your day-to-day development means writing code that's easy to understand and maintain. Start by naming with intent. A function called calculateInvoiceTotal() tells you far more than a vague process(), and that clarity pays dividends in debugging and review. Don't hide behavior behind defaults. If a function changes based on a magic input, make that

CASE STUDY

At Basecamp, the product and engineering teams have long emphasized simplicity, clarity, and intentional design in both interface and implementation. Their backend services, primarily written in Ruby, reflect a disciplined application of principles like "explicit over implicit" and pure function design. One major initiative involved refactoring legacy billing logic that had grown opaque over time. Originally built with loosely named methods like *processAccount()* and *updateStatus()*, the system bundled logic and relied heavily on implicit defaults.

To regain control, Basecamp engineers decomposed the codebase into smaller, more focused units. Each function was rewritten to reveal intent. For example, *calculateLateFee()* replaced vague handlers, and defaults like grace periods were passed explicitly, not inferred. Side effects such as logging and email notifications were extracted to the edges, while core logic remained pure and testable. This shift improved test coverage and onboarding speed and allowed the team to improve customer billing with clarity and self-assurance.

What made this successful was Basecamp's cultural alignment with the principle. Engineers were encouraged to write readable, expressive code, and routinely reviewed pull requests for signs of hidden behavior or cryptic logic. As a result, the billing system became easier to extend and debug and was far less prone to regressions.

visible. Keep side effects under control by isolating I/O (input/output), state changes, and external dependencies; these belong at the system's edges, not its core.

When writing business logic or calculations, use pure functions that are deterministic and side-effect-free. Let structure reflect behavior: a function that fetches and saves data should be named fetchAndSaveUser(), not something misleading like getUser(). If you're working with code full of side effects, refactor it. Break it down into pure and impure parts so you can test the logic independently. Make every state transition visible; avoid silent mutations and favor explicit, traceable updates. Don't write functions that do more "just in case." Let each one do a single job well, and keep your system grounded in clarity, not "just in case" code that adds bloat to your codebase.

COMMON PITFALLS

These are the traps that quietly undermine clarity and predictability. Cryptic naming forces readers to guess what the code does; vague terms like doWork() or handle() obscure intent instead of clarifying it. Hidden side effects, such as logging or saving to a database, often lurk in functions that appear simple on the surface. These actions should be explicit, not concealed.

Mutating shared state, especially through global variables or shared references, introduces subtle, hard-to-reproduce bugs. Overusing defaults, like optional parameters or auto-instantiated objects, may seem convenient but often lead to surprising and inconsistent behavior. Code that relies on hidden state or performs multiple tasks becomes difficult

Figure 02 – Explicit over Implicit

to test and maintain. Finally, while pure functions are powerful, not everything should be pure. Operations like sending emails or writing logs are valid side effects, but they should be clearly separated from core logic. Good code doesn't ban side effects. It just makes them obvious.

SUCCESS INDICATORS

You'll notice this principle taking root when code becomes easier to follow, and questions about behavior disappear. Developers stop asking "What does this function really do?" because the answer is already in the name. Unit tests become simpler to write because logic is isolated. Bugs tied to shared state or side effects drop sharply.

Code reviews focus on business logic, not detective work. Refactoring becomes less risky because you know what each function touches (and doesn't). Teams move faster without compromising quality because systems behave as expected.

SUMMARY

Designing for clarity and purity means writing code that tells the truth. It does what it says. It behaves the same way every time. This keeps complexity out in the open, where it can be seen and managed. When code is both explicit and pure, developers can move faster, test more confidently, and maintain systems with less risk. Whether you're writing a small script or a large, distributed service, these principles make your software more understandable and far easier to scale.

REFERENCES

R. C. Martin, *Clean Code: A Handbook of Agile Software Craftsmanship*, Prentice Hall, 2009.

J. Hughes, "Why Functional Programming Matters," *The Computer Journal*, vol. 32, no. 2, pp 98–107, 1989.

J. Fried, "Launch: Basecamp 3," *Signal v. Noise*, Nov. 3, 2015.

03 · Fail Safe, Fail Fast, Fail Loud

"What you do not see, you cannot correct." — Chanakya

INTRODUCTION

Failures don't age well. They only get harder to find and more expensive to fix. If something's wrong, you want to know immediately and be alerted before the problem spreads. That's the essence of "fail fast, fail loud." When combined with defensive programming practices, this principle forms a powerful foundation for resilient, fault-tolerant software. You detect problems early and build guardrails into your code so nothing silently breaks or corrupts downstream.

In large systems, minor errors can snowball. The earlier you catch them, the less damage they do. When errors are detected in places designed to fail fast, your system can remain healthy even when parts of it aren't.

KEY CONCEPT

Fail fast, fail loud is about surfacing errors immediately and refusing to proceed in invalid states. If something's broken, your system should stop, tell you precisely what broke and why, and give you everything you need to fix it. Defensive programming complements this by preparing the code to expect the unexpected. The goal is to catch things like invalid inputs, untrusted data, and handle them safely without crashing or corrupting anything else. Note, you can't eliminate all failures; that's impossible. Instead, work to make failures visible, and containable. When you pair early detection with safe fallback behavior, you give your team the two very helpful things: a clear signal and code that defends itself.

WHY IT MATTERS

Quite often, system failure happens because of a series of small things that no one noticed until it was too late. A null value gets silently ignored or an exception is caught and discarded. These minor issues pile up until the whole system becomes unstable and nearly impossible to debug. Fail fast, fail loud flips that pattern. When something goes wrong, you hear about it immediately and, ideally, at the source. That lets you fix the problem before users notice and downstream systems get bombarded. Defensive programming supports this by making the code itself more resilient. In the process, inputs are validated, boundaries are enforced, and faulty behavior is anticipated. Basically, every assumption is questioned, so code knows when it's in trouble and is able to either address it or ask for help.

IN PRACTICE

Applying the principles of fail fast and fail loud alongside defensive programming means writing code and building systems that catch problems early and report them with enough detail to fix them. You begin by validating everything at the point of entry. This includes type checks, range validations, length constraints, or pattern matching to catch errors before they propagate. You never trust the client blindly, and treat every boundary as an opportunity for validation and enforcement. During development and testing, you assess preconditions aggressively. If a function is misused, it should crash immediately, not silently allow a bad state to spread. You are better off catching them in staging than in production. You also treat warnings as errors; they often signal misalignments between assumptions and reality. Logging should be structured and valuable. When something fails, avoid vague phrases like "unexpected error." Log what went wrong, where it happened, and why.

Similarly, never suppress exceptions without a clear fallback. If you catch an error, do something with it, or let it crash and alert. If you reject an input, log it, and count it. These rejections often uncover systemic issues upstream. Also, pay attention to anomalies; things like heartbeats and sanity validations should be monitored as closely as primary metrics. Even the absence of expected signals should trigger an investigation.

Finally, document assumptions and failure modes. If a function depends on certain invariants, make them explicit in code or comments. When these practices come together, they create code corpora that are designed to break in ways that are detectable and recoverable.

COMMON PITFALLS

Even strong systems falter when fail-fast and defensive programming principles are misapplied. A common pitfall is to have broad catch blocks that handle every exception the same way. Instead of vague error messages like "unexpected error," logs should include context on what failed, where, and with what input. Swallowed exceptions are another trap; catching errors without acting on them hides failures that should trigger a response. However, logging alone isn't enough; pair logging with connected monitoring so issues do not go unnoticed.

CASE STUDY

Stripe integrates fail-fast and defensive programming deeply into its payment infrastructure. Every API request is strictly validated. Missing or malformed fields are rejected with clear and actionable errors before any logic runs. During development, assertions catch misuse early, especially in areas like currency handling and transaction states.

To prevent cascading failures, Stripe uses guard clauses, circuit breakers, and timeouts around third-party services. If an external API fails, the system degrades gracefully rather than hanging or crashing. Logs include full context with request IDs, sanitized inputs, and stack traces so incidents are fast to debug. This disciplined approach helps Stripe catch issues early and recover without user impact.

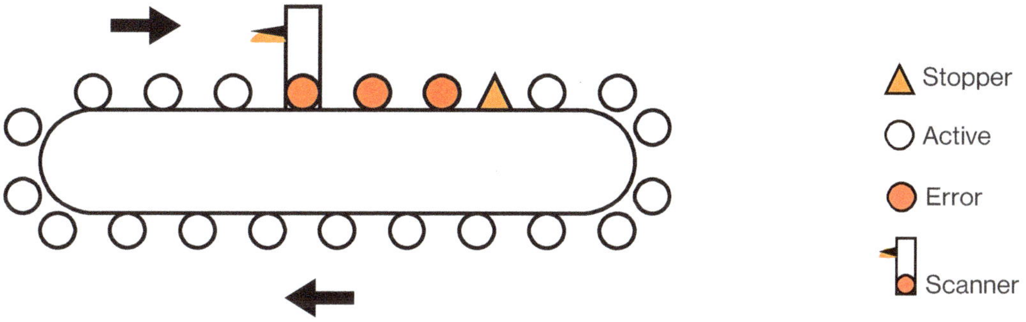

Figure 03 – Fail Safe, Fail Fast, Fail Loud

Similarly, always pair fast failure with graceful degradation, like retries (within a limit) or defaults. However, be judicious in alerts, as alert fatigue is real. If every minor issue triggers an alert, teams start ignoring all of them. Prioritize and tune alerts so they stay meaningful.

SUCCESS INDICATORS

You'll know this principle is working when your system starts exposing issues you weren't even looking for. It will surface them early, close to the source, and with enough clarity to fix them quickly. Errors don't trickle through layers of abstraction; they appear right where they happen, with clean logs and informative stack traces that point directly to the root cause. When something fails, it's contained and easy to recover from. Developers spend less time digging through ambiguous behavior and more time solving real problems. QA reports fewer strange, hard-to-reproduce edge cases because those are now caught and clarified sooner in the development cycle. Recovery becomes faster since each failure is well-understood and doesn't require guesswork or firefighting. Teams move faster knowing the system has strong boundaries and clear guardrails. When things go wrong behind the scenes, users experience minimal disruption because your system and code fail gracefully, and in the right direction.

SUMMARY

Fail fast, fail loud is about surfacing problems clearly, containing them early, and designing software that defends itself. Combined with defensive programming, it creates a development discipline that anticipates failure, handles it, and keeps your system stable no matter what the world throws at it. These principles are technical AND cultural. They help catch bugs before they spread and recover gracefully when things go wrong. If your system fails, it should tell you immediately and give you everything you need to make it right.

REFERENCES

M. Nygard, *Release It! Design and Deploy Production-Ready Software*, Pragmatic Bookshelf, 2007.

Patterson, D. A., et al. (2002). *Recovery Oriented Computing (ROC): Motivation, definition, techniques, and case studies.* University of California, Berkeley.

04 · The Boy Scout Rule

"We are what we repeatedly do. Excellence, then, is not an act, but a habit." — Aristotle

INTRODUCTION

The Second Law of Thermodynamics states that in an isolated system, entropy will either increase or stay the same over time. It never decreases. Codebases follow the same trajectory, and quite often, an increase in entropy comes from gradual neglect. Small problems get left unaddressed, awkward logic is preserved out of habit, and clutter is tolerated in the name of urgency. The Boy Scout Rule exists to counter that. It encourages you to make small, opportunistic improvements every time you touch a file. The idea is simple: whenever you touch code, you leave it a little better than you found it. Not perfect. Just better.

This principle is about paying attention. Maybe you can rename a misleading variable. Maybe you reword a confusing comment, or remove a line of dead code. These actions are tiny, but they compound quickly. The Boy Scout Rule works because it requires no special planning, budget, or buy-in beyond a shared commitment to quality. Over time, it turns maintenance into momentum.

KEY CONCEPT

The Boy Scout Rule is about deliberate, local improvement. If you're already in a file to fix a bug or add a feature, take a few moments to notice what else can be improved. These changes are safe, incremental, and directly adjacent to the task at hand. They might clarify logic or reduce duplication. The goal is to be thoughtful and consistent.

The effect is cumulative. Codebases age more gracefully. Technical debt shrinks quietly. Teams spend less time navigating outdated structures and more time solving actual problems. When everyone follows this practice, quality stops relying on cleanup sprints, fire drill efforts, or major rewrites. It becomes part of the everyday rhythm of development.

WHY IT MATTERS

As software grows, complexity grows with it. Every edge case patched, and every workaround added, pushes the system closer to a jumbled mess. Without regular care, these small compromises become structural liabilities. The Boy Scout Rule offers a way to push back without disrupting delivery. When you make improvements in the flow of your work, the system gets better without anyone having to pause or ask permission. A muddled function, a misleading

CASE STUDY

At Shopify, engineers were facing the growing complexity of a large monolithic codebase. Instead of launching sweeping rewrites or delaying feature work for refactors, they adopted the Boy Scout Rule as an everyday discipline. The approach directly reflected the principles outlined above. Developers were expected to fold in small improvements as part of regular work, fixing typos in docs, renaming confusing variables, deleting dead code, or simplifying conditionals. These weren't treated as distractions. They were the work. Code reviews praised cleanup efforts, and internal tooling surfaced outdated patterns and suggested improvements in-line during development. There was a change and improvement in culture as well. Engineers weren't waiting for time to clean up. They cleaned as they built. Over time, even the most complex corners of the codebase became more readable and resilient. Developers moved faster because they weren't constantly tripping over legacy quirks. The payoff matched the principle: small fixes, done routinely, led to a healthier system.

comment, or a broken abstraction: all these get gently improved. These small actions reduce long-term risk and increase short-term clarity. They make onboarding smoother, testing easier, and the architecture more aligned with how the software actually works. The Boy Scout Rule ensures that maintenance happens continuously, not eventually.

IN PRACTICE

You see this principle in small, everyday choices. You remove a deprecated import while updating an endpoint. You notice repeated logic during a review and suggest pulling it into a helper. You update a *README* that still mentions an old flag. If something looks confusing or out of place, fix it while you're there. If you're unsure, comment or flag it for review. These aren't dramatic fixes. They're part of showing up and working with care. Code reviews play a significant role here. When code reviewers recognize and encourage small improvements, the practice spreads. The cost is low, and you get the lifetime benefit of building a good habit of paying attention. Over time, they change the culture.

COMMON PITFALLS

The Boy Scout Rule only works when it's applied with judgment. Sometimes developers get carried away, changing code that works just fine because they prefer a different pattern. That's not helpful. Every cleanup should make the code easier to understand, not just different. If the result is harder to understand or introduces unnecessary risk, it's not in the spirit of this principle.

Another issue is uneven adoption. If only a few team members clean as they go while others leave things as-is, improvement stalls. The system stays patchy. For this rule to work, the whole team has to value it and participate. Everyone must recognize that quality is everyone's job, not just QAs or the Tech Leads'. Last, there's a risk of conflating code cleanup with code perfection. The Boy Scout Rule isn't about making things pristine. It's about thoughtful, incremental change. Small steps forward, made often.

Figure 04 – The Boy Scout Rule

SUCCESS INDICATORS

You'll see the results in the way your team works. Fewer comments appear in reviews ask why something looks outdated or broken. Less time is spent debugging legacy code that no one wants to touch. New developers find their footing faster because the codebase reflects current best practices instead of forgotten ones. Cleanup sprints become rare because there's less mess to clean up. Teams move faster because changes feel less risky.

SUMMARY

The Boy Scout Rule is about building momentum through care. While it is not a heroic principle, when it's practiced consistently, it transforms writing code from something static to a continuous improvement practice. You get there by showing up and cleaning up every time you work on your codebase. Every improvement, no matter how small, becomes a step toward a healthier, more sustainable codebase.

REFERENCES

M. Feathers, *Working Effectively with Legacy Code,* Prentice Hall, 2004.

R. C. Martin, *Clean Code: A Handbook of Agile Software Craftsmanship*, Prentice Hall, 2008.

J. DeWyze. "The 25 Percent Rule for Tackling Technical Debt." *Shopify Engineering Blog,* February 16. 2023. https://shopify.engineering/technical-debt-25-percent-rule

A Chang. "Refactoring Legacy Code with the Strangler Fig Pattern." *Shopify Engineering Blog,* March 11, 2020. https://shopify.engineering/refactoring-legacy-code-strangler-fig-pattern

05 • Commit Meaningful Changes

"The faintest ink is better than the best memory." — Chinese proverb

INTRODUCTION

Every commit is a conversation with your past self, your future self, and your team. When that conversation is clear, code reviews are faster and project history reads like a well-structured narrative instead of scattered notes. The Commit Meaningful Changes principle uplevels version control into a tool for just tracking to one that promotes clarity. It transforms your git history into a dependable source of truth.

KEY CONCEPT

A meaningful commit is atomic, intentional, and traceable. It introduces a single, coherent change: a bug fix, a feature, a refactor. It doesn't mix concerns, surprise reviewers, or hide logic changes in formatting tweaks. It should explain what changed, why it changed, and how it ties into the broader context, like issues or design decisions. Each commit is a checkpoint and a note for the future, so it is important to make sure that the message is clear.

WHY IT MATTERS

Meaningful commits enable better engineering. When a bug slips into production, atomic commits can help pinpoint the issue in seconds. When a release breaks something, small commits let you roll back the right part without losing everything else. When a teammate joins mid-project, your commit messages become the best onboarding guide they never asked for. Sloppy commit practices, on the other hand, lead to blocked reviews, botched rollbacks, and hours lost deciphering what "fix stuff" actually means.

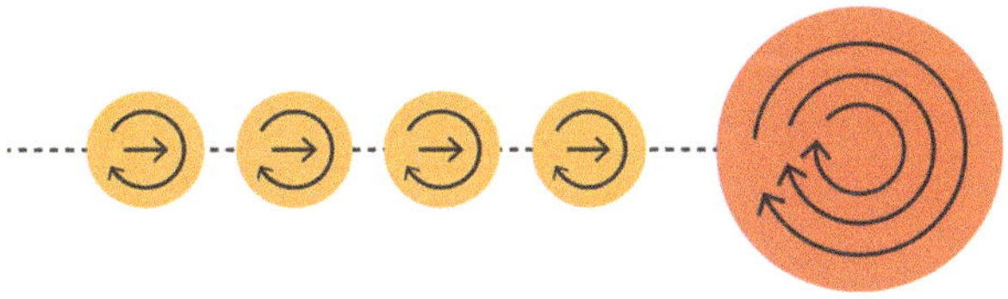

Figure 05 – Commit Meaningful Changes

IN PRACTICE

This principle begins with discipline. You commit only when your work represents a clear, logical change. Avoid mixing unrelated fixes. When you write commit messages, use the imperative. Say "Fix validation bug," not "Fixed a bug." Add a brief explanation if it adds context, and links to issues or pull requests when it helps trace the change.

Keep the code trunk green and never commit code that breaks tests or introduces a known regression.

CASE STUDY

With over 20,000 contributors and millions of lines of code, the Linux Kernel is a model of how version control clarity can scale. Its development process enforces atomic commits: each must do one thing and one thing only. Contributors are expected to describe what changed, why it changed, and how to reproduce the issue it fixes. Commit messages link back to mailing list discussions, bug trackers, and sometimes even hardware specifications. There is no room for vague messages or bundled updates. The result is a repository that spans decades yet remains navigable. When regressions appear, you can find the root cause effectively because the commit history was written with care.

Before you merge, fold micro-fixes like typos or comment tweaks into the original commit. You're aiming for a history that's traceable and easy to roll back when needed.

COMMON PITFALLS

The usual pitfall involves large, unfocused commits because they increase cognitive overload. Reviewers can't isolate logic changes from formatting, and if a revert is needed, it pulls down unrelated fixes with it. Vague messages like "update code" or "final edits" that provide no useful history, especially when debugging or mixing whitespace tweaks with logic changes, clutter diffs and hide bugs. Another trap is micro-commits: things like "typo" or "oops" flood the history and bury meaningful work. If left unsquashed, they fragment understanding. In all scenarios, you will have to ensure that you don't break the build; every commit should leave the system in a deployable state. Anything less disrupts the feedback loop.

SUCCESS INDICATORS

When this principle is working well, the commit history becomes a timeline of clear, isolated changes. Developers trust version control as a debugging tool. Rollbacks are surgical, not destructive. Every commit message communicates enough context to understand what changed without opening the diff. Teams begin to review changes faster, with fewer misunderstandings. For new engineers, the commit log doubles as documentation, explaining the system's evolution one message at a time.

SUMMARY

Version control is the story of how your code got here. By committing meaningful changes, you write that story clearly and help every engineer who reads it. One commit, one purpose. That's how you keep your codebase understandable and ready for change.

REFERENCES

Torvalds, L. (2005). Git: A version control system for the Linux kernel. *Git SCM.* https://git-scm.com/book/en/v2/Getting-Started-A-Short-History-of-Git

Atlassian Community. (2021, March 9). *Git best practices.* Atlassian. https://community.atlassian.com/forums/Bitbucket-articles/Git-Best-Practices/ba-p/1628803

06 • Avoid Premature Optimization

"Nature does nothing in vain."— Aristotle

INTRODUCTION

Every developer wants their code to run fast. That instinct isn't wrong however, optimizing before the system works, or you know where it's slow, adds complexity and weakens the code. Premature optimization begins when teams pursue speed before the software even works reliably. Code gets changed in the name of efficiency without understanding the cost or context. Most of the time, it makes the code harder to read and change later.

This principle is simple: make it correct and maintainable first. If and only if real performance problems show up, address them based on profiling data. Otherwise, focus on clarity, modularity, and architecture.

KEY CONCEPT

Premature optimization means solving a problem that doesn't exist and may never appear. It shows up when you write a complicated algorithm to save milliseconds on a task that runs once a day, or when you reach for obscure language features in the name of speed, even though no one has measured any performance issues. Sometimes, you avoid using simpler, more readable code because it "might be inefficient," even though there's no evidence of an actual bottleneck.

Real optimization is deliberate. It starts with profilingand it targets actual performance issues. It follows after working, maintainable code, not before. It happens when the code is stable enough that changes are safe and verifiable. Instead of guessing, observe real usage. Let production show you where the slow parts are, then fix what matters.

WHY IT MATTERS

When you optimize prematurely, you sacrifice clarity and flexibility before you've even delivered something useful. The code becomes harder to understand due to tweaks aimed at "speeding things up," even though there's no evidence they're needed. Developers end up spending valuable time tuning parts of the system that offer no measurable performance benefit. Bugs creep in through unnecessary complexity, often in subtle, hard-to-detect ways. These early decisions can lock you into architectural patterns, making the system harder to change later.

By contrast, optimizing only when it's truly necessary leads to real, lasting advantages. The code stays readable, which makes it easier to test, debug, and maintain. Improvements are driven by actual usage

CASE STUDY

When Facebook launched in 2004, it ran on a plain PHP codebase. At the time, speed wasn't the priority. Rightfully, they focused on releasing fast and shipping features that helped them stand out. As usage grew into the hundreds of millions, they ran into scale issues. Looking at data and diagnostics, they noted that server CPU usage spiked primarily from PHP's runtime overhead. Instead of guessing or rewriting everything, Facebook profiled production systems and identified the scripting engine as the core issue. Their response was targeted. In 2010, they launched HipHop, a PHP-to-C++ transpiler (a type of compiler that translates source code from one programming language to another) that slashed CPU usage by 50%. Further tuning delivered a 1.7× throughput boost, enabling them to serve 70% more traffic on the same hardware, all without halting product development or rewriting unaffected code.

The key was restraint and avoiding premature optimization. They didn't optimize based on instinct. They waited for data, then acted surgically. It worked because they knew exactly where the pain was and focused there. Twitter learned the same lesson the hard way. Their early outages ("Fail Whales") led to assumptions that switching languages would help. However, it was smarter caching and queue design, not a rewrite, that made the system 100× faster. Both of these examples show that you should optimize only when metrics demand it, and when you do, opt for focusing on data-driven and confirmed bottlenecks.

patterns, ensuring optimization effort is focused where it counts. Your team zeroes in on meaningful, high-impact changes, and speculative constraints do not burden your team.

IN PRACTICE

You apply this principle by starting with clarity and correctness. Your top priority should be clean, readable code that works. Optimization is irrelevant if the system doesn't function, or if no one understands it well enough to extend or maintain it safely. After that, refactor your code, since a cleaner structure makes performance problems easier to spot and fix. Once the code is solid, turn to data. Use profiling tools to measure what matters, be it latency, memory, CPU usage, or throughput, and only then decide where to optimize.

For actual improvement, note that larger architectural changes often produce bigger gains than local tweaks, so optimize at the right level. If the database is the bottleneck, tuning a loop won't help. Avoid optimizing temporary code altogether. There's no benefit in tuning a script that's meant to be thrown away. Favor general improvements over clever hacks. For example, caching a result is more effective than inlining a function. A better algorithm will usually outperform minor tweaks to loops or control flow. Measure every change. When an optimization adds complexity, isolate it by keeping the core logic simple, so that you can separate performance trade-offs into modular sections that can be

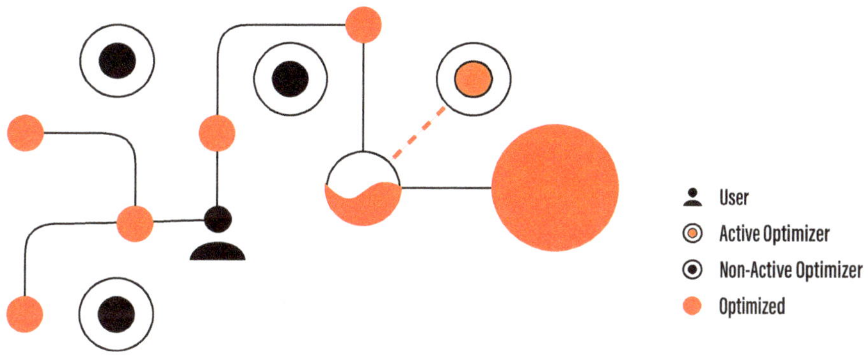

Figure 06 – Avoid Premature Optimization

swapped or removed later. That's how you keep your system fast without giving up maintainability.

COMMON PITFALLS

Teams often get optimization wrong by focusing on the wrong problems, jumping into code changes without data, or prioritizing micro-efficiencies over maintainability. One common mistake is optimizing non-issues. In the name of engineering excellence, developers may spend hours trying to speed up something that hasn't been identified as a bottleneck. If a slowdown hasn't been measured or reported, it probably isn't real. Another trap is making code unreadable for imagined gains. Using obscure tricks or dense syntax might eke out a slight speed boost, but it comes at the cost of clarity. That trade-off rarely pays off.

Skipping profiling entirely is another classic pitfall. Trying to optimize without measuring first turns every tweak into guesswork. You might fix the wrong thing or waste time where it doesn't matter. Likewise, developers often focus on the wrong layer. They may obsess over application logic when the real culprit is a slow, unindexed database query or unnecessary API calls.

Early architecture decisions can also backfire. Picking a performance-optimized structure too soon often locks teams into a rigid design that's hard to change as requirements evolve. Flexibility is more valuable than marginal performance gains during the early stages of a project. Finally, teams may over-generalize. Just because one part of the system has a bottleneck doesn't mean the whole thing needs optimizing. Fix what's broken, not everything around it. Optimization should be deliberate, data-driven, and balanced.

SUCCESS INDICATORS

You'll know you're avoiding premature optimization effectively when most of your performance improvements are driven by profiling data or real usage insights, not guesses. Even in performance-critical sections, your code stays readable and approachable. You rarely find yourself undoing over-optimized code that turned out to be unnecessary or unused. When performance bugs arise, your team addresses them with targeted, efficient fixes rather than broad rewrites. The optimizations you apply touch only small portions of the codebase but result in significant gains. Development velocity remains high. Each optimization feels deliberate and justified, not reflexive or overcautious.

SUMMARY

Premature optimization is seductive. It feels like engineering mastery to squeeze every last drop of speed from your code. However, if you do it too early, before you've built the product and measured it, you'll spend your time solving the wrong problems and making your code worse in the process. The best teams follow a different rhythm. They make it work, then make it clean, and only then make it fast if it actually needs to be faster. With that mindset, you build software that performs when needed, stays readable over time, and evolves with intent.

REFERENCES

D. E. Knuth, "Structured Programming with Go to Statements," *ACM Computing Surveys*, vol. 6, no. 4, pp. 261–301, 1974.

Fowler, M. (2009). Yet another optimization article. *IEEE Software*. https://www.martinfowler.com/ieeeSoftware/yetOptimization.pdf

Meta (Facebook) Engineering. (2011, March 30). HipHop for PHP: More optimizations for efficient servers. *Meta Engineering Blog*. https://engineering.fb.com/2011/03/30/web/hiphop-for-php-more-optimizations-for-efficient-servers/

07 • Orthogonality

"Good fences make good neighbors." — Robert Frost

INTRODUCTION

Great software is flexible. Orthogonality is the principle that makes this possible. It encourages you to keep parts of your system independent, so that one change doesn't ripple through unrelated components. When your modules do one job each and communicate through well-defined, minimal interfaces, you reduce risk, and enable faster development.

Orthogonality matters at every level. You see it when utility functions stay decoupled from application logic, when APIs are shaped around their domain, or when a microservice can be replaced without rewriting its consumers. When code modules and systems are orthogonal, boundaries stay clean, changes remain local, and they are easy to make.

KEY CONCEPT

Orthogonality means that components behave independently and do not rely on one another's internal workings. A module is orthogonal when its function is self-contained (with clear responsibilities) and its interface is stable. It can be changed or replaced without requiring changes elsewhere. The value of this principle lies in the separation of purpose.

You apply orthogonality by designing components to be loosely coupled yet cohesive. A data store doesn't need to know which interface renders its results. A payment processor doesn't care whether the transaction was initiated from a mobile or a desktop. These systems share contracts, not context. Orthogonality enables reuse without tight coupling and change without regression. It also supports long-term adaptability by limiting the blast radius of change. It draws strong lines between roles and keeps logic isolated.

WHY IT MATTERS

Systems that lack orthogonality are hard to change. A seemingly innocent change in one module unexpectedly breaks functionality in another. Bug fixes become regressions. Onboarding slows down because no one knows what can be changed safely. By contrast, orthogonal systems are resilient. When modules are independent, developers can test them in isolation, work in parallel, and evolve their code without fear of unintended consequences. Teams can build faster, ship safer, and maintain more with less coordination.

Orthogonality also improves the experience of reading code. When components are clearly bounded and named according to what they do, developers don't have to wonder about hidden dependencies or side effects. They can trace problems directly to where they originated and understand what needs to change. In a well-structured system, each function and service answers one question and one question only.

IN PRACTICE

You apply orthogonality by first giving every component a narrow, intentional responsibility. A data parser should not log errors or write results to a database. A controller should route requests, not validate business logic. When responsibilities are clear, you reduce friction between components. Then, you design interfaces to be explicit and stable. Components expose what they need and nothing more. They don't leak internal state or make assumptions about how others behave. When systems interact, they do so through clean contracts, not implicit behavior. Shared mutable state is kept to a minimum, and when it's necessary, access is controlled and predictable.

Orthogonality also calls for architectural discipline. You have to structure your code to reflect real separation of concerns. For example, don't let configuration bleed into business logic, or side effects blur the boundary between functional and imperative code. As your system grows, revisit your boundaries. Watch for modules that start doing too much or relying on too many external details. Refactor early and design with replacement in mind. A truly orthogonal system welcomes change because change doesn't come with hidden dependencies or unpredictable fallout.

COMMON PITFALLS

When orthogonality is misunderstood or ignored, systems accumulate hidden dependencies and unintended complexity. Blurred module boundaries lead

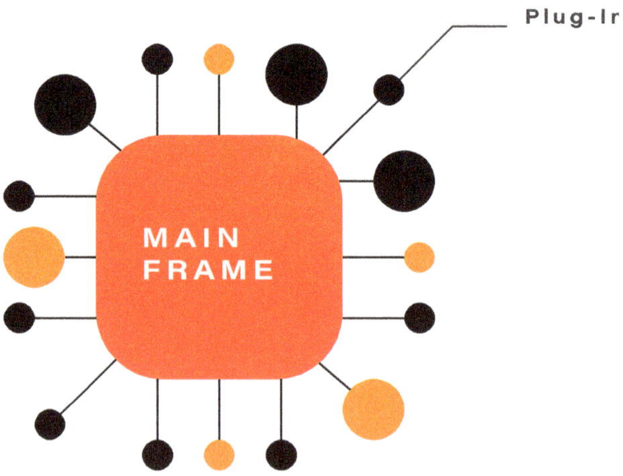

Figure 07 – Orthogonality

to logic that grows without structure. Shared state becomes a liability, causing components to behave differently based on who touched the data last. Attempts to over-generalize too early often produce abstractions that are leaky and unfit for reuse.

Teams sometimes mistake premature abstraction for orthogonality, introducing indirection that increases cognitive load instead of reducing it. Others fall into the trap of runtime coupling services that look separate in code but cannot operate without each other in production. These systems are prone to cascading failures and high coordination costs. Even with good intentions, the absence of regular refactoring and dependency audits allows drift to turn clean designs into tangled networks over time.

SUCCESS INDICATORS

You know orthogonality is working when changes are localized and predictable. Developers edit one module without triggering concern across the system. Tests become faster because there's less need for scaffolding. Features roll out incrementally, and rollbacks are

CASE STUDY

Datadog, a leading observability platform, demonstrates orthogonality at scale. As the company expanded its offerings beyond monitoring into incident management, security analytics, and application profiling, its platform architecture had to evolve rapidly without slowing teams down or causing regressions.

Each feature module within Datadog is built to operate independently with a clear API boundary. The log management module, for example, processes and stores structured log data without requiring context from the application performance monitoring or infrastructure monitoring layers. When a new capability like real-time collaboration was introduced, Datadog's orthogonal design meant it could be layered across existing features with minimal disruption. Teams didn't need to update core modules. They added capabilities through integration points that already respected existing contracts. This made cross-cutting feature delivery faster and safer, while maintaining the reliability expected by large-scale enterprise users. The clarity and safety of their architectural boundaries allowed Datadog to grow its product surface without bloating its codebase or increasing dependencies. Orthogonality became the operational backbone that enabled velocity and quality at once.

rare. Collaboration across teams improves because responsibilities are clear, and boundaries are respected. Over time, the system grows in capability without losing agility and flexibility.

SUMMARY

Orthogonality turns software into a system of parts that play well together without stepping on each other. It allows teams to move faster by making code easier to read, change, and replace. It minimizes risk and lays the groundwork for scaling growth. Clean, clear interfaces and single-responsibility components are your first line of defense against entropy. Build with orthogonality, and your codebase will last longer and get better with age.

REFERENCES

A. Hunt and D. Thomas, *The Pragmatic Programmer: Your Journey to Mastery,* 2nd ed., Addison-Wesley Professional, 2

E. Gamma, R. Helm, R. Johnson, and J. Vlissides, *Design Patterns: Elements of Reusable Object-Oriented Software,* Addison-Wesley Professional, 1994.

S. Mazzone, "Observability in Event-Driven Architectures," *Datadog Architecture Center,* November 20, 2024.

II THE ARTIST'S WAY

"First, you master the instrument. Then you forget the instrument. Then the music happens." — Charlie Parker

In engineering, we're taught to chase precision. Find the cleanest solution, pick the right abstraction, and trust that somewhere out there, the best answer exists. Sometimes, with enough clarity and care, you do find the perfect answer. There are practices that have earned their place. Patterns so effective that they're almost universal. In those cases, following them is just smart.

Unfortunately, not all decisions work that way. In the real world, you'll often face two paths that both seem reasonable, and no analysis, however deep, will guarantee which one will last. In those situations, technical skill alone isn't enough. You can't optimize your way through it. You need to approach the work like an artist.

That doesn't mean being loose or whimsical. The artist's discipline is about noticing what others have made and using that as raw material. That mindset, starting with what's known and shaping something of your own, is just as relevant in software as it is in any other craft. The principles that follow, such as DRY, Separation of Concerns, SOLID Design, and Concurrency vs. Parallelism, are not the destination. You learn them so they become second nature. You practice them until they no longer need to be at the front of your mind. When things get interesting, you draw on them without having to stop and think. They support the early stages of good design. Eventually, they should fade into the background.

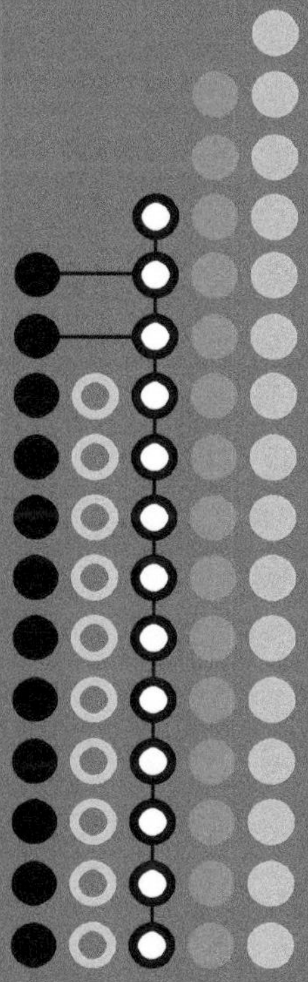

That's what mastery looks like, not perfection, just fluency.

As you read the principles ahead, treat them the way a musician treats scales. You don't memorize them to perform them exactly. You absorb them so you can improvise with clarity. Let them tune your ear, then move past the rules into the work itself. Ask questions like: Am I repeating myself here? Is this logic in the right place? Will someone else be able to follow what I've built? Beyond these principles, structure can also be borrowed from fields outside of software, like architecture, painting, and engineering. Basically, any discipline that deals with form, function, and flow could be helpful.

Over time, my sincere wish is that, eventually, you let go of the need to be right and stop worrying about whether your decision is perfect. You focus instead on whether it's strong enough to move forward. In the end, building is the only truth, and it is the only way to figure things out. You won't find certainty before you begin. What is likely to happen is that if you stay with it, you'll shape something solid enough to stand. That's how the craft (any art) works, and that's how you will design and build good software.

08 • Don't Repeat Yourself (DRY)

"A man with one watch knows what time it is. A man with two is never sure."— Proverb

INTRODUCTION

You know the feeling. You're tracking down a bug or making a simple update, and suddenly you're editing the same logic in five different files. That's the mess DRY helps you avoid. The Don't Repeat Yourself principle, first introduced in The Pragmatic Programmer, is rooted in a simple belief: every piece of knowledge should have a single, unambiguous representation in your system. When duplication creeps in, whether it's logic, configuration, or structure, errors multiply, and maintenance becomes a chore. Beyond avoiding extra work, DRY also helps protect your codebase's integrity.

KEY CONCEPT

Applying DRY means you resist the urge to reimplement or recopy. Instead of duplicating logic, you centralize it. When you see similar patterns across components, models, or services, you extract and abstract carefully. The goal is not to create overcomplicated utility layers, but to capture shared knowledge in ways that are easy to understand and easy to maintain.

Picture a scenario where three different forms validate emails. If each has its own slightly different validation rule, a change in one leaves the other two inconsistent. Instead, you define the rule once. That one function becomes the source of truth, and every form reflects the same logic automatically. The result is less work, fewer bugs, and a clearer path forward.

DRY doesn't only apply to code. It extends to configuration files, documentation, test data, and even infrastructure. When you duplicate knowledge across environments, teams, or layers, you increase the chances that it will fall out of sync. DRY asks you to think carefully about where each piece of logic or information should live and how to ensure it stays authoritative.

WHY IT MATTERS

Ignoring DRY leads to systems that grow in size but shrink in clarity. As duplication spreads, inconsistencies become inevitable. Small fixes and refactors take longer than they should. New team members struggle to tell which version of a function or rule they should trust. DRY gives you a cleaner mental model of your system. When logic changes, you know exactly where to go. When something breaks, you don't have to hunt through variations. You isolate the issue and resolve it with precision.

Following DRY also improves collaboration. Everyone moves faster when your team works in a codebase with well-defined, centralized patterns. Pull requests

CASE STUDY

At GitHub, engineers noticed a pattern: new internal services constantly reinvented the wheel. Each team had its own way of structuring endpoints, configuring timeouts, handling authentication, and deploying infrastructure. These weren't wild deviations, but the small inconsistencies added up. Teams spent time fixing the same issues in slightly different ways, and configuration drift became a silent source of bugs.

To address this, GitHub leaned into the DRY principle. They created an internal services platform that codified shared logic, standardizing how services were scaffolded, logs were formatted, and infrastructure was provisioned. Configuration files were centralized and version-controlled, allowing updates to propagate consistently across teams. Even documentation templates were consolidated to prevent fragmentation across wikis.

This directly reflects DRY in action: identifying repeatable patterns, extracting them into shared components, and maintaining a single source of truth. When a logging policy changed, teams didn't need to update ten different scripts. They updated one. When a new service was launched, it started from a trusted template, reducing setup time and eliminating guesswork. DRY raised the baseline quality of every service by ensuring consistency from day one.

are easier to review. Debugging sessions are shorter. Testing becomes more focused, since you only need to validate a behavior in one place, not three or four. The benefits stack up over time, giving your project resilience and your team room to focus on real progress rather than repetitive fixes.

IN PRACTICE

Applying DRY well means knowing when repetition is harmless and when it signals a deeper problem. You don't need to refactor after copying one line, but when a pattern shows up three or four times, step back and extract it into a shared module or helper. When you do write it, name it clearly so the intent is obvious. As noted in other principles, abstractions should feel familiar, not clever. Similarly, when configurations like timeouts, limits, or keys live in multiple places, every update carries risk. Moving these into a single config file or service helps you avoid the "forgot to change it everywhere" problem. As your system grows, that consistency becomes essential.

Watch for repetition in documentation, too. When you copy and paste explanations across wikis or repos, they get out of sync. Link to a single source instead and keep that up to date. The same applies to infrastructure scripts, API contracts, and schemas. Every duplicate is a risk. Every well-named source of truth is a safeguard.

COMMON PITFALLS

Like any principle, DRY works best when balanced with judgment. Not all repetition is harmful. Sometimes what looks like duplication is actually different logic expressed in a similar form. Blindly abstracting too early can make code harder to follow and maintain. You want clarity and reuse, not straitjacket-type one-size-fits-all solutions.

Another risk is applying DRY too aggressively across service boundaries. In microservice architectures, trying to unify everything can create tight coupling. Each service should remain independently deployable, even if that means repeating small bits of logic. DRY should not compromise autonomy.

Finally, don't confuse DRY with cleverness. Simple, repeated logic may be easier to understand than a shared abstraction that hides important differences. The right abstraction should feel obvious. If it doesn't, it might not be the right time to extract it yet.

SUCCESS INDICATORS

You'll know DRY works when updates feel predictable and when a change to business logic requires a single edit, not a sweeping patch across the codebase, when your team moves faster because there's less guesswork, less duplication, and fewer inconsistencies. When bugs tied to diverging implementations simply stop appearing. Your codebase starts to feel more modular, more expressive, and easier to work with. Even onboarding gets smoother because everything is in its right place and clearly defined.

SUMMARY

The Don't Repeat Yourself principle reminds you that software is easier to scale and maintain when every idea has one home. By centralizing logic and structure, you reduce friction and make your system easier to understand. You spend less time fixing bugs introduced by inconsistency and more time solving the problems that matter. Using the DRY principle avoids repetition and moves you toward writing better software and working as a better team. The effort you put into consolidating today becomes the stability and speed you can leverage tomorrow.

REFERENCES

A. Hunt and D. Thomas, *The Pragmatic Programmer,* Addison-Wesley Professional, 1999.

M. Fowler, "Technical Debt Quadrant," *martinFowler.com* (blog), 2009.

GitHub, "GitHub's Engineering System Success Playbook," *GitHub Resources,* 2025. https://resources.github.com/engineering-system-success-playbook/

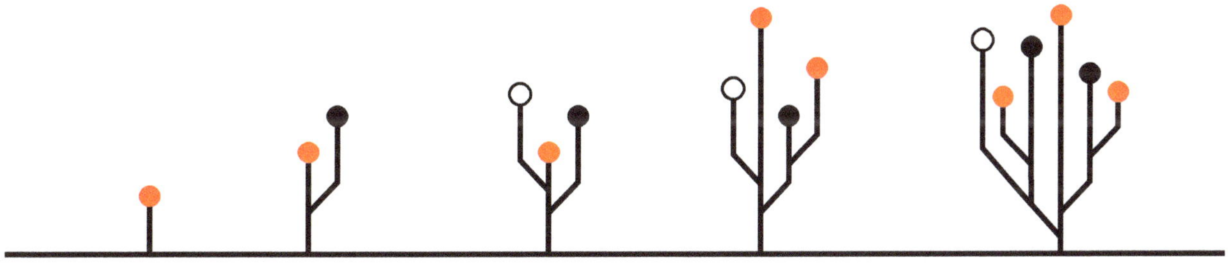

Figure 08 – DRY: Don't Repeat Yourself

09 · Separation of Concerns

"He who tries to do everything does nothing well." — Thomas Aquinas

INTRODUCTION

When systems grow, it's easy for boundaries to blur. UI components start pulling in business logic, backend services reach into presentation layers, and data access code starts including validation rules. The principle of Separation of Concerns (SoC) is a deliberate response to that code sprawl. It encourages you to isolate responsibilities so that each part of your system has a single, focused purpose. The result is software that's easier to evolve and maintain over time. SoC isn't about abstraction for its own sake. It's a safeguard that keeps changes contained, prevents overlap between teams, and makes behavior easier to understand and trust.

KEY CONCEPT

The Separation of Concerns principle helps you manage complexity by drawing clear boundaries between distinct responsibilities. Each module, service, or class should do one job and do it well. A UI layer renders views and handles input. A business logic layer makes decisions and applies rules. A data layer interacts with persistent storage. When you organize your code with clear boundaries, your system becomes easier to navigate and safer to modify. A reporting module, for instance, doesn't need to know how the data got there; it should only know how to display it. Similarly, a payment service doesn't need to care about which frontend form submitted a transaction, just whether the data it received is valid and complete. This modularity allows you to move faster without introducing risk.

WHY IT MATTERS

When concerns are tangled and cross-dependent, every change feels risky. Updating a validation rule breaks the UI, or fixing a rendering bug corrupts the database state. These problems aren't always visible until they hit production; by then, they're expensive to resolve. SoC prevents this entanglement by guiding you toward a structure where logic lives in the right place, and nothing else has to know how it works. The benefits of SoC are immediate. Systems become easier to read because each component tells a single story. Teams can divide work cleanly, with fewer merge conflicts and overlapping responsibilities. As your application grows, you can scale the parts that need it without rewriting everything else.

Separation of concerns also strengthens your APIs. When modules only communicate through well-defined interfaces, you reduce the risk of shared-state bugs and keep internal logic flexible. You can upgrade, optimize, or replace internals without breaking the rest of the system, because your contracts stay intact.

CASE STUDY

As Airbnb grew from a travel booking site into a global platform supporting experiences, payments, messaging, and fraud detection, its original monolithic Rails application became increasingly difficult to scale. Teams often found themselves stepping on each other's toes, changes to pricing would unintentionally affect booking flows, and analytics logic was scattered across modules that also handled business logic.

To regain control, Airbnb restructured around the principle of Separation of Concerns by adopting a domain-driven microservice architecture. Core business capabilities like search, reservation, pricing, messaging, and payments were isolated into their own bounded context, with dedicated teams responsible for the code and the underlying data models. Instead of centralizing all logic in one place, each service became a self-contained unit with a well-defined API contract. Booking services didn't touch the recommendation engine. Fraud detection had its own models and infrastructure, separate from transaction processing. Teams stopped patching shared logic and started evolving services independently.

This separation extended to their deployment pipelines and continuous integration (CI) workflows. Since concerns were decoupled, services could be tested, deployed, and scaled independently. Airbnb saw fewer incidents caused by unintended side effects. By embedding SoC into both its architecture and organizational structure, Airbnb built a foundation for continuous product evolution at scale.

IN PRACTICE

Applying SoC begins with structural intent. You choose an architecture that supports separation, be it layered, hexagonal, or microservice, and within that structure, you group logic by responsibility, not by technical type. A controller and a service that serve the same domain live together, while unrelated utility classes go elsewhere.

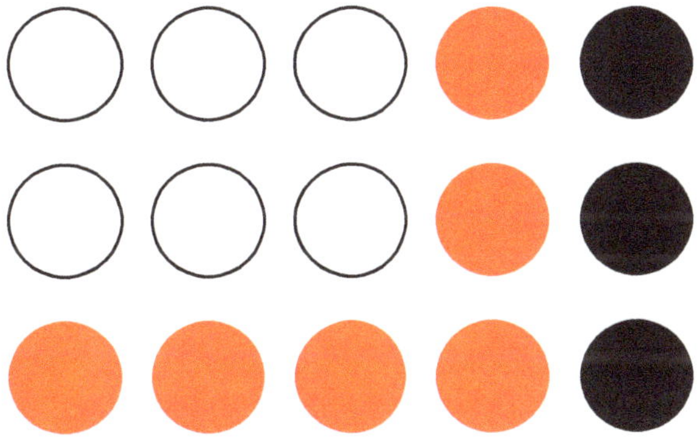

Figure 09 – Separation of Concerns (SOC)

You draw boundaries in code and ownership. If two developers routinely modify the same module for unrelated reasons, that module is doing too much. The goal is to create self-contained units of logic that can be tested and deployed independently. Interfaces serve as contracts between modules. They define what each component exposes and what it hides. You don't expose database internals to your UI, just as you wouldn't ask a payment gateway to format HTML. You protect every layer's internal detail so each can evolve on its own terms.

Separation of concerns is not a one-time setup. As your system evolves, boundaries will blur, especially when shortcuts are taken to meet deadlines. Refactoring is part of the discipline. You revisit the structure, realign responsibilities, and make sure concerns stay isolated as complexity grows.

COMMON PITFALLS

You can overdo SoC. Breaking every feature into its own abstraction may satisfy architectural purity, but it can overwhelm new contributors and slow down velocity. A balance must be struck. You separate concerns to simplify reasoning, not to create academic elegance. On the other hand, tight coupling can also masquerade as convenience. Modules that share internal state, bypass interfaces, or lean too heavily on global configuration violate the spirit of SoC. These shortcuts create heavy dependencies that are hard to scale.

SUCCESS INDICATORS

You know the separation of concerns is working when development becomes more fluid. Features move faster because engineers aren't wading through unrelated logic. Bugs become easier to trace because responsibilities are contained. Testing becomes more focused because each module has a narrow purpose. Refactoring becomes welcoming because the code is well-encapsulated and safe to reshape.

On the people side, ownership becomes clearer. Collaboration becomes easier. Systems evolve without regressions or rewrites. Separation in action will start influencing how your team thinks about the product.

SUMMARY

Separation of Concerns is a foundation for sustainable software. It's the difference between systems that sprawl and systems that scale. This principle gives your system the structure it needs to grow, adapt, and stay dependable. When responsibilities are clearly defined and thoughtfully enforced, code becomes easier to change and own. You spend less time untangling logic and more time building what matters. As your software expands, SoC ensures the system doesn't collapse under its own weight.

REFERENCES

L. Constantine and E. Yourdon, *Structured Design: Fundamentals of a Discipline of Computer Program and Systems Design,* Prentice Hall, 1979.

M. Richards and N. Ford, *Fundamentals of Software Architecture: An Engineering Approach,* O'Reilly Media, 2020.

F. Buschmann, R. Meunier, H. Rohnert, P. Sommerlad, and M. Stal, *Pattern-Oriented Software Architecture: A System of Patterns*, Wiley, 1996.

S. Liu, "Airbnb at Scale: From Monolith to Microservices" [Video]. InfoQ/QCon Plus 2022, YouTube, posted 2023. https://www.youtube.com/watch?v=PIw1WF1UXNc

10 • Command-Query Separation

"Clear is kind. Unclear is unkind." — Brené Brown

INTRODUCTION

This principle extends *Separation of Concerns* by focusing specifically on read and write operations. The Command-Query Separation (CQS) principle, first articulated by Bertrand Meyer, emphasizes a simple but powerful rule: separate operations that modify state from those that merely retrieve information. By maintaining a clear distinction between commands and queries, CQS enhances software systems' predictability, readability, and maintainability. When each method or service has a single, well-understood responsibility, systems become easier to follow and ultimately more robust.

CQS can be compared to the natural order in a restaurant. Asking what is on the menu is fundamentally different from ordering a dish. One is informational, the other triggers a change in the kitchen. Mixing the two leads to mistakes. In the same way, software that fails to separate commands from queries causes hidden side effects and increased complexity.

KEY CONCEPT

At its core, command-query separation draws a hard line between two types of operations. Commands perform actions that alter the system's internal state but do not return data. Queries retrieve data without changing any state. Following this separation ensures that when a method is called, its behavior is immediately predictable: either it changes the system or reads from it, but never both.

Consider a method like *createUser*. As a command, it modifies the state by adding a new user to the database. In contrast, *getUserById* is a query that safely retrieves user information without affecting the system's internal structure. Problems arise when a method attempts to do both. A method named *getAndLogUserActivity* might appear harmless, but it could introduce side effects by writing access logs or updating statistics behind the scenes. This violates CQS, leaving the caller uncertain whether multiple invocations are safe.

By adhering to CQS, methods like *getUserActivity* remain pure queries, free from hidden consequences, while actions like *logUserAccess* are isolated as explicit commands. This transparency makes system behavior clear and intentional, forming a foundation for reliable, maintainable codebases.

CASE STUDY

The clear implementation of CQS principles can be seen in Netflix's internal API structures. Managing millions of user profiles, watch histories, and preferences requires a system that can handle vast read and write traffic reliably and at scale. To address this, Netflix segregated operations cleanly. APIs handling user profile updates were strictly command-based and responsible for validating and mutating stored data without returning more than minimal confirmation responses. Separate read APIs retrieved profile data without side effects, ensuring that applications could cache and optimize queries without risking data corruption.

This strict adherence to CQS allowed Netflix to scale user personalization features confidently. New services consuming user data could rely on consistent, non-mutating reads. Update flows became simpler to audit and understand. Ultimately, Netflix's clear separation between commands and queries helped maintain high system reliability, rapid development velocity, and a seamless user experience at a global scale.

WHY IT MATTERS

Uncertainty is one of the greatest enemies of reliable software development. When developers cannot easily discern whether a method mutates state or simply retrieves data, the entire system becomes difficult to understand, test, and debug. The CQS principle eliminates this ambiguity at its source. Clear separation reduces hidden side effects. Tracing and understanding system mutations become straightforward when every state change is confined to an explicit command. Debugging improves as developers no longer need to chase subtle state alterations hidden within seemingly safe read operations.

Predictability also drives faster development. Engineers can immediately tell whether it is safe to call a method repeatedly, cache its result, or integrate it into asynchronous workflows. Queries become naturally idempotent and safe for repeated execution, while commands clearly signal their impact.

Testability also improves substantially. Read-only queries are easy to verify independently, without complex setup or teardown. Commands can be tested in isolation for their effect on state, allowing for more focused, meaningful unit tests.

Finally, CQS aligns naturally with broader architectural practices. In RESTful APIs, for instance, *HTTP GET* maps directly to queries, while *POST*, *PUT*, and *DELETE* align with commands. Following CQS internally reinforces these external interfaces, creating coherent, predictable systems both inside and out.

IN PRACTICE

Implementing CQS isn't about rewriting your entire system. It's about practicing a design discipline as you build. Start by auditing your method signatures. Look for methods that do more than one thing, and refactor them into clear, separate operations. Any method that returns data should avoid causing side effects. Any method that changes state shouldn't also return retrieved data.

During development, bring this up in code reviews. Ask explicitly whether each method is purely a command or purely a query. That habit raises awareness across the team and keeps the principle front of mind. Reflect the same clarity in your API design. Use *HTTP GET* for reads only. Use *POST*, *PUT*, or for commands that change state. When your API behavior is consistent, you make life easier on both the client and the server. On the frontend, the same rule applies. Functions that fetch data shouldn't also update UI state, trigger animations, or dispatch logs. Keeping retrieval pure and separating change-driven actions makes your UI more predictable and consistent.

In larger systems, CQS can grow into CQRS (command-query-responsibility segregation), where you separate entire read and write models to improve scalability and performance. You don't always need that extra weight. Still, the foundation is the same: one operation, one purpose.

COMMON PITFALLS

Applying CQS can go wrong if misunderstood or overapplied. One common mistake is overengineering small systems by introducing CQRS patterns prematurely. In simple create, read, update, and delete (CRUD) applications, the overhead of completely separate read and write models may outweigh the benefits. CQS should guide design, but the principle must be applied pragmatically.

Another pitfall is inconsistency between method naming and behavior. If a method's name implies a query but actually causes side effects, you are breaking the CQS. Developers calling such methods cannot rely on their intuition, leading to mistakes and debugging difficulties. On the frontend, mixing retrieval and mutation in UI components remains a frequent source of subtle bugs. Fetching data should not accidentally trigger state transitions, workflows, or logs. Keeping user interface actions and data access separate preserves clarity and prevents confusing side effects.

SUCCESS INDICATORS

The benefits of adopting CQS manifest clearly over time. Debugging becomes more surgical, as developers can focus directly on either read paths or write paths without second-guessing hidden effects. Code reviews accelerate because intent is visible at a glance, commands modify state, queries do not. Unit tests become cleaner and more focused, targeting single responsibilities without sprawling setup require-

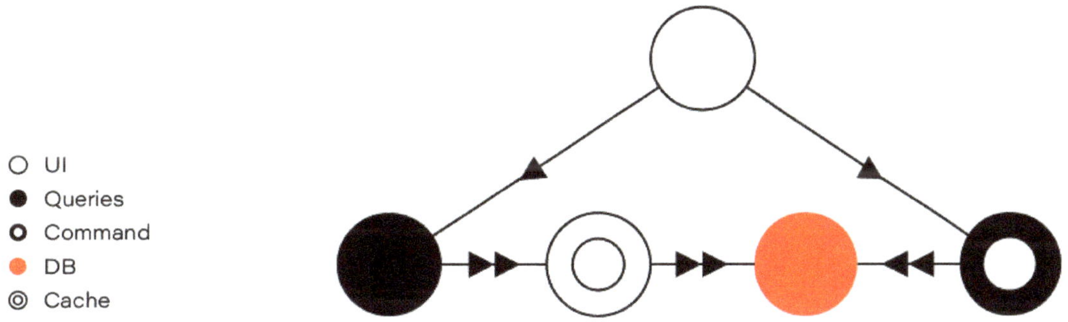

Figure 10 – Command, Query, Responsibility, Segregation (CQRS)

ments. System performance also improves, as reads and writes can be optimized separately when needed.

In large-scale systems, the transition from CQS to CQRS enables architectures that scale reads horizontally without burdening write operations, supporting better throughput and responsiveness. Above all, clear separation of commands and queries builds a deep, systemic trust within the engineering team. Developers work faster and safer because they know, intuitively and reliably, what their systems are supposed to do.

SUMMARY

The Command–Query Separation principle fosters predictability, testability, and maintainability by clearly distinguishing between methods that alter state and those that only retrieve information. Whether designing backend services, frontend logic, or APIs, applying CQS clarifies system behavior, reduces hidden side effects, and strengthens long-term system health. Over time, this discipline supports scalable architectures and accelerates development. Clear intent leads to clear execution, and clear execution leads to reliable software.

REFERENCES

B. Meyer, *Object-Oriented Software Construction*, 2nd ed., Prentice Hall, 2000.

E. Yemelyanau and J. Grice, "Netflix Tudum Architecture: From CQRS with Kafka to CQRS with RAW Hollow," *Netflix TechBlog*, 2025. https://netflixtechblog.com/netflix-tudum-architecture-from-cqrs-with-kafka-to-cqrs-with-raw-hollow-86d141b72e52

11 • High Cohesion and Low Coupling

"The parts must be adapted to the whole but not enslaved by it."— Marcus Aurelius

INTRODUCTION

High cohesion and low coupling are two foundational principles that guide software toward being more maintainable and scalable. They build on the Separation of Concerns principle, and often appear side by side with it because they reinforce each other. Cohesion is about how well a module's responsibilities align. Low coupling is about how little it depends on other parts of the system. Used together, they promote modular design and increased flexibility.

When cohesion is high, everything inside a module serves a single, focused purpose. When coupling is low, that module can be changed or replaced without untangling half the system. Together, they form the backbone of systems that are modular and easier to evolve safely.

KEY CONCEPT

A cohesive module focuses on one responsibility and handles it fully. It doesn't blur boundaries or mix unrelated concerns. A well-structured *UserAuthService*, for example, manages logins, password resets, and token handling, all of which are closely related concerns. Those operations share a purpose and are easier to test and improve together. By contrast, putting login, user profile editing, and analytics tracking in the same class would spread focus and dilute clarity.

Coupling is about dependency. A tightly coupled module might rely on another's internal logic or data structures, making both harder to modify. Loose coupling avoids that by using clean interfaces and reducing shared knowledge. Instead of directly calling a method buried in another service, a module relies on a stable contract. This makes interactions predictable, and changes in one part don't cascade through the rest.

Together, cohesion and coupling give you leverage. High cohesion improves internal clarity. Low coupling improves external flexibility. You gain modules that are easier to build and swap out.

WHY IT MATTERS

High cohesion and low coupling localize risk. When a module does one thing well, it's easier to read, test, and refactor. When that module has minimal ties to others, changes become safe and predictable. Debugging improves because issues have more precise boundaries. Teams move independently, without stepping on each other's work.

You don't need perfect cohesion or perfect decoupling to see the benefits. Even incremental moves toward better separation reduce overhead and improve pliability in the system.

IN PRACTICE

You start by designing each module with a single, clear purpose. That intent should come through in its name, the scope of its methods, and the responsibilities it holds. You don't mix unrelated concerns just because it feels convenient. For example, a product inventory module shouldn't handle pricing logic. A notification handler shouldn't perform user lookups. That separation gives your system room to grow.

Keep modules isolated through interfaces. When one part of the system needs to call another, it should go through an abstraction. That way, the caller doesn't care how the work gets done. It only depends on the contract. If the implementation changes later, the interface shields the rest of the codebase.

As your system evolves, refactor as needed before the code settles into the wrong shape. During reviews, ask if the responsibilities are focused and if the dependencies still make sense. If needed, you group related logic together, even if it means creating a new file, class, or service. The goal is to structure your software so that one part can change without sending others into failure. That's how cohesion and coupling turn into real-world leverage.

COMMON PITFALLS

Even good intentions can backfire if misunderstood. Sometimes teams split logic too aggressively, creating fragmented modules that make it harder to trace a feature end-to-end. Over-abstraction can also introduce unnecessary complexity. Keep the focus on clarity. Modules should be small enough to understand and large enough to be useful. Even interfaces can become a source of coupling when changes ripple

CASE STUDY

As Slack scaled its core messaging platform, engineering teams faced growing pains from early design decisions. Originally, much of the messaging logic, like delivery, formatting, presence status, and notification triggers, was intertwined in a shared messaging service. New features like threads and workflows slowed releases, made debugging harder, and blurred team ownership.

To address this, Slack re-architected its system around high cohesion and low coupling. The messaging pipeline was decomposed into well-defined, single-purpose services. One service handled message persistence and delivery. Another managed formatting and markdown parsing. A third controlled notifications and user presence. These components were highly cohesive. Each focused on a narrow concern with tightly related logic and communicated through clear, versioned APIs. This separation allowed teams to iterate independently. The notifications team could add "do not disturb" logic without touching core message delivery. The formatting engine could evolve to support new block elements without a risk of introducing delivery regressions. Internal service boundaries became contracts, and changes within one module rarely impacted others.

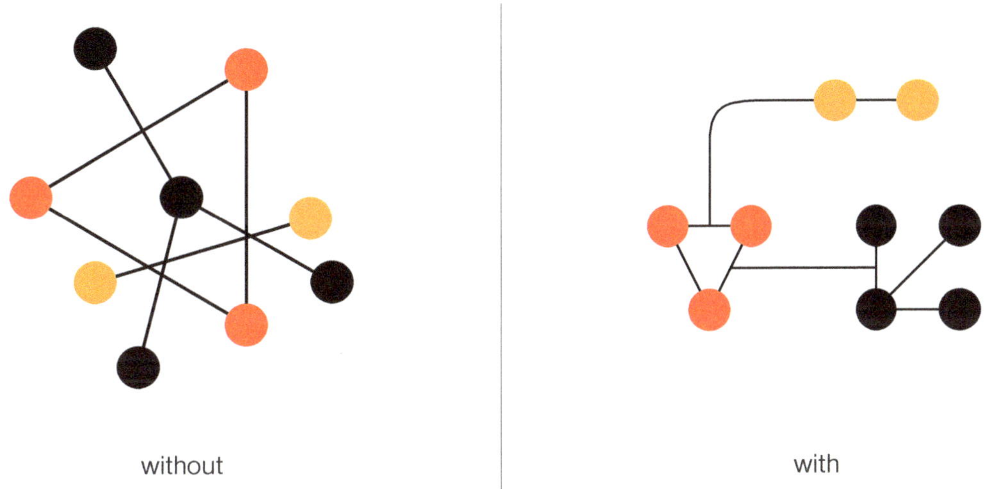

Figure 11 – High Cohesion & Low Coupling

through them often. You reduce this risk by keeping interfaces stable and limited to essential communication only. A subtler issue is interface leakage, when a module exposes too much of its internals to others, forcing dependent code to understand details it shouldn't care about. Watch for this during code reviews. Encapsulation is essential for preserving low coupling over time.

SUCCESS INDICATORS

Teams applying high cohesion and low coupling don't need elaborate coordination to work in parallel. Features move faster because changes stay confined. Testing becomes easier with well-scoped units and fewer dependencies to mock or manage. Refactors happen more frequently, not because they're needed urgently, but because they feel safe. Over time, the codebase remains healthy, complexity grows at a controlled rate, and every part of the system has a clear place and purpose.

SUMMARY

High cohesion and low coupling make software easier to understand, easier to test, and safer to evolve. Cohesion gives each module a clear, focused purpose. Coupling determines how safely modules can work together without stepping on each other. When you apply both principles, your code becomes more flexible and future-proof.

REFERENCES

L. Constantine and E. Yourdon, *Structured Design: Fundamentals of a Discipline of Computer Program and Systems Design*, Prentice Hall, 1979.

K. J. Lieberherr, I. Holland, and A. J. Riel, "Object-oriented Programming: An Objective Sense of Style," *ACM SIGPLAN Notices*, vol. 23, no. 11, pp. 323–334, 1988.

S. Panichella, M. I. Rahman, and D. Taibi, "Structural Coupling for Microservices," *arXiv*, 2021. https://doi.org/10.48550/arXiv.2103.04674

E. Stiller, "Real-Time Messaging Architecture at Slack," *InfoQ*, 2023. https://www.infoq.com/news/2023/04/real-time-messaging-slack/

12 · SOLID Design

"What is well planted cannot be uprooted." — Laozi, Tao Te Ching

INTRODUCTION

The SOLID principles offer a set of approaches for writing code so systems can stay simple and organized as features and the user base grow. By following the five object-oriented design guidelines described below, you can create systems that are easier to understand, extend, and maintain over time.

KEY CONCEPT

The SOLID acronym represents five key principles that encourage modular, flexible, and resilient design. Each one addresses a specific challenge that arises as systems scale. You will notice some overlap with earlier principles, and that's because they are pointing in the same direction.

The *Single Responsibility* principle states that each class or module should have exactly one reason to change. If a class handles logging, metrics, and API interaction all at once, it is doing too much. Separating those responsibilities into focused units makes testing and extending logic easier.

The *Open-Closed* principle guides us in designing software that is open for extension but closed for modification. Instead of editing existing code when requirements shift, you build on top of stable abstractions. This preserves existing functionality while making space for new behavior.

The *Liskov Substitution* principle ensures that subclasses behave in ways consistent with their parent classes. If a function accepts a base class, it should also accept any subclass without producing errors or altering the intended behavior. This consistency keeps inheritance relationships safe and reliable.

The *Interface Segregation* principle encourages the creation of small, focused interfaces instead of large, general-purpose ones. Classes should never be forced to implement methods they don't need. Smaller contracts reduce the surface area for bugs and improve code readability.

The *Dependency Inversion* principle promotes a shift from depending on concrete implementations to depending on abstractions. High-level modules should rely on interfaces or abstract classes, not specific services or tools. This separation makes systems easier to test and more flexible to adapt when requirements or technologies change.

When used together, these principles reduce tight coupling, enforce clear responsibilities, and support maintainability across a growing system.

CASE STUDY

Stripe's engineering team embraced SOLID principles incrementally, starting where it mattered most: payments. With dozens of providers to integrate, from Visa to Apple Pay to Klarna, they recognized that hardcoded logic would quickly become unmanageable. So instead of writing classes that directly depended on specific providers, they introduced interfaces that defined shared behaviors like charge authorization, refund processing, and error handling.

This aligned directly with the Open-Closed principle: core services remained stable while new payment providers were added as plug-in modules. It also demonstrated the Dependency Inversion principle, where high-level business logic depended on abstractions, not concrete implementations. Refactoring toward this design allowed Stripe to launch region-specific payment options quickly, test integrations in isolation, and evolve internal services without cross-system breakage. These weren't massive rewrites; they were deliberate, SOLID-aligned decisions made one interface at a time. This led to a payment platform that's fast to iterate, safe to scale, and easy to trust.

WHY IT MATTERS

Software that ignores these principles tends to calcify over time. Instead of evolving gracefully, the system resists change and slows progress. Each part of the SOLID design offers a growth path, and they compound with each other. The cumulative result is code that supports progress. Developers make changes with more freedom and agility. New features launch faster. Testing becomes more targeted, and the system evolves with intent instead of clutter.

IN PRACTICE

You don't adopt SOLID principles all at once. You grow into them through mindful refactoring, thoughtful architecture, and regular team alignment. Start by reviewing your codebase. Look for classes that are trying to do too much. Split them by responsibility. For example, separate data formatting from business logic and extract concerns like logging, authentication, or data persistence into their own modules or services.

As you introduce new features, resist the temptation to reach into existing classes and pile on more behavior. Instead, extend through composition or new implementations of existing interfaces. Create abstractions that reflect how your system needs to evolve. Design interfaces based on real use cases, not imagined flexibility. And wherever possible, write code that depends on behavior, not implementations. Testing can serve as a guide. If a class is difficult to mock or test in isolation, it may be doing too much or depending on too many details. The easier it is to test a component, the more likely it is to align with SOLID principles.

COMMON PITFALLS

While the SOLID principles are helpful, sometimes teams fall into the trap of adding abstractions too early before the system's needs are clear. Overusing inheritance, creating unnecessary interfaces, or prematurely fragmenting code can introduce more complexity.

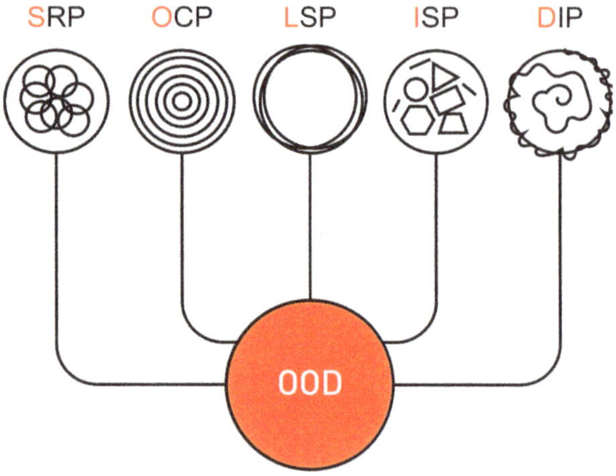

Figure 12 – SOLID: SOLID Design, Solid Systems

Also, inheritance itself should be leveraged carefully, as it can carry a lot more cognitive burden than initially realized.

Another common issue is neglecting the Single Responsibility principle in small but compounding ways. It often starts with a helper method or a one-off tweak. Before long, a class built for one task is doing three. These shifts feel harmless at the time, but eventually create convoluted logic. The solution isn't to apply SOLID dogmatically. It's to use each principle with judgment. The right time to refactor is when a pattern emerges. The right abstraction is the one that simplifies your current needs without hiding intent.

SUCCESS INDICATORS

When the SOLID principles are working, your system feels calm even under change. Developers can fix bugs and add features without tracing through cross-dependencies. Unit tests become precise and reliable because they target components with clear responsibilities. Interfaces are descriptive and minimal. Swapping out services or reusing logic in new contexts becomes routine, not risky.

The team spends less time asking, "What will this break?" and more time asking, "What should this do?" As software grows, the structure holds. That structure gives your team freedom to build, to adapt, and to move forward with speed.

SUMMARY

The SOLID principles aren't rules for perfect code. They are tools for creating sustainable software. By designing components that are focused, extensible, substitutable, and modular, you build systems that grow alongside your business needs. These principles help you reduce friction and isolate complexity. Good software design makes change easier and faster. That's the long-term value of SOLID.

REFERENCES

R. C. Martin, *Agile Software Development: Principles, Patterns, and Practices*, Prentice Hall, 2002.

M. Richards and N. Ford, *Fundamentals of Software Architecture*, O'Reilly Media, 2020.

B. Smith, "Introducing Stripe Workflows: Tailoring Payments to Your Business Needs," *Stripe Dev Blog*, May 7, 2025.

13 • Write Code That Writes Code

"The craftsman employs his tool; the wise man, his mind." — Seneca

INTRODUCTION

You didn't become a software engineer to repeat yourself manually. Yet without automation, that's often what happens. The principle of Write Code That Writes Code helps you step out of that loop. Instead of solving the same problem repeatedly, you encode the solution once and let the system replicate it. Whether you're generating APIs, spinning up infrastructure, or templating workflows, you replace repetition with automation and free your team to focus on what truly needs human insight.

This automation is about building leverage into your engineering practices. You shift your mindset from solving isolated problems to designing repeatable solutions. Over time, that shift speeds things up and, just as indispensably, it creates consistency and resilience in how your systems grow.

KEY CONCEPT

The heart of this principle lies in replacing repetitive manual work with systems that generate it for you. In practice, that might mean using command-line tools to scaffold services with standardized structure, building reusable templates for configurations, or adopting a declarative format like YAML to define system behavior. You might reach for metaprogramming, letting the code modify itself through decorators or macros. In more complex domains, it could mean defining a small internal language that abstracts intent and automatically generates implementation.

The expected outcome is always the same. Instead of rethinking the same file structure, test setup, or API signature, you rely on well-designed tools to do that part for you. Teams gain time and scale while reducing variability. The codebase begins to reflect intentional architecture, not a one-off effort, and every fix to a generator becomes a fix that ripples through the entire system.

WHY IT MATTERS

Automation is about saving time, and equally important, it's about protecting consistency and unlocking scale. When your team starts from shared scaffolding or templates, code becomes easier to read and debug. When structure is standardized, there are fewer places for edge-case bugs to hide and fewer reasons to revisit brittle, duplicated code. Automated generation also improves maintainability. Instead of fixing the same logic in twenty files, you fix it in one generator. That change propagates, reducing the cost and cognitive load of updates. Even subtle quality improvements like renaming a field or adjusting a security header become feasible at scale when they don't require a dozen manual edits.

This principle supports and reinforces others like DRY (Don't Repeat Yourself), infrastructure as code, and immutable infrastructure. It encourages a mindset of treating your system like a product: versioned, repeatable, auditable. When you build from a foundation like that, you are saving time and building something that scales cleanly and behaves predictably under growth.

IN PRACTICE

Applying this principle begins by identifying the patterns you repeat most often. When you notice developers spending time copy-pasting or recreating something that already exists, that's a sign that automation can help. Once you notice them, you start small. For example, you automate setting up a new service, defining an endpoint, or writing a test. You build or adapt a generator that encapsulates that structure and makes it easy to spin up a new instance with minimal effort.

Templates are just as powerful. Maintaining a central template repository ensures consistency across teams for recurring configurations, test cases, or document formats. These templates evolve with the project, becoming smarter and more aligned with your architecture over time. Declarative formats are another effective tool. Instead of scripting behavior step by step, define the desired outcome and let the tooling handle the details. Infrastructure-as-code platforms follow this model. They translate clean declarations into predictable, reproducible results.

Metaprogramming can also reduce boilerplate, but it demands caution. Macros, annotations, and decorators can simplify codebases, but when overused or poorly documented, they obscure logic and raise the cost of debugging. Apply them where they improve clarity, and always ensure the generated behavior is easy to inspect.

Across all of this, the key is transparency. Generated code should be clear, inspectable, and version-controlled. Developers need to understand what is generated, why it exists, and how to override it when necessary. That's what transforms automation from an opaque process into a trusted tool.

CASE STUDY

GitHub's engineering teams encountered the same repetitive setup challenges that were common across organizations. For example, creating new microservices, documentation sites, or CI workflows often meant copy-pasting from past projects and tweaking by hand. Recognizing this inefficiency, they leaned into the principle of Write Code That Writes Code by adopting template repositories. Templates were predefined, version-controlled starting points for different types of projects.

These templates acted as transparent generators. Each one encoded organization-wide standards across file structure, naming conventions, starter logic, and security checks, so that every new project began with the right foundation. As the company evolved, these templates were updated like any other code: versioned and continuously improved.

This aligned tightly with their shift toward declarative setup, automation-first culture, and scalable onboarding. New engineers could get a service up and running in minutes, not days. Templates reduced boilerplate, avoided inconsistencies, and helped teams focus on product logic instead of setup friction. GitHub codified best practices into reusable assets, turning automation into institutional memory.

COMMON PITFALLS

The power of this principle can quickly become a liability if not managed carefully. One risk is starting with unstable patterns. If your templates or generators are based on logic that's still evolving, automating them too early can lock in bad decisions or cause wide-reaching regressions. It's better to wait until the pattern is proven and repeatable before encoding it into tooling.

Lack of transparency is another risk. When developers don't know where the code came from or how to modify it, frustration builds, and trust in the system breaks down. Every automated path must be documented and understandable to the team maintaining it. There's also the danger of neglect. As systems evolve, so must your templates and generators. If the tooling lags behind your actual architecture, it creates fragmentation rather than consistency. Regular reviews and tight integration with your CI workflows can help avoid this.

Also, not every problem needs a domain-specific language or generator. Start with simple, useful automation and let it grow organically from actual need. When your automation supports the team instead of hobbling it, you know you've struck the right balance.

SUCCESS INDICATORS

You'll notice this principle working when developers stop dreading repetitive tasks and start focusing on meaningful ones. Bootstrapping a new service or feature feels fast and predictable. Fewer bugs appear in early development because foundational logic comes pre-validated. Your test coverage improves because tests follow a consistent structure. Reviews become easier because the structure no longer varies arbitrarily. Your team begins to think more like system designers than one-off implementers and focuses on building tools that build solutions.

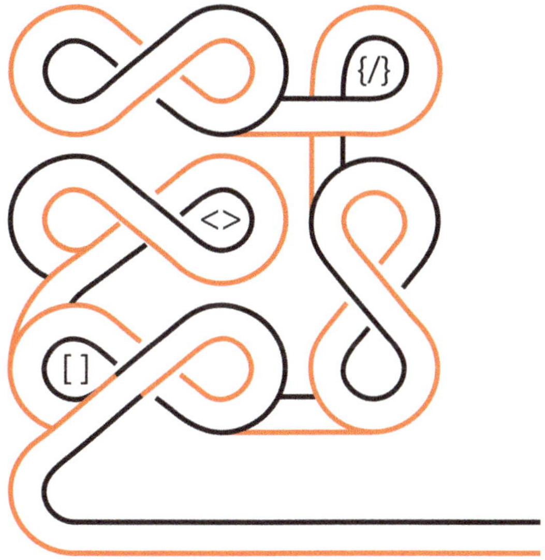

Figure 13 – Write Code That Writes Code

SUMMARY

Write Code That Writes Code is a principle rooted in efficiency, consistency, and long-term scale. It helps teams encode repeatable patterns, remove human error, and focus on meaningful work. By automating the predictable, you free yourself to solve the complex. Good developers write clean code. Great developers build systems that write it for them.

REFERENCES

E. Murphy-Hill, C. Parnin, and A.P. Black, "How We Refactor, and How We Know It," *IEEE Transactions on Software Engineering*, vol. 38, no. 1, pp. 5–18, 2012.

K. Hotta, Y. Sasaki, Y. Sano, Y. Higo, and S. Kusumoto, "An Empirical Study on the Impact of Duplicate Code," *Advances in Software Engineering*, pp 1–22, 2012.

GitHub, "Creating a Template Repository," *GitHub Docs*, retrieved July 25, 2025, from https://docs.github.com/en/repositories/creating-and-managing-repositories/creating-a-template-repository.

14 • Don't Reinvent the Wheel

"If I have seen further, it is by standing on the shoulders of giants."— Isaac Newton

INTRODUCTION

In software development, originality isn't always the goal. Reinventing existing solutions wastes time, increases risk, and pulls focus away from what matters most: delivering distinct value. The Don't Reinvent the Wheel principle encourages teams to reuse proven technologies, patterns, and systems instead of building everything from scratch. When done thoughtfully, this approach frees up time and energy for solving the unique problems that actually set your product apart.

KEY CONCEPT

This principle is about reuse over reinvention. Core systems like authentication, logging, orchestration, caching, and configuration appear in nearly every application. Unless your business depends on rethinking them, you're better off adopting what's already battle-tested. Libraries, frameworks, cloud platforms, open-source tools, and internal shared services exist for a reason: they reflect decades of hard-earned engineering lessons. When you adopt them, you inherit their maturity, community support, and optimization without paying the cost of building and maintaining them yourself.

The core value should come from what you build on top of this foundation, not from rebuilding the foundation itself.

WHY IT MATTERS

Reinventing the wheel wastes effort, and it adds long-term drag. Custom tools require more documentation, testing, training, and bug fixes. Even well-intentioned reinvention introduces fragmentation across teams. One group might build a custom scheduler, another a bespoke logging system, and neither will interoperate cleanly with the rest of the stack. In time, duplication becomes tech debt.

Adopting proven tools helps avoid these issues. It keeps systems leaner, faster to build, easier to debug, and more predictable at scale. Better yet, shared tools create shared knowledge. It's easier to align teams, accelerate onboarding, and transfer institutional knowledge.

IN PRACTICE

When you start, assume a solution already exists. Before designing a new system, ask whether an open-source library, internal utility, or platform service already solves the problem. Evaluate existing tools against your needs and choose the one that fits best without jumping to customization. If a tool covers

Figure 14 – Do Not Reinvent The Wheel

most of what you need, use it. Build your own only when the problem is central to your product and the alternatives clearly fall short.

Promote shared practices across teams. Create internal libraries and reusable modules to reduce duplication. Encourage teams to document and share solutions that prove useful more than once. Use loosely coupled interfaces so tools can be swapped out when they no longer fit. However, avoid blind adoption. Every dependency should be monitored and maintainable. The point of reuse is to keep your effort focused where it makes the most impact.

CASE STUDY

When Netflix faced scaling challenges during its global expansion, the team didn't default to building proprietary infrastructure. Instead, they applied the reuse mindset systematically. Rather than reinvent compute, storage, or delivery pipelines, Netflix migrated to Amazon Web Services and adopted EC2, S3, and CloudFront as foundational building blocks. These services covered the bulk of their needs with minimal customization.

For distributed systems, Netflix reused proven technologies like Apache Cassandra for database scaling, Apache Kafka for streaming data, and Spring Boot for microservices. Even its approach to failure testing followed this pattern. Chaos Monkey, originally an internal tool, was built on top of the existing ecosystem and later shared with the open-source community.

This allowed Netflix engineers to spend less time solving solved problems and more time focusing on improving their product. The company's ability to innovate at scale came not from building everything itself, but from reusing well-established tools and extending them only where it truly added value. Netflix's approach is a good example of the principle in action. Reuse first, reinvent only when necessary.

COMMON PITFALLS

Sometimes, teams over-customize adopted tools until they become as difficult to maintain as homegrown solutions. Others skip due diligence and adopt tools that don't scale or lack support. Still others build something bespoke without realizing a shared internal tool already exists. These traps all stem from the same issue: not pausing to ask, "Has someone already solved this well?"

Avoiding reinvention doesn't mean giving up control. It means recognizing that originality should be reserved for what makes your software special, not for the plumbing beneath it.

SUCCESS INDICATORS

You'll know this principle is working when systems are easier to maintain, onboarding is faster, and teams focus more on product features than on rewriting common infrastructure. Teams spend less time chasing bugs in homegrown code and more time tuning performance, improving UX, and shipping features that move the business forward. Shared libraries and standard tooling become accelerators. The engineering organization feels aligned because everyone speaks the same technical language.

SUMMARY

Don't Reinvent the Wheel is about engineering focus. When you rely on proven solutions, you give your team room to build what really matters: experiences, features, and logic unique to your users. With DRW, use what works, adapt when needed, and invent only when it creates clear value.

REFERENCES

P. Mohagheghi and R. Conradi, "An Empirical Software Reuse Benefits in a Large Telecom Project," *ACM Transactions on Software Engineering and Methodology*, 17(3), 1–31, 2008. https://doi.org/10.1145/1375642.1375644

E. Gamma, R. Helm, R. Johnson, and J. Vlissides, *Design Patterns: Elements of Reusable Object-Oriented Software*. Addison-Wesley Professional, 1994.

N. Hunt, "Netflix Case Study: Netflix Innovation with AWS," *Amazon Web Services*, 2016. https://aws.amazon.com/solutions/case-studies/netflix-case-study/

15 • Concurrency vs. Parallelism

"Order is heaven's first law."— Alexander Pope

INTRODUCTION

Concurrency and parallelism are often mentioned together but treating them interchangeably leads to inefficiency and unpredictable systems. Concurrency is about structuring software so that multiple tasks make progress without blocking each other. It manages the logical complexity of multitasking. Parallelism is about achieving speed and executing multiple tasks simultaneously across cores or machines to maximize hardware utilization. These are not rival ideas. They are distinct strategies that, when applied thoughtfully, create performant and scalable systems. Mastering this distinction is vital for building applications that grow with reliability and resilience.

KEY CONCEPT

Concurrency structures tasks to move forward independently, even if not simultaneously. It is the art of making progress on multiple activities through scheduling, context switching, or interleaving without requiring them to finish simultaneously. Parallelism, by contrast, is the physical reality of performing computations simultaneously, leveraging multiple processors or machines to achieve greater throughput. Concurrency organizes. Parallelism accelerates.

Understanding this distinction matters because concurrency without careful management often leads to shared state issues. It can cause multiple threads or functions to interfere with one another, causing race conditions or subtle, hard-to-reproduce failures. This is why a shared mutable state is considered a fundamental hazard in concurrent systems. Systems should avoid it wherever possible. This approach dramatically reduces complexity by isolating concerns, making concurrent systems easier to understand and scale.

WHY IT MATTERS

Without mastering concurrency and parallelism as separate concerns, teams build systems that fail under load, spend excessive effort debugging concurrency issues, or lose the ability to evolve confidently. Conflating task organization with execution speed creates architectures where scaling becomes unpredictable, and simple failures balloon into major outages. Proper concurrency management improves responsiveness and reliability. Harnessing parallelism correctly unlocks raw performance gains without creating instability.

When concurrency is modeled carefully and actors manage encapsulated state, systems remain predictable under pressure. When parallelism is layered correctly onto a concurrent structure, throughput improves without hidden risks. These principles become even more critical at scale.

IN PRACTICE

Building concurrency into a system starts by selecting frameworks and languages that support non-blocking execution models. Teams use concurrency primitives like *async/await*, futures, and coroutines to schedule task execution cleanly, without assuming those tasks will run simultaneously. Parallelism comes into play when applications leverage multi-core processors or distributed systems to run computations in true parallel.

Choosing the right model also means minimizing shared state. Immutability, defensive copying, and explicit message-passing patterns reduce the chance of silent conflicts. One proven strategy for safe concurrency is the actor model. Instead of allowing free access to shared memory, actors encapsulate their state and communicate exclusively via asynchronous message passing. Systems that embrace the actor model structure concurrency as a series of isolated actors communicating asynchronously, making coordination predictable and local. Effective parallelism uses tools that understand the hardware. Libraries like OpenMP, CUDA, or Java's forkJoin framework execute tasks across cores or GPUs only when the underlying concurrency structure supports safe, independent execution.

Even in highly parallel systems, observability is essential. Teams must monitor thread saturation, contention rates, and queue backlogs to validate that concurrency remains healthy under load. Sophisticated applications treat concurrency as first-class architecture and parallelism as an optimization layer, not the other way around.

CASE STUDY

At Twitter (X), handling millions of concurrent interactions and real-time computations across a massive user base forced the company to design for concurrency and parallelism as distinct, complementary challenges. To manage user requests, including tweets, likes, retweets, and notifications, the engineering team structured their services to handle concurrency through asynchronous programming models, ensuring that user-facing interactions never block one another unnecessarily. They adopted Scala's Akka framework, bringing the actor model to the forefront and enabling services to handle concurrency without relying on shared mutable state.

On the parallelism front, computationally intensive tasks such as timeline generation, spam detection, and real-time analytics were distributed across thousands of cores and machines. By parallelizing workloads like ranking tweets or analyzing trends, Twitter achieved performance at a global scale. The clear separation of concerns meant that concurrency management reduced internal contention, while parallelism delivered high throughput for batch and real-time computations. As a result, Twitter could provide low-latency interactions to millions of users while scaling horizontally with growing demand.

Their experience showed that systems achieve both reliability and speed not by treating concurrency and parallelism as synonyms, but by respecting their unique contributions and designing for both.

Figure 15 – Concurrency & Parellelism

COMMON PITFALLS

Mistaking concurrency for parallelism leads to logically messy and physically inefficient architectures. Developers who assume that asynchronous scheduling automatically means faster execution often overlook bottlenecks at the CPU or network level. Systems built without isolating shared state suffer from race conditions that only surface under high concurrency, creating debugging nightmares. Excessive reliance on locks, mutexes, and semaphores adds complexity that chokes performance instead of helping it. Ignoring frameworks like the actor model, favoring raw thread management introduces unnecessary coordination challenges. Ultimately, these mistakes accumulate into sickly systems that neither scale well nor fail gracefully.

SUCCESS INDICATORS

The successful application of these principles helps achieve predictable behavior under heavy concurrency. Requests and operations do not interfere with one another, even at peak load. Performance profiling shows increased throughput when tasks are parallelized correctly. Incidents of race conditions or deadlocks sharply decline because the shared state is minimized or eliminated. Teams can roll out new services and features without major regression, knowing that concurrency is well-managed and parallelism is used as an actual performance enhancer. Over time, the system supports greater scale, faster deployments, and more resilient operations without increasing complexity.

SUMMARY

Understanding and respecting the difference between concurrency and parallelism is a key skill for building modern software systems. Concurrency organizes tasks so work progresses without blocking, while parallelism accelerates that work across available compute resources. Systems that avoid shared state and embrace isolation patterns like the actor model benefit from greater stability, faster debugging, and easier scaling. Mastering this distinction separates systems that survive under load from those that stumble with scale. By building concurrency into your architecture and layering parallelism on top, you design systems ready for the future, irrespective of how fast that future arrives.

REFERENCES

C. Hewitt, "Actor Model of Computation: Scalable Robust Information Systems," *arXiv*, 2010 (last revised 2015). https://doi.org/10.48550/arXiv.1008.1459

Scrums.com Editorial Team, "Parallelism and Concurrency in Engineering," *Scrums.com*, 2024. https://www.scrums.com/software-engineering/parallelism-and-concurrency-in-engineering

S. Kumari, "How Twitter Leverages Scala Programming for its Massive Platform!" *LinkedIn*, 2024. https://www.linkedin.com/pulse/how-twitter-leverages-scala-programming-its-massive-platform-kumari-wkmxc

III THE INVISIBLE ARCHITECTURE

"The music is not in the notes, but in the silence between."
— Wolfgang Amadeus Mozart

Every system has a structure you can see. The interfaces are named, the modules are clear, and the components are drawn on design diagrams. These choices are discussed and documented. That's the part of the design that's easy to point to. Every system also has a structure you can't see, and that part matters just as much.

In visual art, negative space helps define the image. In writing, pauses and white space shape how the message lands. In systems, the same principle applies. The invisible choices shape how the whole thing behaves, especially under the strain of new features or increased system load.

You won't always find these decisions in documentation. You'll notice them in how easily something can be changed, scaled, or understood, how one module stays insulated from another, or in how a boundary absorbs complexity without letting it leak into the rest of the system.

Make no mistake, these invisible choices define the experience for both customers and engineers, even if they rarely get called out. That's the invisible part of the architecture. The better you are at it, the less likely anyone is to notice. It won't draw attention or accolades, but it's the kind of design that stands the test of time.

The people who will recognize this work are the ones who've spent time in it. They've built things, fought through outages, and fixed code they didn't write. They know what it takes to build something resilient. They understand the value of thoughtful separation, even when it isn't obvious or visible right away.

Mastering this kind of design means paying attention to what's not said. You may start noticing how teams get work done, where code gets reused, and where responsibility lives. You take these and other insights and design for function, but also for space.

This is why certain principles matter more than they first appear. For example, encapsulation, abstraction, the Law of Demeter, composition over inheritance, dependency injection, and inversion of control are just different ways of protecting the space around each part of the system so other parts have room to grow.

As you go through the principles ahead, I hope you remember this unstated, hard-to-pinpoint elegance. When you're deciding how much context a component needs to do its job, or when you're managing how much one part should know about another, aim to create conditions that make future work easier, not harder.

Over time, as your skills grow, I hope you begin to notice the empty space and the boundaries that keep things clean just as clearly as what's on the design diagram. Those spaces and boundaries hold systems together. In the end, it's both: the work you can and can't see working together produces the work that lasts.

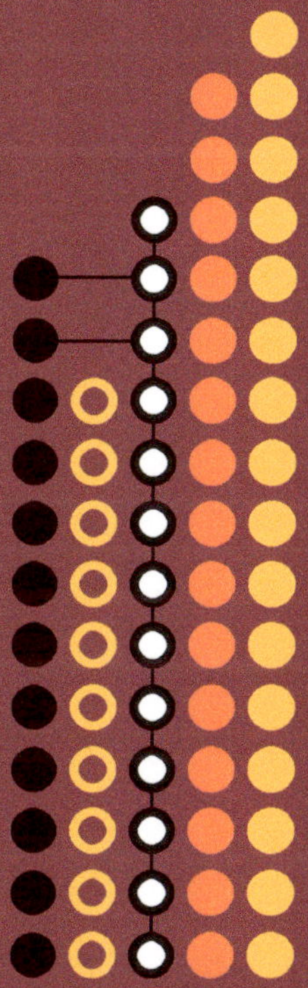

16 • Encapsulate with Abstractions

"The height of wisdom is to conceal it."— Baltasar Gracián

INTRODUCTION

You do not need to understand how a microwave converts electricity into heat to operate it. You simply set a timer, press Start, and trust it will work. Software should offer the same simplicity. When systems expose only what is necessary and hide the rest, they become easier to use and easier to change. That is the essence of this principle.

Encapsulation and abstraction, when combined thoughtfully, build systems with clarity and flexibility. Abstractions allow you to interact with a system through predictable interfaces without knowing internal complexities. Encapsulation protects these complexities, ensuring that internal changes do not ripple outward and create dependencies with other components. In fast-moving teams and evolving systems, this structure reduces defects and enables safe iteration. You can replace or improve internals without touching every part of the codebase. Respecting the boundary between what should change and remain stable becomes the foundation for building systems that last.

KEY CONCEPT

Abstraction defines what a system does, while encapsulation protects how it does it. Together, they encourage software structures where users and other systems interact through minimal, clear interfaces, without needing, or being able, to tamper with underlying mechanics. Proper encapsulation hides volatile details, minimizes the surface area for failure, and enables isolated improvements. A well-designed module defines clean inputs, outputs, and responsibilities while safely keeping business rules, data structures, and internal logic behind those contracts. Effective abstraction also avoids leaking internal decisions through names or behaviors, focusing instead on role and intent. When built well, these structures resist accidental misuse and make correct usage the natural, easy path.

WHY IT MATTERS

Systems that expose internal implementations create easy-to-break cross dependencies. Changing one component often triggers unexpected failures elsewhere, slowing development and making changes risky. Without strong encapsulation, systems grow increasingly shaky as they scale. Every improvement demands more coordination, regression testing, and defensive coding against invisible contracts.

Abstractions and encapsulation counter this by defining clear interfaces and shielding internal mechanics. Teams gain the ability to change or replace components independently. Testing becomes simpler because mocks or stubs can target predictable con-

CASE STUDY

When MediaTek, a Taiwanese fabless semiconductor company, entered the mobile chipset market, it faced a key challenge: enabling rapid product development for phone makers with limited engineering resources. Instead of exposing the full complexity of modem firmware and hardware integration, MediaTek encapsulated these layers behind a tightly controlled set of abstractions.

They offered a complete package, reference hardware, plus a proprietary software platform that spanned the OS to dialer functions. This lets manufacturers build and ship customized phones quickly, using clean APIs and ready-to-use templates without needing to understand the internals.

Crucially, this approach enabled both speed and control. MediaTek could upgrade core components like modems or codecs without disrupting downstream partners. By hiding complexity behind stable interfaces, MediaTek scaled to support hundreds of device variations, showing how abstraction and encapsulation can power fast, flexible innovation.

tracts. Collaboration improves as different teams work confidently behind shared, stable boundaries without stepping on one another's work. Code review shifts from inspecting internal to verifying external behavior. Ultimately, abstraction and encapsulation transform the codebase from a web of thin threads into a network of clear, maintainable parts that evolve safely over time.

IN PRACTICE

Applying this principle in practice means treating an interface as a promise that stakeholders and future systems can rely on without needing to know implementation details. It starts with you defining roles before any code is written. You design classes, modules, and services around what they provide, not how they deliver it. You keep the interface surfaces minimal, exposing only what collaborators truly need. Details like algorithms, data storage, and operational sequences remain private and protected behind these contracts.

You use naming conventions to reinforce boundaries and describe behaviors or roles, not internal mechanics. Internal names and structure stay flexible and can evolve without breaking external use. Patterns like Factory, Strategy, and Adapter can help you here because they promote clear encapsulation and interchangeable abstractions.

Internally, you and your team stay disciplined with access modifiers, modular file structures, and version-controlled public APIs so that you can keep improving and adjusting without affecting others. Interfaces change slowly by design, giving consumers stability while the code behind them continues to evolve.

COMMON PITFALLS

Poorly applying abstraction and encapsulation often causes more harm than good. Building interfaces for parts of the system that do not yet require flexibility creates a maintenance burden without a tangible benefit.

Premature generalization clutters the codebase with indirection and guesswork about future needs. Similarly, leaky abstractions occur when interfaces fail to hide important details. If a module exposes brittle data formats, or operational assumptions, callers must still understand internal workings, defeating the point of abstraction. Systems also suffer when interfaces expose too much, offering wide, unfocused APIs that confuse rather than clarify usage.

Neglecting interface stability can introduce hidden coupling. If interfaces change frequently, consumers lose the benefit of insulation and are forced to track internal shifts. True abstraction and encapsulation are about restraint: exposing only what is necessary, hiding what is likely to change, and maintaining that discipline as the system grows.

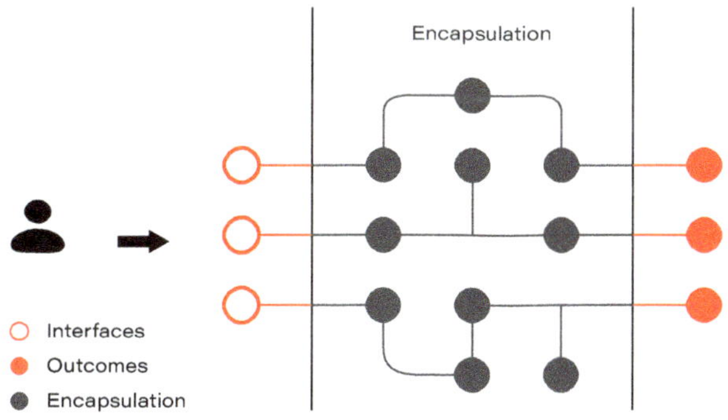

Figure 16 – Encapsulate with Abstraction

SUCCESS INDICATORS

You know encapsulation and abstraction are working when you can modify internals without needing to notify or update consuming modules. Teams can refactor or swap out implementations with minimal coordination. Unit tests operate against interfaces, not concrete classes, making tests simpler and more durable. Integration failures decline because the system resists tight coupling by design. When breaking changes happen, they are deliberate, versioned, and communicated early. Over time, the codebase feels modular and ready to adapt at speed.

SUMMARY

Encapsulation and abstraction are not mere academic ideals. They are practical tools for building software that thrives with growth and scaling pressure. By committing to clear, focused interfaces and hiding internal changes, you create flexible and maintainable systems even as complexity increases. The less you expose today, the more you can change tomorrow without breaking.

REFERENCES

E. Gamma, R. Helm, R. Johnson, and J. Vlissides, Design Patterns: *Elements of Reusable Object-Oriented Software*, Addison-Wesley Professional, 1994.

R. C. Martin, *Clean Code: A Handbook of Agile Software Craftsmanship*, Prentice Hall, 2008.

W. Shih, "Increasing the Level of Abstraction as a Strategy for Accelerating the Adoption of Complex Technologies," *Strategy Science* 6(1), 2020. https://doi.org/10.1287/stsc.2020.0116

17 • The Law of Demeter

"Loose lips sink ships." —WW II, US Office of War Information

INTRODUCTION

The Law of Demeter gets its name from the Demeter Project at Northeastern University from the late 1980s, focused on adaptive programming and aspect-oriented programming. Now, often called the principle of least knowledge, advocates for minimizing coupling between modules to build software that stays maintainable as it grows. It states that a unit of software, whether a class, function, or module, should only interact with its direct collaborators. It should not reach through one object to manipulate or depend on another's internals. Systems designed with minimal knowledge boundaries scale more easily, break less often, and support faster development over time. Rather than relying on deep object hierarchies, developers focus on clear, narrow interfaces, encouraging cleaner, more predictable software.

KEY CONCEPT

The Law of Demeter defines clear boundaries for communication. A given module should only interact with itself, objects it directly creates, objects passed to it as parameters, or well-defined external interfaces. The goal is to prevent deep object navigation (code like *order.getCustomer().getAddress().getCity()*) that reaches too far across internal structures. Deep coupling of this kind creates flimsy systems where small internal changes can show up unpredictably across unrelated modules.

Maintaining shallow, direct communication enables stronger encapsulation, clearer abstractions, and greater modularity. In highly complex systems, the right architectures can further decouple components by having them communicate indirectly through a shared information space. In everyday code or advanced distributed systems, minimizing coupling remains a fundamental design practice for achieving resilient, scalable software.

WHY IT MATTERS

Excessive coupling makes software into rigid knots that resist change. Teams slow down, burdened by unintentional dependencies, and every addition feels like a big undertaking because touching one part can disturb many others. When the Law of Demeter is applied well, these problems shrink. Maintenance becomes easier because modules remain focused and isolated. Testing becomes simpler because dependencies are narrow and explicit, reducing the need for extensive mocking. Scalability improves because systems can grow organically, adding new capabilities without needing to rewrite stable ones. Failures become localized rather than systemic. When one piece breaks, it does not necessarily bring the entire structure down. Over time, decoupled systems prove more adaptable and less prone to regressions.

IN PRACTICE

Minimizing coupling starts with paying close attention to how you navigate objects. When you find yourself chaining calls across multiple layers to fetch or update data, consider it a sign that something needs to change. Instead of reaching deep into dependencies, design interfaces that give you exactly what you need. For instance, have the *Order* class provide a *getCustomerCity* method rather than exposing *Customer* or *Address* objects. Each class should guard its data and reveal only what's necessary through simple, stable contracts.

Use dependency injection to keep relationships clear. Rather than pulling from global state or discovering dependencies at runtime, declare what you need up front. When you pass dependencies through constructors or parameters, your code becomes easier to understand and test.

As your system grows, look to patterns like facades and mediators to coordinate behavior without building tight links. A facade gives you a clean, simple interface over complexity. A mediator helps module communication without the parties needing to know each other directly. In highly dynamic systems, you can go further by avoiding direct calls altogether. Instead, publish facts or events into a shared space and let components react to what they see. This is how you keep coupling low while letting the system adapt and grow.

COMMON PITFALLS

Blindly applying the Law of Demeter without considering context can increase complexity without adding real protection. Not every chained method call demands a new interface. Moving deep object chains into new getter methods, rather than truly redefining relationships, simply shifts the problem into a new form. Similarly, favoring shared global types instead of narrow, context-specific abstractions can reintroduce hidden coupling across modules.

Occasionally, there are performance trade-offs as well. Excessive delegation between shallow modules can introduce minor overhead. However, in most systems, the long-term maintainability benefits vastly outweigh these small runtime costs. A common pitfall is letting interfaces drift. Without disciplined ownership and regular review, abstractions expand to expose more and more internal details. Once callers depend on internals again, the benefits of decoupling evaporate.

CASE STUDY

Citibank's global finance platform had grown into a complex system with tightly coupled components, making updates risky and time-consuming. The goal was to improve maintainability and resilience by reducing interdependencies across modules. The architecture team adopted the Law of Demeter as a guiding principle, restructuring services to expose only what was necessary, enforcing strict module boundaries, and introducing intermediaries like facades to decouple communication. This shift led to smoother deployments, fewer cascading failures, and faster onboarding for new developers. Over time, Citibank's systems became more adaptable to regulatory and market changes, without requiring large-scale rewrites.

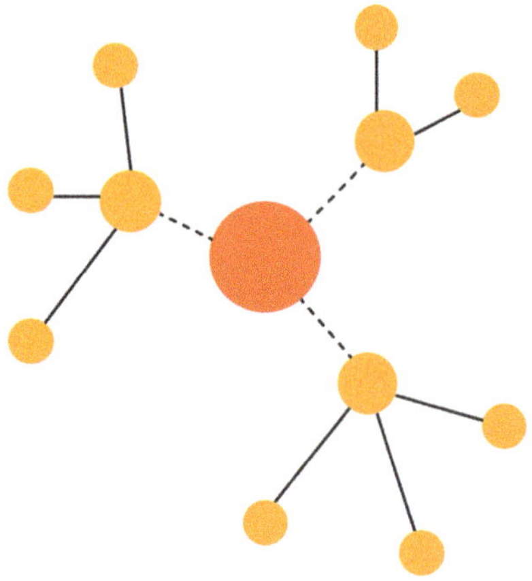

Figure 17 – Minimizing Coupling for Maintainable Software

SUCCESS INDICATORS

This principle is working well when modules change independently without requiring sweeping updates across the codebase. Test setups grow simpler because collaborators are shallow and clear. Refactors happen without huge regression tests because direct contracts protect downstream modules. Systems become more resilient as partial failures remain contained. Developer onboarding improves because understanding a module's interface no longer requires tracing deep dependency chains. Collaboration improves across teams because well-defined boundaries eliminate the need for hidden knowledge. Over time, a decoupled system simply feels cleaner and safer to evolve.

SUMMARY

Minimizing coupling through the Law of Demeter and related practices allows systems to scale more easily, change more safely, and recover gracefully from failures. By limiting knowledge, embracing dependency injection, leveraging facades and mediators, and applying blackboard models[5] where needed, developers build architectures that grow stronger with time instead of becoming more brittle. Every decision to hide unnecessary detail and expose only stable contracts reinforces the foundation for sustainable, high-quality software.

REFERENCES

L. D. Erman, F. Hayes-Roth, V. R. Lesser, and D. R. Reddy, "The Hearsay-II Speech-Understanding System: Integrating Knowledge to Resolve Uncertainty," *ACM Computing Surveys*, vol. 12, no. 2, pp. 213–253, 1980.

E. Gamma, R. Helm, R. Johnson, and J. Vlissides, *Design Patterns: Elements of Reusable Object-Oriented Software*, Addison-Wesley Professional, 1994.

FOOTNOTES

5 See glossary.

18 • Composition over Inheritance

"Rigidity is death. Flexibility is life." — Miyamoto Musashi, The Book of Five Rings

INTRODUCTION

Software grows faster and stays healthier when it is built from modular, interchangeable parts instead of rigid hierarchies. The principle of Composition over Inheritance encourages teams to assemble behavior by combining small, focused components, rather than stacking functionality through deep class inheritance. While inheritance often feels natural at first for reusing code, it tends to create rigid dependencies that slow change and amplify risk as systems evolve. Composition, on the other hand, offers a flexible alternative. It lets developers plug in behavior at runtime instead of hardwiring it during design. By choosing composition, teams avoid the traps of hard base classes and cross overrides.

KEY CONCEPT

Composition shifts focus from building elaborate class trees to assembling simple, independent modules. Instead of extending a base class to inherit behavior, developers compose objects from small components that each do one job well. These components, whether services, strategies, or helpers, hide their internal logic and expose only the minimal behavior needed. Since they operate through explicit contracts rather than an inherited structure, they can be freely replaced, combined, or upgraded without affecting the surrounding system. This modularity transforms maintenance and feature growth from costly rewrites into predictable, localized changes. Deep inheritance chains lock you into decisions made long ago. Composition gives you escape hatches, letting software evolve gracefully without rewriting foundations. Every module remains self-contained and predictable, while new functionality emerges by assembling these stable pieces in new ways.

WHY IT MATTERS

Inheritance often starts clean but becomes a liability as requirements change. Developers bend base classes to accommodate new features, stacking conditionals and adding gating flags. Small changes in parent classes cascade through layers of subclasses, causing unpredictable breakages. Testing becomes more difficult because the behavior of any subclass depends on distant ancestors. Debugging and refactoring gets harder since failures can originate anywhere in the inheritance chain and behavior is hidden in relationships rather than being explicit at the point of use.

Composition solves these problems by keeping behavior local and explicit. When new behavior is needed, developers introduce a new component rather than rewriting a shared ancestor. Tests stay simple and feature growth accelerates because each piece can be verified independently. Systems that embrace composition over inheritance stay adaptable longer, avoiding the slow decay into rigidity that affects older software.

IN PRACTICE

Applying the Composition over Inheritance principle starts with focusing on behavior instead of structure. Rather than embedding functionality into base classes, you define clear interfaces and inject them where needed. Your objects stop hardcoding behavior and instead depend on collaborators you can swap out at runtime. When you need different behavior, you pass in a new strategy rather than building another subclass. Delegation becomes your tool of choice. Instead of extending a parent just to override a method, you hand off work to a helper component built for that responsibility.

COMMON PITFALLS

Even sound principles can be misapplied. The most common mistake in composition is excessive fragmentation. If every behavior is broken into tiny, trivial pieces, systems can become hard to understand because no single module does anything meaningful alone. Clear boundaries are essential, but cohesion matters too. Another risk is poorly defined contracts. Without clear interfaces and predictable behavior, swapping components becomes unpredictable, undermining the benefits of composition. Sometimes, in an effort to avoid inheritance altogether, teams ignore cases where it is actually the better tool. Modeling simple "is-a" relationships through inheritance, when behavior differences are minimal, can avoid unnecessary complexity. Dogmatic avoidance of inheritance serves no one. The key is to prefer composition because it leads to better modularity, not because of a rigid rule.

CASE STUDY

This approach played a transformative role at Unity Technologies, the company behind the Unity game engine. Early versions of Unity suffered from deep inheritance hierarchies for game object behavior. As the engine matured, developers found that inheritance-based design made the system inflexible. Adding new features or modifying existing ones often requires invasive changes across unrelated classes.

To address this, Unity shifted toward a composition-based architecture. In the new model, a *GameObject* was simply a container that held components, each responsible for a single behavior like rendering, physics, or animation. Developers could dynamically add or remove components at runtime, composing behavior on the fly without relying on rigid hierarchies. This modular architecture improved maintainability and scalability and empowered developers to prototype and build complex behaviors quickly. By composing behaviors rather than inheriting them, Unity created a system flexible enough to support millions of developers across wildly different genres and platforms.

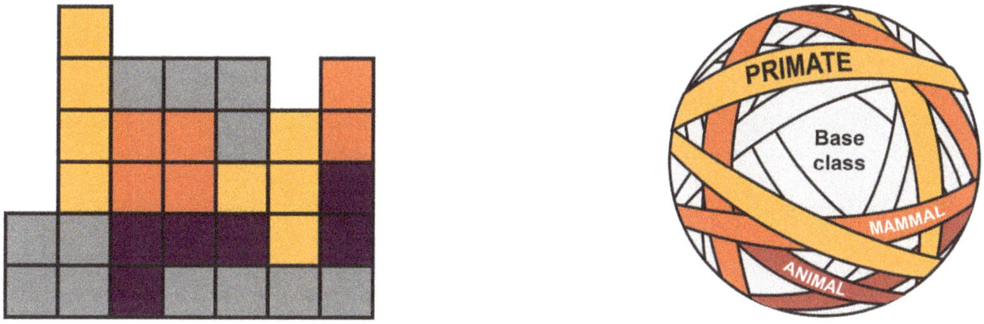

Figure 18 – Composition Over Inheritance

SUCCESS INDICATORS

When Composition over Inheritance is practiced well, software becomes easier to navigate and evolve. Developers introduce new behavior by adding or swapping components rather than modifying core classes. Systems stay modular and flexible. Testing accelerates because units are small and predictable. Debugging becomes easier and teams deliver features faster and refactor with less uncertainty because the blast radius of any change remains small. Over time, the system continues to grow without feeling rigid. Composition becomes the quiet architecture that supports sustainable, confident software evolution.

SUMMARY

Choosing Composition over Inheritance unlocks a more modular, resilient way to build systems. Instead of committing functionality to rigid class hierarchies, teams assemble behaviors through collaboration and clear contracts. This approach keeps code easier to understand, faster to change, and safer to scale. As requirements evolve, instead of untangling brittle base classes, new behaviors emerge by plugging in new pieces. Well-designed composition fosters better testing and more reliable deployments. Teams build software that stands the test of time by snapping behaviors together instead of stacking them vertically.

REFERENCES

E. Gamma, R. Helm, R. Johnson, and J. Vlissides, *Design Patterns: Elements of Reusable Object-Oriented Software*, Addison-Wesley, 1994.

K. Fedoseev, N. Askarbekuly, E. Uzbekova, and M. Mazzara, "A Case Study on Object-Oriented and Data Oriented Design Paradigms in Game Development," *preprint*, 2020. DOI:10.13140/RG.2.2.16657.66405

Unity Technologies, "Introduction to Components," *Unity Documentation*, retrieved May 3, 2025, from https://docs.unity3d.com/Manual/Compoents.html.

19 • Dependency Injection

"The mind is not a vessel to be filled, but a fire to be kindled."— Plutarch

INTRODUCTION

Dependency Injection (DI) is a principle that improves software flexibility, testability, and maintainability by externalizing the provision of an object's dependencies. Instead of hardwiring dependencies inside a class, DI ensures that all external components like services, collaborators, and configurations are passed into the object from the outside. This simple change in mindset creates enormous benefits: objects become easier to understand, easier to reuse, easier to test, and easier to replace. Rather than forcing an object to know how to build or find what it needs, DI lets the object focus solely on what it does with those dependencies. It decouples construction from behavior, leaving code more modular and systems more adaptable.

KEY CONCEPT

At the core, the Dependency Injection principle separates two concerns: how an object gets what it needs, and what the object actually does. Instead of an object creating or discovering its collaborators internally, it accepts them through its constructor, methods, or properties. This practice clarifies roles and boundaries. The object becomes a consumer of behavior, not a builder of it. By shifting dependency management outward, DI enables loose coupling between components. Changes to one service or class no longer impact the broader system. Tests can substitute real services with mock implementations. Systems can swap different dependency configurations based on environment or feature toggles. DI empowers flexibility not by reducing dependencies to zero, but by making them explicit and replaceable

WHY IT MATTERS

Without dependency injection, objects tightly couple themselves to the specific details of their collaborators. They often create new instances internally, rely on global state, or embed assumptions about how dependencies should behave. This pattern quietly turns small design decisions into long-term liabilities. Every new requirement becomes more complicated to implement because classes resist change. Testing becomes more difficult because objects cannot easily substitute real services for mocks. Systems become more rigid over time as components entangle their construction and logic.

By applying dependency injection, software stays loosely coupled and resilient to change. Developers gain the freedom to rewire or replace services without rewriting consumers. Codebases become easier to onboard because every object's dependencies are visible at the surface, not hidden deep inside. Testing accelerates because mocks, fakes, and stubs can be injected effortlessly. Configuration becomes dynamic because dependency graphs can change based on environment, runtime conditions, or system load. Over time, DI supports faster iteration, cleaner architecture, and more reliable delivery.

IN PRACTICE

The practical application of dependency injection starts when you notice an object needs external behavior. Instead of constructing that behavior inside, you inject it. Use constructors to pass in required services so your objects get what they need up front. For optional behaviors, inject them through setter methods or configuration properties. Stop letting objects reach out to gather what they need. Let them wait for collaborators to come through their public interface.

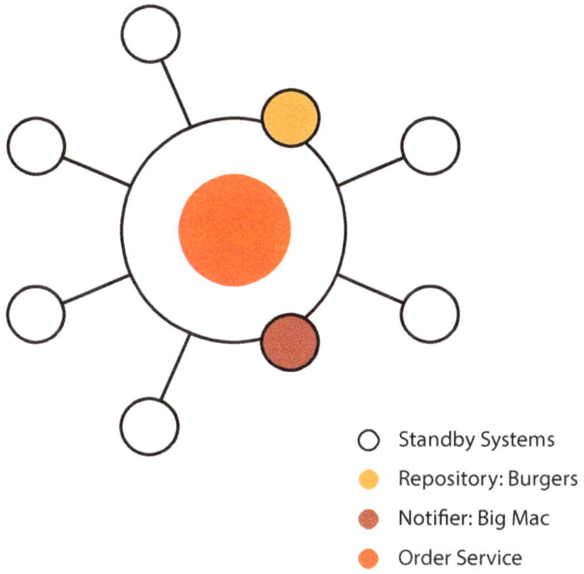

Figure 19 – Dependency Injection - From Outside

CASE STUDY

A real-world example comes from how Uber re-architected its dispatch platform. Early versions of Uber's backend relied heavily on objects that created their own database connections, routing engines, and configuration readers. As the system expanded globally, this approach began to fail. Any slight change in one dependency caused ripple effects across dozens of classes. Testing required setting up full backend environments, which slowed development and masked bugs until late in the cycle.

To fix this, Uber adopted a rigorous dependency injection model. Every service, from geolocation to pricing, had its dependencies explicitly declared and injected. A central dependency graph defines how services relate to each other, and different graphs could be created for testing, staging, or production. The result was a significant reduction in deployment risk. Engineers could now test dispatch logic in isolation using fake services. New features like dynamic pricing models could be introduced by swapping injected strategies, not rewriting the dispatch code. Performance tuning became easier because caching layers or databases could be reconfigured without touching the core service logic. Dependency injection turned Uber's dispatch system from a maze of assumptions into a resilient, adaptable architecture that supported hypergrowth without constant rewrites.

COMMON PITFALLS

Like any powerful principle, dependency injection can be misapplied. The most frequent mistake is over-injection, where objects receive dozens of dependencies they barely use. This signals poor design at a higher level, often a sign that responsibilities have blurred or modules have grown too large. Another pitfall is hiding dependency wiring deep inside frameworks or containers without clear visibility. When DI happens by magic, developers lose track of what an object really needs, leading to debugging nightmares. Poorly scoped dependencies can also create hidden coupling if injected services themselves manage broad swaths of unrelated behavior. Finally, premature optimization can turn DI into unnecessary complexity if small, simple systems adopt heavy injection frameworks before the need truly arises.

SUCCESS INDICATORS

When dependency injection is used well, code becomes easier to follow because every object's collaborators are listed up front. Constructors are short and declarative, showing exactly what each class depends on. Testing is fast and focused, requiring minimal setup to inject mocks or fakes. Refactoring becomes less stressful because changing one service's internal behavior does not break downstream consumers. Systems feel less brittle because dependency graphs can evolve without touching business logic. Cross-team development improves because teams can build against stable contracts rather than tangled implementations. The net effect is a codebase that grows naturally without hardening into inflexible shapes.

SUMMARY

Dependency injection transforms software architecture by separating the creation of dependencies from their use. It encourages modular design, makes testing easier, reduces coupling, and speeds up maintenance. Rather than letting objects reach outward and gather what they need, DI ensures that dependencies arrive in a controlled, visible, and swappable manner. This boundary between construction and behavior fosters healthier systems that grow with minimal friction. In a world where requirements shift constantly and speed matters, dependency injection offers the structure for building codebases that stay flexible.

REFERENCES

M. Seemann and S. Deursen, *Dependency Injection Principles, Practices, and Patterns*, Manning Publications, 2019.

P. Sun and D.-K. Kim, "Analyzing Impact of Dependency Injection on Software Maintainability," *arXiv*, ˆ2022. https://doi.org/10.48550/arXiv.2205.06381

A. Kolawole, "Taming the Dependencies: Mastering Dependency Injection in Go with UberFx," *Medium*, 2024.

IV SYMPHONY OF SYSTEMS

"An orchestra full of stars can be a disaster unless one brings harmony out of chaos." — Kurt Masur

When you're first learning to design systems, it's natural to focus on individual pieces (let's say, the APIs, the data stores) with the expectation that if each part behaves well, the system as a whole will work as expected. At a smaller scale, that often holds true. You can get by tuning individual services in isolation, fixing problems as they arise, and trusting that the structure you've drawn on paper won't fall too far from how it performs in production. However, as systems grow, the nature of the challenge also changes. Scale has a way of revealing weaknesses that can skate by on a smaller scale. What ends up happening is that scale exposes timing mismatches, shared dependencies, and small delays or retries that compound into something larger. In many cases, one failure becomes several.

Designing for scale requires a different way of thinking. You're no longer just optimizing for correctness inside a service boundary. You're thinking across the entire system. You're considering how the pieces interact, how they recover, how the system handles each piece moving independently, and how they share responsibility. This shift requires you to move beyond individual implementation and start seeing yourself more as a conductor. You still choose the right instruments, like stateless services, durable queues, and scalable data stores, but you also focus on the timing, the tempo, and the handoffs between each part of the system.

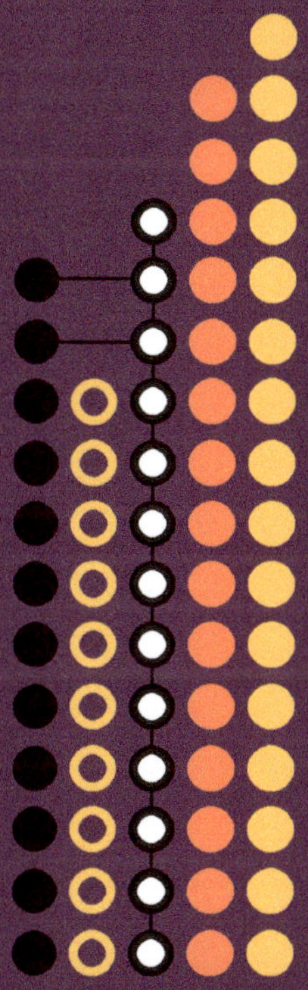

You will have to start paying attention to how retries are spaced, how timeouts are handled, how failures are logged and surfaced, and how gracefully components can degrade when their dependencies are unavailable. Your work becomes about shaping a system that expects disruption and makes room for it. When you take in the principles that follow service decomposition, shared-nothing architecture, multi-region redundancy, eventual consistency, autoscaling, and circuit breakers, seek to see them as a whole rather than as individual pieces that you can drop into your design diagram. Each one plays a role in shaping how a system holds up under pressure. Some add stability. Others enable recovery. A few create the slack needed for everything else to keep functioning.

The key point is that harmony in systems is something you design toward with intent. If you begin thinking of your systems as a living performance, you will build an intuition for architectural balance. With that intuition, you are more likely to build a system that is truly well-composed and balanced, where all components work together and where the system serves its intent faithfully and beautifully in the real world.

20 • Service Decomposition

"The mark of a great mind is the ability to divide without destroying." —Plutarch

INTRODUCTION

As software systems grow, so does the friction between development speed and structural complexity. The Service Decomposition principle addresses this tension by shifting the focus from technical components to business capabilities. Instead of organizing code by controllers, helpers, or layers, this principle encourages breaking systems down into autonomous services that align with what the business actually does. Each service maps to a real-world function such as billing, authentication, or reporting. It owns its logic and data. When applied with discipline, this approach transforms a tightly coupled monolith into a set of independent, focused services that are easier to scale and evolve.

Decomposition helps reshape the architecture around meaningful, testable boundaries. It reduces overhead and ambiguity, teams gain autonomy, and releases happen faster. Since failures stay contained, systems become more adaptable.

KEY CONCEPT

At the heart of this principle is the idea that systems should be structured around capabilities, not technical convenience. A service should reflect something the business does, not something the codebase happens to expose. For instance, "invoicing" is a capability. "Utilities," as a grab-bag of helpers, is not. Decomposed services should encapsulate their logic and manage their data independently. They should interact through explicit APIs and evolve on their own timelines. There's no shared database. No undocumented side channels. Communication is intentional, and the responsibilities are clear.

A good decomposition respects boundaries. It doesn't split code arbitrarily or fragment functionality just for its own sake. It begins with an understanding of the business domain, not a checklist of microservices. Each service should be independently deployable and testable. It should solve one thing completely and defer everything else. The goal is not isolation for its own sake, but modularity that enables safe change and steady progress.

WHY IT MATTERS

Monoliths are easy to build but hard to grow. When everything lives in one codebase, dependencies creep in unnoticed. Over time, complexity grows faster than the business. The system becomes harder to maintain, harder to debug, and harder to trust.

Decomposition is how that complexity gets solved. It turns broad systems into manageable pieces. Development becomes parallel instead of sequential. Failures become isolated instead of contagious. Releases happen more often and with ease. Teams gain actual ownership over how their software behaves in production. A well-decomposed system maps to the organization's structure and scales with it.

IN PRACTICE

Applying the Service Decomposition principle begins when you think about what the system does in business terms. You start by noticing which parts change often, where bottlenecks slow you down, and where responsibility feels scattered. These observations reveal seams, places where one function ends, and another begins. From there, you decompose gradually. Pull out one domain at a time, rebuild it as a service, and reroute traffic through clear service boundaries. APIs become your only interface. The services stand on their own and don't depend on internal details from neighbors. This lets other teams build integrations or contribute without touching the core logic. You also have to think carefully about communication. More services often mean more points of failure. If you rely too much on synchronous calls, you create latency and new failure paths.

CASE STUDY

Walmart's original e-commerce platform was tightly coupled (monolithic), hard to scale, and hard to change. During peak traffic, like Black Friday, it struggled to handle increased load (2.5 million requests per second). Since the system was tightly coupled, small changes required full regression, slowing down feature releases, and failure in one component risked full-site outages. Scaling an individual component also meant scaling the whole stack. Around the mid-2010s, Walmart made a clean architectural change. They decomposed the monolith into domain-aligned microservices. Services like product catalog, search, checkout, and returns were rebuilt as independent components, each owning its own logic, API, and database. Node.js replaced legacy code in many areas. Services were containerized and deployed to the cloud for on-demand scaling. An API gateway provides centralized routing and authorization, while new features are shipped as microservices. This change was not easy; it required dealing with the complexity of integration and operational consistency across services and cultural change.

Post-decomposition, Walmart saw immediate gains; both scalability and resilience improved in a meaningful way. For example, on Black Friday, the new architecture handled 500 million page views without a hitch. Teams scaled individual services like checkout without touching unrelated systems. Failures became isolated. A broken recommendation engine no longer risked taking down checkout. Services were shipped faster, without waiting on a global release cycle. Each team owned its code, data, and deployment, allowing them to move independently. Infrastructure costs dropped through right-sized provisioning. The architecture now mirrors the business, enabling them to serve their business and users better.

Event-based interactions and eventual consistency let services collaborate without needing everything to be available at once. This manages complexity rather than removing it.

Ownership is also essential. A service with no clear owner will rot quickly. Decomposition isn't just architectural. It's also about how you structure your teams. Each service needs a purpose, a known owner, and a well-defined contract.

COMMON PITFALLS

One of the most common mistakes with service decomposition is fragmenting the system too early. When decomposition happens without a deep understanding of the domain, teams create services that are too small, generic, or interdependent. Instead of true modularity, they end up with tightly coupled services in smaller containers. Another failure mode is shared state. Teams sometimes split services logically but keep a shared database underneath. This breaks encapsulation and turns every schema change into a system-wide negotiation. It also makes failure isolation nearly impossible. A real decomposition means owning your data and recovery paths.

Some systems fall into the trap of using synchronous calls for everything. They replace local function calls with remote service calls and expect the same speed and reliability. As a result, latency grows, dependencies stack, and cascading failures become more likely. Decomposition requires a shift in how coordination happens toward asynchronous flows, decoupled contracts, and tolerance for partial progress.

SUCCESS INDICATORS

A successful decomposition shows up in how teams work. Releases move faster and require fewer cross-team meetings. When something breaks, the blast radius is small, and recovery is local. Each team can confidently answer questions about its service and knows what to do when things go wrong. Logs and dashboards are focused, service-specific, and meaningful. Metrics reflect business outcomes rather than low-level technical events.

As the system evolves, adding new features doesn't require revisiting old ones. New services plug into existing flows with little friction. Teams don't have to choose between speed and stability. They get both because the architecture supports the pace of change.

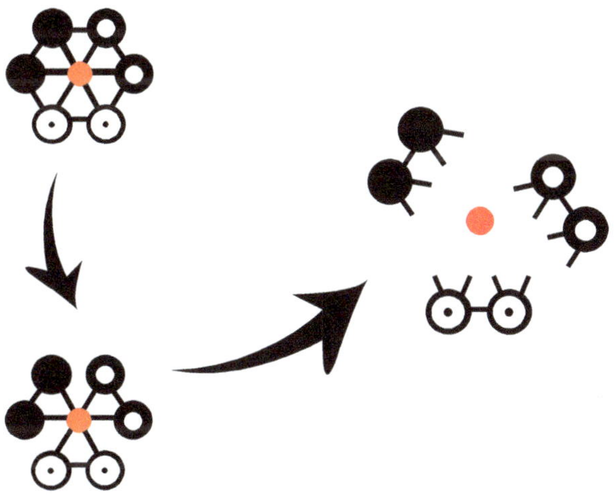

Figure 20 – Decomposition

SUMMARY

The Service Decomposition principle provides a pathway to long-term system sustainability. It doesn't promise simplicity, but it does offer clarity, autonomy, and the ability to evolve without rewriting everything. When teams shape services around what the business actually does, the architecture starts to serve its purpose: enabling people to move fast without breaking anything. When you decompose deliberately, assign ownership, and embrace asynchronous flows, you create a foundation that's both flexible and durable.

REFERENCES

E. Evans, *Domain-Driven Design: Tackling Complexity in the Heart of Software*, Addison-Wesley Professional, 2003.

D. Eldenk and H. A. Çetin, "Incidents During Microservice Decomposition: A Case Study," *arXiv*, arXiv:2505.09813, May 2025.

Golden Owl Solutions, "Microservices for eCommerce: A Smarter Choice than Monolith? (2024)", *Golden Own Blog*, 2025.

21 • API Gateway Pattern

"He who opens the gate, controls the city."— Ancient proverb

INTRODUCTION

In service-oriented architecture (SOA), splitting applications into independent services brings flexibility, scalability, and modularity. However, it also introduces significant complexity. Clients must now communicate with multiple endpoints, manage authentication flows, and coordinate responses across different services. This fragmentation can burden teams with non-value-added work and increase operational and security risks.

The API Gateway Pattern principle solves these challenges by providing a single, centralized entry point for all client interactions. Acting as the unified front door to the system, the API gateway streamlines communication, handles authentication, enforces security policies, and abstracts backend complexity. By presenting a simplified, consistent interface to clients, the API gateway pattern allows systems to grow or change internally without affecting external consumers.

KEY CONCEPT

The essence of the API gateway pattern is centralization. Instead of exposing each service directly to external clients, a dedicated gateway mediates all communication. This gateway routes incoming requests to the appropriate internal service, validates credentials, enforces authorization rules, and can even aggregate responses from multiple sources into a unified payload.

An API gateway improves both security and operational control. It logs traffic, enforces rate limits, applies governance policies, and can shape or transform requests and responses as needed. By consolidating these concerns into a single, strategically placed component, the system gains a clean, auditable perimeter while maintaining flexibility behind the scenes. In effect, the gateway abstracts the complexity of a distributed backend and presents clients with a coherent, predictable API surface. It enables microservices to evolve independently while shielding users from the fragmentation inherent in distributed systems.

WHY IT MATTERS

As systems grow, the cost of direct client–service interaction compounds rapidly. Every exposed service endpoint becomes a potential security risk, a maintenance burden, and a source of client-side complexity. Without an intermediary, rolling out updates, managing versioning, or enforcing consistent authentication policies becomes challenging. The API gateway pattern addresses this challenge by acting as a central point for access control, ensuring that authentication and authorization happen uniformly. It improves scalability by absorbing traffic surges, balancing load, and applying rate limits before requests reach backend services.

Equally important, it enhances developer experience. Frontend and mobile teams no longer need to adapt to backend changes. Instead, they interact with a stable, client-centric API. Service teams gain autonomy as they can iterate, deploy, and even replace internal services without disrupting external clients. The API gateway decouples internal system evolution from external system stability, a critical property for any organization seeking to scale with peace of mind. Beyond technical benefits, an effective gateway also strengthens the product experience. It provides users with a reliable facade, turning a collection of services into a unified, trustworthy system.

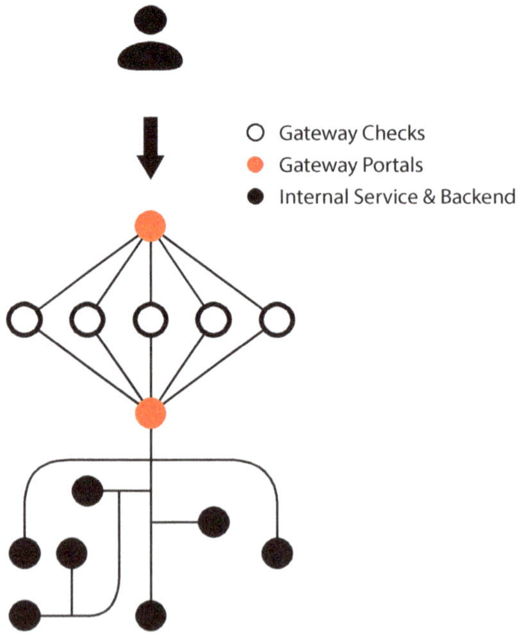

Figure 21 – API Gateway Parallel

IN PRACTICE

Designing an effective API gateway starts with focusing on what clients need, not how your internal services are structured. Organize your APIs around logical operations and use cases. Group-related actions should be put into clear interfaces instead of exposing raw service boundaries. You also have to make security a top priority. Centralize authentication, token validation, and authorization checks at the gateway so you avoid inconsistent policies across services. Route requests dynamically based on paths, headers, meta-

CASE STUDY

Wix, a leading website development platform, has effectively implemented the API gateway pattern to manage its extensive microservices architecture. As Wix transitioned from a monolithic system to microservices, the need for a centralized entry point became evident to streamline communication between clients and services. By adopting an API gateway, Wix was able to handle routing, authentication, and response aggregation efficiently, ensuring a seamless experience for both developers and end users. This approach not only enhanced security and scalability but also simplified the development process by providing a unified interface for all client interactions.

data, or user attributes. This is also the place to handle versioning, A/B testing, and tenant-specific routing.

Use response aggregation when it makes sense, but be careful. Combining calls from multiple backend services can add latency and reveal downstream weaknesses. You can reduce this risk with timeouts, fallbacks, and caching. Treat your gateway as a first-class component. Use versioning, testing, and automated deployments so changes are deliberate and reversible. Once in place, your gateway should fade into the background for users and become a powerful tool for your team.

COMMON PITFALLS

A poorly managed gateway becomes a single point of failure. When every client request flows through the gateway, ensuring high availability, redundancy, and rapid failover is non-negotiable. Remember that the gateway's role is coordination, not computation. Introducing domain logic at this layer increases coupling, making systems harder to evolve and maintain. Business rules belong in services, not gateways. If you include aggregation (for response payload) at the gateway, make sure it is necessary and backed by timeout management and fallback strategies.

Security enforcement at the gateway must be consistent and robust. Weak validation or inconsistent authorization checks expose the entire system to risk. Authentication and policy enforcement should be treated as core gateway responsibilities, not optional enhancements.

Finally, contracts between the gateway and backend services must stay in sync. If the gateway deviates from backend capabilities, clients experience broken functionality and inconsistencies in expected responses.

SUCCESS INDICATORS

The value of the API Gateway Pattern principle becomes visible in multiple dimensions. Clients experience a stable, predictable API surface even as backend services evolve independently. Frontend development accelerates because teams no longer wrestle with fragmented service interactions or shifting authentication models. Service teams gain the freedom to refactor, scale, and evolve their services behind the gateway without disrupting external consumers. Releases become safer, more incremental, and less coupled to client deployment cycles. Security also improves dramatically, with a clear perimeter for authentication, authorization, and traffic shaping. Operational observability strengthens, offering real-time insights into system performance and client behavior.

The overall system becomes easier to understand, troubleshoot, and improve. The API gateway serves as a strategic enabler of system coherence and organizational agility.

SUMMARY

A well-designed gateway transforms a distributed set of services into a cohesive product experience. It empowers teams to move faster, deploy more safely, and deliver consistently better experiences at scale. An effective API gateway improves security, enhances observability, and simplifies client and service development.

REFERENCES

C. Richardson, *Microservices Patterns: With Examples in Java*, Manning Publications, 2018.

T. Nguyen and T. T. Nguyen, "API Gateway in Microservices Architecture: A Systematic Review," *Journal of Information Systems and Technology Management*, vol. 16, no. 3, pp. 1–18, 2019.

N. Silnitsky, "How Wix Accelerated Open Platform Dev with Standardized APIs & Schemas," *Wix Engineering*, March 11, 2023.

22 • Shared Nothing Architecture

"Divide your forces, but never your strength" —Napoleon Bonaparte

INTRODUCTION

The closer your data is to the code that needs it, the faster your software runs. The more independent your components are, the more resilient your system becomes. Shared nothing emphasizes isolating services so that no two parts of the system share memory, storage, or tightly coupled state. Data locality minimizes the physical and logical distance between data and computation.[6] Applied in tandem, these principles create systems that move quickly, recover gracefully, and scale predictably as demands grow.

KEY CONCEPT

Shared nothing is about architectural independence. Each component owns its own state, manages its own persistence, and exposes well-defined APIs for interaction. Components do not share databases, memory structures, or session states unless absolutely necessary. They are designed to survive and evolve independently. When one node fails, the others continue unharmed. When traffic surges, you add replicas without worrying about hidden bottlenecks. Data locality is about proximity. Locality determines latency, whether you are caching hot keys inside a CPU, co-locating storage with compute in cloud platforms, or scheduling Spark tasks where the relevant Hadoop distributed file system (HDFS) blocks reside. Every additional network hop, every extra disk seek, deducts from performance. Systems that respect locality finish jobs faster, use less energy, and recover from spikes without heroics.

When combined, data locality and shared-nothing architecture reinforce each other. Local computation reduces the need for shared access. Independent nodes lessen the need for constant synchronization. The system becomes a constellation of self-reliant services. Each is fast on its own, and stronger together.

WHY IT MATTERS

Moving data across a network is costly. Every cross-node read adds latency, consumes bandwidth, and introduces risk. The more distributed your system becomes, the more critical it is to minimize these costs. Poor locality shows up as slow page loads, missed service-level agreements (SLAs), and bloated operational bills. At the same time, tight coupling across services turns small changes

6 Data locality is also covered later in more detail in "Data Locality and Stack Flattening."

into large incidents. One schema update, one overloaded service, can cascade into outages far beyond the original scope. Centrally coordinated systems buckle under the weight of normal failures.

Data locality and shared nothing prevent this. Systems built with these principles run faster because they minimize travel. They fail less because they reduce dependencies. They scale naturally because you can add new nodes without reengineering old assumptions.

IN PRACTICE

Applying these principles means making deliberate design decisions. You start by partitioning data intelligently. Whether you work with relational databases, key-value stores, or event logs, segment data so each service or node handles its own slice. Avoid cross-partition joins unless they are absolutely necessary. Align computation with storage whenever you can. If you run batch jobs, keep them close to the data they process. For web services, put backend logic near the data stores it needs, ideally in the same availability zone. Use aggressive local caching. Keep frequently accessed data at the edge, in memory, or in replicas close to users so you cut round trips and keep the hot path fast.

Give each service its own database or schema. Sharing a monolithic database might feel efficient early, but it builds hidden connections that slow scaling and innovation later. Services that own their data fail independently and evolve without waiting on others. Communicate through APIs, not shared state. Use

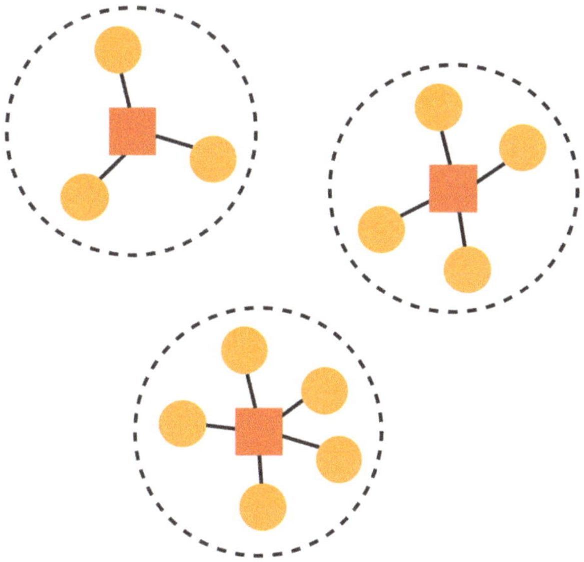

Figure 22 – Shared Nothing Architecture

CASE STUDY

As Uber expanded globally, a centralized architecture struggled to meet the performance and reliability demands of real-time ride matching, dynamic pricing, and trip tracking. To solve this, Uber decentralized key components of its system. Regional services handled local ride data, dynamic pricing was computed closer to the rider and driver, and decision-making was pushed to the edges where needed. Instead of every change flowing through a global control plane, localized services owned their domains and synchronized only when necessary. This shift reduced latency, improved fault isolation, and allowed different regions to operate independently even in the face of partial network failures. By thoughtfully decentralizing control, Uber has kept its platform resilient and adaptable as it scales across thousands of cities worldwide.

REST, gRPC, or message queues to enforce boundaries. Choose synchronous APIs for critical reads and asynchronous events for eventual updates. Build with stateless protocols where you can. Stateless services scale and recover more easily because they don't tie state to one machine. When you do need state, keep it explicit and contained.

COMMON PITFALLS

Over-isolating services sounds good in theory, but it can backfire if the trade-offs aren't managed carefully. Excessive decomposition creates microservices that spend more time talking to each other than doing useful work. Internal calls turn into network calls, adding latency and new failure points. Any system needs constant monitoring and rebalancing to keep the load steady. When one node gets overloaded, the supposed benefits of distribution vanish. The same goes for replication. Push it too far, and you end up with synchronization storms, consistency headaches, and ballooning operational costs. Replication works best when done with intention and restraint.

SUCCESS INDICATORS

When these principles are working, you see fast, consistent performance under real-world load. Application latency shrinks even during peak traffic because the system spends less time waiting for remote data. New services spin up without requiring massive coordination meetings or centralized design changes. Operational incidents stay localized, and rollbacks target only the affected nodes. Scaling feels linear and predictable: double the nodes, double the throughput. Developers move faster, debugging gets simpler, and the system adapts organically as demand grows.

SUMMARY

In modern systems, resilience and speed are table-stakes requirements. Data locality ensures your system moves quickly, even when load surges. Shared-nothing architecture ensures it survives, even when parts fail. Together, they create systems that are scalable, safer, and easier to operate.

If you want your architecture to endure growth, weather failures, and delight users at scale, stop thinking in terms of more hardware or more retries. Think in terms of closer data. Think in terms of independent nodes. Design with distance and independence in mind, and everything else gets easier.

REFERENCES

P. J. Denning, "The Locality Principle," *Communications of the ACM*, vol. 48, no. 7, pp. 19–24, 2005.

J. L. Hennessy and D. A. Patterson, *Computer Architecture: A Quantitative Approach*, 5th ed., Elsevier, 2011.

S. S, Krishnaswamy, M. Matthew, and S. Goyal, "Evolution of Data Lifecycle Management at Uber," *Uber Blog*, August 17, 2023.

23 • Spread Your Infrastructure

"Do not put all your eggs in one basket." — Spanish proverb

INTRODUCTION

When you build systems that serve the world, you cannot assume that any single region will always stay online. Natural disasters, network outages, political events, and infrastructure failures happen without warning. The geographical redundancy principle is about protecting against these realities. By distributing your services, data, and critical workloads across multiple regions, you ensure that your system stays available and responsive even when entire areas go dark. Geographical redundancy safeguards against failure, improves user experience by reducing latency, and supports compliance by enforcing data residency laws.

KEY CONCEPT

Geographical redundancy means that no single regional failure can break your system. It involves replicating infrastructure, databases, and services across distant data centers. When one region goes offline, others automatically take over, maintaining uptime without requiring emergency heroics. This can be achieved through active-active designs, where multiple regions serve live traffic simultaneously, or active-passive setups, where backup regions stand ready to activate when needed.

Distribution also improves performance. By serving users from the nearest healthy region, you shorten response times and deliver a smoother experience. At its core, geographical redundancy separates business continuity from geographic fate. It ensures that failures stay local while your system stays global.

WHY IT MATTERS

When you design for geographical redundancy, you ensure that disruption in one place does not become disruption everywhere. Systems without geographical redundancy break when their single region fails. Redundancy also supports growth. As your user base spreads across continents, so should your systems. Distributed deployments provide faster service delivery, help meet local regulations, and position your infrastructure to scale gracefully. Disaster recovery becomes a routine part of the system's DNA rather than a special-case afterthought. By spreading your infrastructure early, you move from reactive firefighting to proactive resilience.

IN PRACTICE

Applying geographical redundancy begins with understanding where your users are and where your risks lie. You plan deployments across diverse regions using cloud platforms that support multi-region replication. Your storage and databases are synchronized across centers, your application instances are deployed redundantly, and your load balancers know how to reroute traffic seamlessly if a region fails.

Failover must be automated. For example, DNS routing, health checks, and traffic management systems should detect issues and divert traffic without human intervention. Similarly, your monitoring must extend across all regions, tracking availability and failover readiness. To ensure effectiveness, run regular disaster recovery drills. These tests expose weaknesses and help address them before they become real issues. Designing for distribution means designing for eventual consistency and graceful degradation when needed. Global systems succeed when local failures are treated as expected scenarios, not exceptional emergencies.

COMMON PITFALLS

Multi-region deployments often fail because complexity is underestimated. Managing cross-region consistency, setting up reliable health checks, and coordinating failover mechanisms requires diligent operational work. Poorly tuned replication can cause data drift or latency spikes. Cost management is also critical, as cross-region traffic and duplicate infrastructure expenses can escalate without careful optimization. Teams also fall into the trap of partial redundancy, replicating application servers but leaving critical dependencies, like databases, locked to a single region. True resilience requires that every major system component survives regional failure, not just those that are easy to move.

SUCCESS INDICATORS

You know geographical redundancy is working when regional failures feel well-managed, not catastrophic. Failover happens automatically and is tested regularly. Users experience minimal to no disruption, even

CASE STUDY

Duolingo, the world's leading language learning platform, serves millions of users in dozens of countries. To ensure uninterrupted learning, even during regional outages, Duolingo adopted a multi-region deployment strategy. They replicated their backend services across geographically distinct cloud regions, used global load balancers to route users to the closest healthy zone, and implemented active-passive failover for critical databases to minimize data loss during transitions.

When an unexpected cloud provider outage temporarily impacted one region, Duolingo's systems rerouted traffic automatically, and users experienced no disruption. Over time, this approach protected uptime and improved lesson load times globally. The team's investment in geographical redundancy turned infrastructure resilience into a competitive advantage, allowing them to scale safely and deliver consistent experiences anywhere on earth.

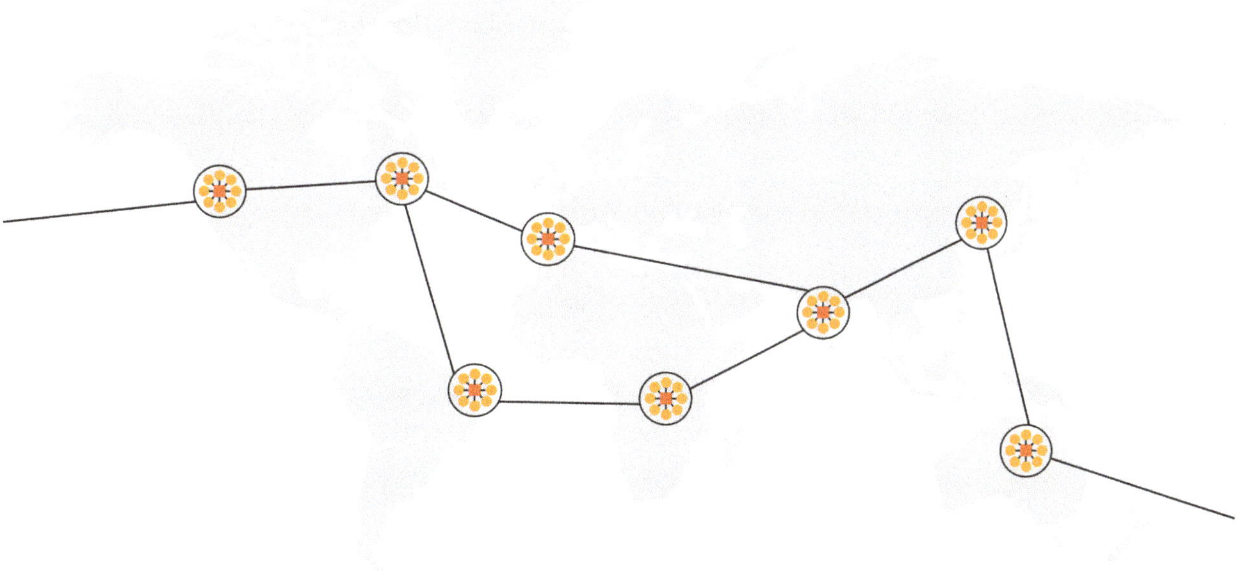

Figure 23 – Spread Your Infrastructure

during cloud outages. Latency stays low worldwide, as users are served from optimal regions. Business operations continue without panic when problems occur, and post-incident reports confirm that availability objectives are consistently met. Geographical redundancy keeps problems small and local so that the business can stay big and global.

SUMMARY

Geographical redundancy is the blueprint for continuous service. Distributing your infrastructure across multiple regions protects your business and lays the foundation for sustainable growth. By designing for distribution early, you create systems that survive and thrive, no matter where the next failure strikes. Spread your systems wide, and you'll stand firm everywhere.

REFERENCES

E. Chisom, et al., "Disaster Recovery in Cloud Computing: Site Reliability Engineering Strategies for Resilience and Business Continuity," *International Journal of Management and Organizational Research*, 3(1), 36–48, 2025.

A. Ajibola, "Cloud-Native Reliability Engineering: A Comprehensive Guide to Failure Resilience Patterns in Distributed Systems," *SSRN*, 2025. http://dx.doi.org/10.2139/ssrn.5260195

S. Kabbour, "How Duolingo Reduces AWS Compute Costs by 60%," *Renova Cloud*, retrieved on July 31, 2025 from https://renovacloud.com/en/how-duolingo-reduces-aws-compute-costs-by-60/.

24 · Batch Processing

"Nature does not hurry, yet everything is accomplished." — Laozi, Tao Te Ching

INTRODUCTION

When data does not need real-time processing, the Batch Processing principle offers a path to scalable, cost-effective solutions. This principle centers on executing large, periodic data jobs in a non-interactive, automated fashion, allowing massive datasets to be processed efficiently without constant human intervention. Systems collect and process information in structured cycles instead of reacting instantly to each data point. Frameworks like Hadoop and Spark are built on this model, providing the structure, fault tolerance, and efficiency needed for large-scale analytics and data transformation. In a world where data volume grows faster than hardware capacity, batch processing is practical and essential for sustainable growth.

KEY CONCEPT

Batch Processing fundamentally means orchestrating large data workloads into discrete, manageable operations. These jobs run on a schedule, not user demand, allowing systems to optimize computation, storage, and throughput at scale.

Technologies like Hadoop popularized this model through MapReduce, splitting work into a "Map" phase for parallel processing and a "Reduce" phase for aggregation and synthesis. Spark modernized the paradigm further with in-memory computations and resilient distributed datasets (RDDs), allowing faster batch jobs without sacrificing fault tolerance. At the heart of these systems is the directed acyclic graph (DAG), a structure where each node performs an independent operation, and edges track dependencies, ensuring efficient and reliable execution. Batch frameworks also implement checkpointing strategies, enabling systems to recover gracefully when failures occur rather than restarting from scratch. Together, these techniques turn overwhelming datasets into routine processing.

WHY IT MATTERS

Large-scale batch processing solves three interconnected problems: scale, reliability, and cost. First, it enables efficiency by operating outside the bounds of real-time constraints, allowing systems to optimize resources across long-running jobs. Second, it provides scalability through horizontal expansion; when data volumes grow, you simply add more nodes. Third, it ensures robustness through fault tolerance mechanisms like recomputation (re-runs lost calculations) and checkpointing (saves snapshots), preserving work even if nodes or processes fail midstream. Without batch systems, organizations would struggle to process historical logs, customer transactions, or scientific simulations within reasonable budgets and timelines. Batch processing empowers businesses to generate meaningful reports, power machine learning pipelines, and run periodic transformations without constant manual intervention. At scale, it enables sustainable data-driven operations.

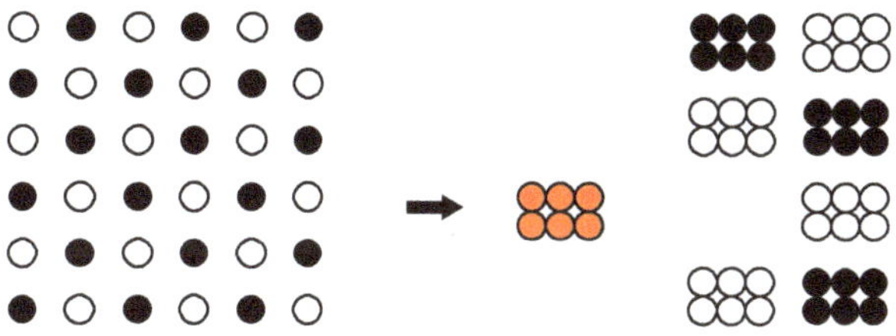

Figure 24 – Batch Processing

IN PRACTICE

Implementing batch processing starts with picking the right infrastructure. You begin by breaking the work into small, parallel tasks laid out in a DAG. That way, you can schedule tasks independently and keep things moving without unnecessary waits. Build fault tolerance from day one. Use checkpointing so you don't lose progress when something fails. Restarting the entire job wastes time and resources.

Think carefully about how you partition data across the cluster. Good partitioning keeps shuffles and I/O bottlenecks from slowing you down. Once your pipeline is live, watch it closely. Track how long jobs run, how of-

CASE STUDY

Yahoo faced the formidable challenge of processing terabytes of web analytics data daily across its advertising, content, and user engagement platforms. Real-time solutions were too costly and inflexible for this volume and variability. The company adopted Hadoop as its batch processing backbone, designing MapReduce pipelines that aggregated, cleaned, and analyzed raw web logs overnight. Partitioning data by time and geography enabled parallelism, while Hadoop's *replication* and *recomputation* features ensured resilience against node failures. Checkpointing allowed partial job completion to be preserved even when individual task trackers failed.

The result was transformative. Yahoo could now generate detailed daily reports on ad performance, page interactions, and search trends without overwhelming its infrastructure or sacrificing reliability. This successful deployment positioned Yahoo as an early benchmark for massive-scale batch processing, influencing many organizations' moves toward Hadoop ecosystems. It proved a key point that smart batch processing could power data-driven insights without the burden of real-time expense or instability.

ten they fail, and how they use resources. As your data grows, adjust schedules and scale resources so jobs stay fast and reliable. That's how you keep the system efficient while demands keep shifting.

COMMON PITFALLS

Despite its strengths, batch processing can go astray if systems are poorly designed. Initial setup and tuning often require significant expertise, and organizations sometimes underestimate the complexity of job scheduling, dependency management, and resource balancing. Delayed feedback is another risk. If bugs or pipeline failures are not detected until the next run or longer, your data decisions are compromised. Without proper resource management, batch jobs can monopolize system bandwidth or storage, causing degraded performance for other applications. Rigid scheduling models also sometimes clash with evolving business needs, leading to inefficiencies if not revisited periodically. Addressing these pitfalls requires disciplined pipeline design, proactive monitoring, and a commitment to continuous tuning and adaptation as data volumes and processing demands evolve.

SUCCESS INDICATORS

Well-implemented batch processing systems exhibit several key signs of success. Batch jobs reliably complete within their target windows without exhausting system resources. Fault tolerance mechanisms function predictably, recovering from task failures without disrupting entire workflows. Systems scale horizontally without drops in throughput as data volumes increase. Cost efficiency is noticeable: organizations spend less on unnecessary real-time systems while still delivering timely insights. Over time, operational overhead shrinks because well-monitored batch pipelines require less firefighting and manual intervention. When these outcomes are visible, it becomes clear that batch processing is doing what it was designed to do: scaling and delivering value at scale.

SUMMARY

Batch processing is the engine behind scalable, efficient, large-scale data operations. By orchestrating tasks through directed acyclic graphs, leveraging checkpointing for fault tolerance, and deploying frameworks like Hadoop and Spark, organizations can transform overwhelming data volumes into manageable workflows. The Batch Processing principle enables dependable, predictable, cost-efficient, data-driven decisions. When designed carefully and tuned continuously, batch systems provide the resilient foundation that modern data-driven enterprises require to operate at scale.

REFERENCES

G. Simuni, "Batch Processing with Apache Hadoop MapReduce: A Performance and Scalability Study," *SSRN*, 2024. https://ssrn.com/abstract=4991394 or http://dx.doi.org/10.2139/ssrn.4991394

K. Shvachko, K. Hairong, S. Radia, and R. Chansler, "The Hadoop Distributed File System," *Proceedings of the 2010 IEEE Symposium on Mass Storage Systems and Technologies*, 2010.

N. Marz and J. Warren, *Big Data: Principles and Best Practices of Scalable Realtime Data Systems*, Manning Publications, 2015.

25 • Saga Pattern

"Little by little, one travels far." — J.R.R. Tolkien

INTRODUCTION

Distributed architectures naturally scale, but they also fragment what used to be single, atomic transactions into multiple, asynchronous pieces. In a microservices ecosystem, trying to execute a traditional end-to-end transaction, such as placing an order, charging a customer, and scheduling fulfillment, can introduce significant risks. Holding locks across services for minutes or even seconds is impractical and makes failures extremely costly. Worse yet, recovering from a half-completed transaction becomes daunting.

The saga pattern offers a powerful solution to address this challenge. Instead of relying on long, tenuous transactions across multiple services, sagas create workflows that are resilient by design. They break down ambitious operations into smaller, reversible actions, allowing systems to move forward confidently even when failures occur. The goal is to expect and control both work and failures, making recovery a deliberate part of system design.

KEY CONCEPT

At its core, the saga pattern structures a large, distributed transaction as a set of smaller local transactions, each of which can be independently reversed if necessary. When a service completes its step, it commits immediately without waiting for global confirmation. If a later operation fails, compensating transactions are triggered to roll back the preceding successful steps, preserving system consistency.

Coordination strategies in sagas typically follow two models. Orchestration uses a central controller to manage the sequence of operations and compensations, ensuring a predictable and tightly managed flow. Conversely, choreography distributes responsibility across services, letting them emit and react to events without centralized control. Each model offers trade-offs between control and flexibility, but both rely on eventual consistency. In sagas, consistency does not mean immediate synchronization but a guarantee that all services will eventually converge to a correct and reliable state.

WHY IT MATTERS

Traditional distributed transactions introduce significant coordination overhead, degrading both performance and resilience. Holding locks across services or enforcing rigid ordering increases latency, tightens coupling, and amplifies failure risks. When a single service becomes unavailable, the entire workflow can stall, creating cascading failures and poor user experiences.

CASE STUDY

A good example of the saga pattern in practice is found at Airbnb. Managing millions of bookings across a decentralized global network of hosts and guests demands careful orchestration of payment processing, calendar updates, and communication workflows. Instead of attempting to enforce a monolithic transaction that locks payment systems and calendars simultaneously, Airbnb applies the saga pattern.

When a guest requests a booking, the system first reserves the calendar slot. It then attempts to authorize payment, and upon success, it triggers confirmation notifications to both guest and host. If payment authorization fails, a compensation flow releases the reserved calendar slot and notifies the involved parties that the booking was not completed. This ensures that stale reservations do not linger, resources are efficiently allocated, and users receive clear, timely feedback. By adopting sagas, Airbnb successfully delivers consistent, reliable operations at a massive scale without sacrificing autonomy or performance across its distributed services.

The saga pattern addresses these weaknesses by decentralizing control and planning for failure from the outset. Each service completes its responsibilities autonomously, improving responsiveness and system availability. If a failure occurs, compensations reverse the impact in a structured, intentional manner rather than leaving recovery to manual intervention or ad hoc scripts.

Beyond technical resilience, sagas offer meaningful business advantages. They reduce the operational risks associated with complex, cross-service workflows. They enable better user experiences by providing clear, transparent transaction outcomes. They empower development teams to build scalable, modular systems that adapt to growth without introducing systemic brittleness. Foremost, sagas shift the engineering mindset from fearing failure to expecting it, a vital transformation in any high-availability environment.

IN PRACTICE

Implementing sagas starts with careful planning. You need to map out the entire transactional flow, define what each step does, which service owns it, and how the system should respond if something fails. For every action, build an idempotent compensation that can bring the system back to a stable state. Even when you can't undo side effects like user notifications, your compensations should still restore business consistency.

Think hard about how you coordinate sagas. Use orchestration when you need tight control, strict sequencing, and centralized error handling. Choreography fits better in event-driven systems where services stay loosely coupled and evolve on their own. No matter which you choose, observability isn't optional. Persist saga state externally, log transitions, and set up alerts so you catch issues fast.

Testing sagas means more than checking the happy path. Simulate failures at every step. Confirm that compensations run correctly and leave the system consistent even when only part of the saga completes.

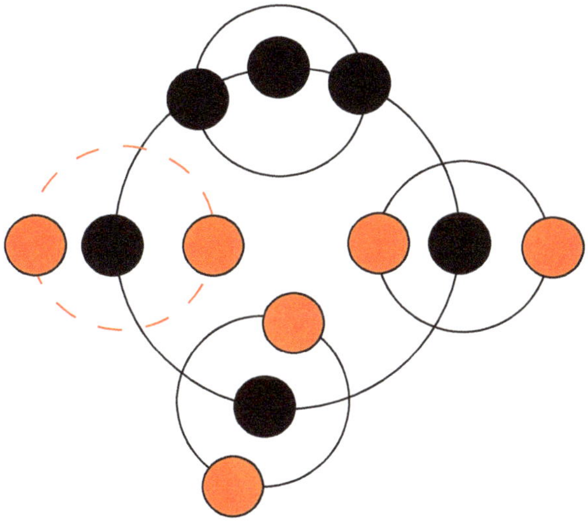

Figure 25 – Saga Pattern

COMMON PITFALLS

Common implementation mistakes can undermine the power of sagas. Missing compensations leave systems vulnerable to partial failures that require manual correction. Over-centralizing orchestration logic introduces bottlenecks and hard dependencies that sagas are meant to avoid. Non-idempotent compensations make failure recovery unpredictable and unsafe, particularly when retries occur. Insufficient saga state tracking can hamper visibility and incident response. Overcompensating for transient or recoverable errors can also cause unnecessary cancellations and degrade the user experience. Avoiding these pitfalls demands a rigorous, disciplined approach to both the technical and business aspects of saga design.

SUCCESS INDICATORS

When sagas are thoughtfully implemented, their impact is unmistakable. Systems demonstrate self-healing behavior, automatically detecting failures and triggering appropriate compensations without external intervention. User-facing operations complete reliably, either succeeding transparently or failing gracefully with clear communication. As the system scales, workflows continue to perform reliably without introducing new bottlenecks or increasing operational risk. Development teams can confidently explain, modify, and extend saga workflows due to their clear structure and modularity. Incident analysis reveals resilient behavior under stress, with failures contained and managed without cascading effects or prolonged downtime. The presence of sagas becomes a hallmark of engineering maturity and operational excellence in any distributed system.

SUMMARY

The saga pattern represents a critical tool of modern distributed architecture. By deconstructing complex operations into local, reversible steps, sagas eliminate the tenuous and inefficient traditional global transactions. They allow services to act autonomously while preserving business consistency, embracing eventual consistency as a practical and reliable reality. Sagas demand careful design, robust observability, and a mindset toward graceful failure recovery. When executed well, they transform uncertainty from a threat into a managed, expected part of system behavior.

REFERENCES

H. Garcia-Molina and K. Salem, "Sagas," *ACM SIGMOD Record*, vol. 16, no. 3, pp. 249–259, 1987.

S. Newman, *Building Microservices: Designing Fine-Grained Systems*, O'Reilly Media, 2015.

J. Bonér, "The Reactive Principles," white paper, 2022, available at https://www.reactiveprinciples.org.

26 • The CAP Theorem

"To choose is to renounce, especially when you're choosing well." — André Gide

INTRODUCTION

Distributed systems fail in parts. Sometimes one node lags, another disappears, and a network hiccup delays or drops messages. In these moments, you're forced to choose: Do you keep the system responsive even if the data might be stale? Or do you prioritize strict accuracy, even if that means some users get no response at all? That's the core tension behind the CAP theorem. The CAP theorem is about practical trade-offs when scaling real-world systems. Understanding CAP helps you choose wisely.

KEY CONCEPT

The CAP theorem, initially proposed by Eric Brewer and formalized by Gilbert and Lynch, lays out a tough reality of distributed systems. You can't guarantee *consistency*, *availability*, and *partition tolerance* all at once. One of them has to give.

Let's break that down. Consistency means every time someone reads data, they get the most recent update, no matter which server they're hitting. Availability means the system always responds to requests, even if it's not the freshest data. Partition tolerance means the system keeps running even when some parts can't talk to each other due to network issues. You can only fully commit to two, and since network partitions are a given in distributed systems, that leaves you choosing between consistency and availability when things go wrong.

Think about running a ride-sharing app. Do you want drivers to keep seeing ride requests, even if they're a little stale? That's availability. Or do you block access until you can confirm the data is fully up to date? That's consistency. Neither answer is wrong, but each leads to a different user experience. The CAP theorem helps you make that choice deliberately, not reactively.

WHY IT MATTERS

Your users don't care how your system works until something breaks. That's when your decisions about consistency, availability, and partition tolerance come into sharp focus. The CAP theorem gives you a practical lens for system design. During design, it becomes a decision-making tool that helps your team navigate trade-offs with clarity. Instead of chasing unrealistic goals like perfect consistency and constant availability simultaneously, you ask better questions: What happens when these two services can't talk to each other? Do we show stale data, block the action, or fail gracefully with a clear fallback?

These conversations shift the culture. Documentation reflects intentional trade-offs, and you have a clear and aligned playbook on how to respond during outages. That mindset creates predictability under stress, and predictability builds trust across your tech stack and stakeholders.

IN PRACTICE

In practice, partition tolerance is a given. The real choice lies between consistency and availability, and you won't make that choice just once. It depends on what part of the system you're building.

Consider payment processing. Here, consistency isn't negotiable. It's better to block a transaction than risk double-charging a customer. That's why companies like Stripe design their systems to reject requests that can't be confirmed across nodes. During a partition, you err on the side of data integrity, even if it means turning away some valid transactions. Now, think about a social media notification system. If a "like" arrives late or shows up twice, most users won't care. In this case, you prioritize availability. Keeping things responsive matters more than perfect consistency.

Mature systems mix these priorities. You choose deliberately, feature by feature. Maybe you allow eventual consistency for user profiles that sync quietly in the background. You demand strong consistency for a checkout flow that handles real money. For analytics logging, you might drop events rather than slow down the app. Each choice reflects how users interact with that part of the system and what kind of failure you're willing to accept.

Resilient teams document these decisions clearly. They don't wait for things to break down to figure out what trade-offs were made. They go into incident reviews asking both what failed and whether it failed in the way they expected. That shift from reacting to predicting builds trust in the system and in you as an engineer.

CASE STUDY

This deliberate, context-aware CAP decision-making is evident in Netflix's infrastructure strategy. When migrating key workloads to the cloud, Netflix adopted Apache Cassandra as its primary distributed data store for services such as video metadata, recommendations, and user activity tracking. For these areas, availability under load is more critical than strict consistency.

Cassandra prioritizes partition tolerance and availability. If a network partition occurs between availability zones or nodes, Cassandra nodes continue accepting writes even if those writes cannot immediately propagate cluster-wide. This ensures the user-facing experience remains responsive, even during underlying infrastructure failures. Netflix embraced this trade-off intentionally. In systems like streaming recommendations, it's acceptable for some data (like recently watched items) to be slightly out of sync, as long as users still get a seamless experience. The system reconciles inconsistencies asynchronously once the partition heals.

This real-world example reinforces the principle that CAP trade-offs aren't abstract. They shape architectural decisions feature by feature. For Netflix, maintaining user experience meant aligning system behavior with availability and partition tolerance because, in their context, speed and uptime were worth more than immediate global consistency.

COMMON PITFALLS

One of the most common mistakes while applying CAP is assuming network failures won't happen. Maybe everything worked fine in staging, so you designed partitions as a rare edge case. When that assumption breaks in production, your system breaks with it. Conversely, some teams go all-in on consistency even for features that don't matter. That adds latency and operational overhead to parts of your product that could've worked just fine with eventual consistency. Then there's the trap of favoring availability at all costs. It feels good to keep the system responsive during a partition, but if you're letting users write data without a plan to reconcile conflicts later, you're just trading short-term uptime for long-term pain.

However, a more subtle failure is thinking of CAP as a rigid, all-or-nothing system-wide rule. It's not. CAP is a lens you apply to each feature, each user path, and each failure mode. When teams treat it as a one-time architectural checkbox, they miss the nuance and the opportunity to design for resilience. These patterns usually emerge when product and engineering aren't aligned, or decisions aren't documented clearly. Note that CAP isn't just a backend concern. It's a product call. It defines how your system behaves under pressure and how your users experience failure.

SUCCESS INDICATORS

You'll know your CAP-related decisions are working when your system behaves predictably in stressful conditions. During a network partition, users can still place orders even if their activity feed lags slightly. Your most critical data remains consistent, never showing two conflicting versions of the same state. Engineers across your team can clearly articulate why each feature leans toward consistency or availability, and product managers are aligned on the trade-offs. Your documentation includes clear fallback strategies and makes those expectations visible to everyone involved.

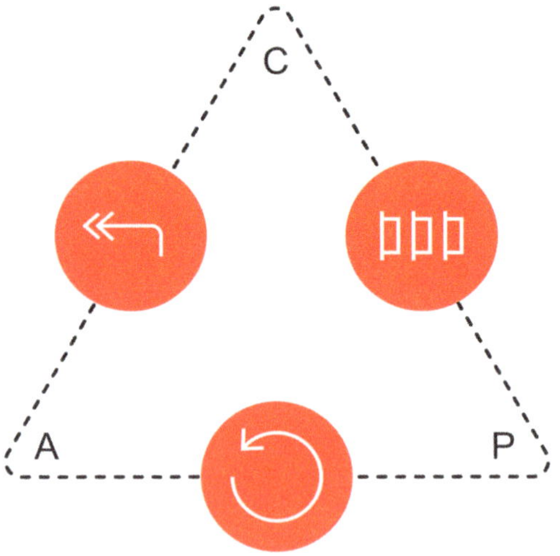

Figure 26 – CAP Theorem

SUMMARY

The CAP theorem is a compass for making deliberate product and user experience choices. It helps you prioritize what matters most in the messiness of real-world systems. By choosing the right trade-offs and documenting them well, you build systems that withstand partitions, meet user expectations, and behave responsibly under stress. You can't have it all, but you can have what your users value most, delivered reliably, even when the network isn't.

REFERENCES

S. Gilbert and N. Lynch, "Brewer's Conjecture and the Feasibility of Consistent, Available, Partition-Tolerant Web Services," *ACM SIGACT News*, vol. 33, no. 2, pp. 51–59, 2002.

E. Brewer, "CAP Twelve Years Later: How the "Rules" Have Changed," *Computer* 45(2), 2012.

A. Lakshman and P. Malik, "Cassandra: A Decentralized Structured Storage System," *ACM SIGOPS Operating Systems Review*, vol. 44, no. 2, pp. 35–40, 2010.

27 • Eventual Consistency

"A delayed result is not a failed one." — Marcus Aurelius

INTRODUCTION

Distributed systems cannot have it all. If you insist on perfect synchronization across nodes at all times, you pay the price in uptime, scalability, and speed. Eventual consistency embraces this trade-off. It allows temporary inconsistencies in exchange for keeping systems fast and available.

Instead of forcing every node to agree immediately, eventual consistency accepts that data may be temporarily out of sync. Updates propagate asynchronously, enabling the system to stay responsive even during failures or network partitions. The goal is to delay full agreement until it is practical. For large-scale applications, this pragmatic mindset often marks the difference between thriving in real-world conditions and failing under idealized expectations.

KEY CONCEPT

Eventual consistency is a distributed systems principle where data replicas can diverge temporarily but are guaranteed to converge to the same state over time. Unlike strict consistency models that require immediate coordination across nodes, eventual consistency permits updates to be made locally and shared asynchronously.

This approach works particularly well in environments that prioritize high availability. Consider a global photo-sharing application. When a user posts a photo, it appears instantly on their feed, even if that update takes seconds or longer to reach other users around the world. The system prioritizes responsiveness, syncing changes across replicas without stalling the user experience.

Databases like Apache Cassandra, Riak, and Couchbase rely on eventual consistency. They allow writes to the nearest or most available node, and instead of halting progress during minor inconsistencies, these systems keep moving while fixing discrepancies in the background. The core idea is to design systems that can handle temporary disorder and the cost of immediate agreement to prioritize availability and responsiveness.

WHY IT MATTERS

Users expect software to feel fast, resilient, and always available. Enforcing immediate consistency across distributed systems undermines that expectation by introducing delays, increasing error rates, and risking total unavailability when one node misbehaves. By embracing eventual consistency, systems stay up and responsive. Even under partial failure or regional network issues, users continue interacting with the platform without disruption. This principle also unlocks horizontal scalability by eliminating the need for global locking or synchronous replication.

At its core, eventual consistency reflects how users interact with the real world. Minor delays in seeing an update are acceptable if it means the system remains fast and functional. Sacrificing perfection in favor of continuous service is a reasonable compromise.

IN PRACTICE

When you build systems with eventual consistency, you balance speed and reliability without making the design too complex. Start by figuring out which workflows can handle temporary inconsistencies and which ones can't. User activity logs, notification systems, and recommendation engines often work well with eventual consistency. Payment processing or inventory management usually needs stricter guarantees.

Use replication and caching to hide synchronization delays. When you serve reads from neasrby replicas and let updates propagate in the background, you give users the sense of immediacy. Clear messages like "Saving..." help set expectations when background syncing is still happening. Conflict resolution is crucial. Techniques like last write wins, version vectors, or custom merge policies let you handle conflicting updates predictably. Often, you mix models, using strong consistency for critical paths and eventual consistency elsewhere.

Keep an eye on synchronization. Monitor lag between replicas, watch for anomalies, and show sync status on internal dashboards so you catch issues early. Done well, eventual consistency turns the challenges of distributed systems into an advantage for your users.

CASE STUDY

Etsy, the online marketplace for handmade and vintage goods, faced the challenge of balancing speed and reliability across a rapidly growing global user base. Rigid consistency models slowed down user interactions and created bottlenecks, particularly as Etsy scaled internationally.

To address this, Etsy adopted an eventual consistency model for non-critical data flows such as product views, likes, and search indexing. When a user favorited an item or updated a shop listing, the local system would accept the change immediately, while background workers propagated updates across data centers asynchronously. Etsy built conflict resolution strategies into its indexing pipelines. It ensured that data reconciled safely even when multiple updates occurred in parallel. Lightweight feedback mechanisms informed users when actions were processing, improving trust without introducing unnecessary friction.

The result was a faster, more resilient platform. Etsy maintained responsiveness during traffic surges like Black Friday or site-wide promotions without compromising core transaction integrity. By intelligently applying eventual consistency where appropriate, Etsy created an experience that balanced user expectations with the realities of distributed system design.

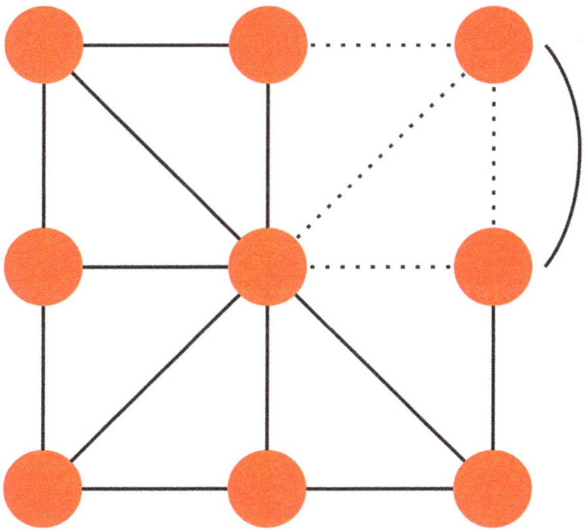

Figure 27 – Eventual Consistency

COMMON PITFALLS

Eventual consistency needs well-defined boundaries, user-focused feedback, and defensive architecture to work effectively. Without that, misapplied eventual consistency often erodes user trust and weakens systems in subtle ways. When services don't communicate synchronization status clearly, users are left wondering if their actions actually worked. Weak conflict resolution can cause data loss, duplication, or corruption. Applying eventual consistency everywhere exposes the business to risks that can outweigh any gains in availability: inconsistent UI behavior, stale data, and gaps between services all chip away at reliability.

SUCCESS INDICATORS

When eventual consistency is implemented correctly, user interactions remain fast and seamless even during infrastructure stress. Error rates related to availability or partition tolerance drop significantly. Conflict resolution happens predictably, without data corruption or rollback incidents. Observability tools track synchronization lag effectively, giving teams real-time visibility into system health. Key performance indicators (KPIs) such as engagement, retention, and customer satisfaction stay strong, even during regional disruptions or backend failures. Trust in the platform grows because users experience reliability, not inconsistency. That is the real measure of successful eventual consistency.

SUMMARY

Eventual consistency is a mature design choice for systems that prioritize resilience, responsiveness, and global reach. By allowing data to settle naturally instead of enforcing strict synchronization at every turn, you create systems that thrive under real-world conditions. Users often value speed and reliability more than instant global agreement, and eventual consistency delivers both when applied with care. When complexity grows and systems stretch across continents, this principle becomes a cornerstone for delivering a great user experience.

REFERENCES

W. Vogels, "Eventually Consistent," *Communications of the ACM*, vol. 52, no. 1, pp. 40–44, 2009.

G. DeCandia et al., "Dynamo: Amazon's Highly Available Key-Value Store," *ACM SIGOPS Operating Systems Review*, pp. 205–220, 2007.

S. Schirmer, "API First Transformation at Etsy—Concurrency," *Etsy Code as Craft*, 2016. https://www.etsy.com/codeascraft/api-first-transformation-at-etsy-concurrency

28 · Single Source of Truth

"If you chase two rabbits, you will not catch either one." — Ancient proverb

INTRODUCTION

Modern software systems often juggle the same data across databases, services, and user interfaces. Without a consistent anchor, data duplicates pile up, values conflict, and teams lose trust in their own system. The Single Source of Truth (SSOT) principle addresses this risk at its core. It asserts that every piece of data should exist in only one authoritative location, and every other part of the system should reference that origin rather than copying or managing its own version.

The SSOT principle is a commitment to reducing errors and simplifying maintenance across every layer of a system. Establishing a clear, consistent truth removes guesswork and enables systems to behave predictably and scale confidently, whether applied to backend databases, frontend applications, or distributed microservices.

KEY CONCEPT

The essence of the SSOT principle is straightforward: there should be only one place where a specific piece of data is stored and updated. All other components or services must reference this authoritative source without creating independent copies. In database design, this shows up through normalization, where relational schemas are structured to avoid duplicated information. Instead of scattering customer addresses across multiple tables, one centralized table ensures that updates occur once and propagate naturally throughout dependent systems.

In frontend applications, an SSOT surfaces through centralized state management. A consistent state store ensures that if a form is saving data, every button, field, and message reflects the same truth, not fragmented perceptions of it. In distributed systems, the principle extends to service boundaries. Each microservice must own its data domain. If multiple services attempt to store and modify the same data independently, version mismatches and reconciliation nightmares show up without fail. The SSOT principle demands that one service manages the canonical version, and others listen for updates or access it through well-defined APIs.

Even configuration management benefits profoundly from an SSOT. Instead of hardcoding environment variables across multiple services, an SSOT ensures that the system reads the same settings from a unified, authoritative source. The guiding idea across all domains remains the same: one data item, one place, one truth.

WHY IT MATTERS

Without a single source of truth, data gets out of sync. Bugs become harder to trace. Teams spend increasing amounts of time reconciling conflicting values rather than building new features. An SSOT brings order to this by re-establishing predictability in the heart of complex systems.

By enforcing an SSOT, systems prevent inconsistencies. When an update occurs, it is made in exactly one location, and every consumer reflects that change immediately or upon refresh. This sharply reduces the risk of stale data bugs that silently degrade system quality.

An SSOT also simplifies reasoning. Engineers no longer have to ask which version of a customer record, configuration setting, or transaction state is correct. The authoritative source is clearly defined, reducing cognitive overhead and accelerating development workflows.

Over time, systems adhering to an SSOT accumulate significantly less technical debt. The need for sync jobs, data migrations, or emergency patches declines because one of the root causes (duplication) is eliminated. As systems grow, the SSOT ensures that they scale cleanly, without services colliding over data ownership or struggling to synchronize fragmented datasets. It is a principle that pays continual dividends across operational, architectural, and business dimensions.

IN PRACTICE

Applying the Single Source of Truth principle starts with making deliberate architectural choices. In your database design, normalize schemas so each fact lives in one place. Reference it using foreign keys instead of copying data across tables. When a customer's address changes, you want one update, not a scatter of manual fixes. On the frontend, centralize state management. Don't let components hold their own versions of state. Instead, have them pull directly from a unified source so the user experience stays consistent and synchronized. In distributed systems, draw clear ownership lines. Make each service responsible for specific data entities. That service becomes the canonical source. Other services read through APIs or

CASE STUDY

The importance of the SSOT principle is illustrated well by GitHub's approach to repository metadata management. As GitHub scaled to millions of repositories, maintaining metadata consistency became a critical operational challenge. Instead of allowing different systems to maintain independent copies of repository information, GitHub centralized the metadata into a unified service.

This service became the single source of truth for repository attributes such as ownership, visibility settings, and access permissions. Other internal systems, from search indexing to notifications to billing, reference this authoritative service rather than duplicating the data. As a result, updates to repository attributes propagate accurately and predictably throughout GitHub's ecosystem. By implementing an SSOT at the metadata level, GitHub improved reliability, reduced operational complexity, and enabled faster development of new features that depended on consistent, trusted data.

event streams rather than managing their own copies. If the billing service owns invoice records, keep them that way. No other service should store independent versions.

Follow this rigorously with configuration, too. Store environment variables, feature flags, and operational settings in centralized systems like AWS Parameter Store, Kubernetes ConfigMaps, or dedicated config servers. Let those centralized values flow consistently everywhere.

The rule is simple. Reference data rather than duplicating it. Whether you're building APIs, subscriptions, or event-driven flows, tie everything back to a single source. That's how you keep your system coherent and trustworthy.

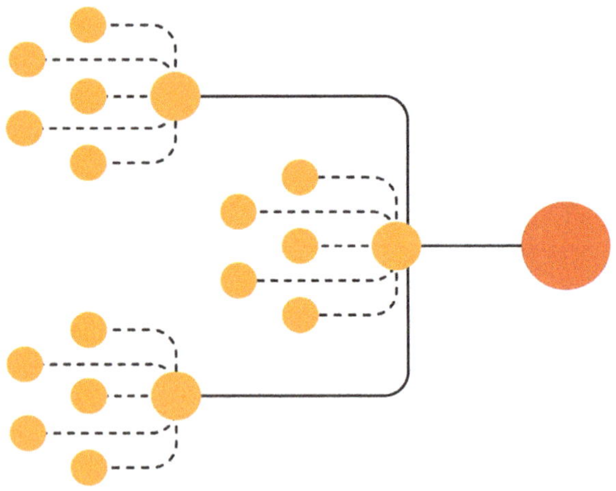

Figure 28 – Single Source of Truth

COMMON PITFALLS

Systems that aspire to an SSOT can still fall into traps. The most common mistake is data duplication, which allows multiple systems or layers to store and modify independent copies of the same data. Attempts to synchronize these copies inevitably fail, introducing version drift and inconsistency. Overzealousness can also backfire. Excessively fragmented schemas may require too many joins at query time, introducing performance bottlenecks that undermine system responsiveness. Judicious, context-aware denormalization may sometimes be appropriate without compromising the spirit of the SSOT principle.

In distributed systems, a lack of a clear ownership model leads to different services maintaining their own unofficial versions of the truth. Without enforced data ownership, version mismatches and reconciliation complexities multiply rapidly. Similarly, poor state management on the frontend, where different components maintain their own versions of user state, leads to buggy or incoherent interfaces.

Configuration sprawl can also defeat an SSOT. Hard-coded values scattered across services and layers make consistent updates nearly impossible, even if the application code itself remains clean. Centralization of configuration must be treated with the same rigor as centralization of domain data.

SUCCESS INDICATORS

When systems successfully implement the Single Source of Truth principle, the benefits become visible at every layer. Data updates propagate smoothly and predictably, with no stale copies or silent inconsistencies. User interfaces remain synchronized, presenting a unified and coherent experience across screens and components. Microservices interact cleanly, trusting each other's data contracts rather than trying to verify or reconcile divergent copies.

Over time, teams spend less time debugging inconsistencies and more time delivering new features. Developers quickly and confidently locate the authoritative source of any data, reducing friction during debugging and development. Configuration updates apply uniformly across environments without needing ad hoc fixes or special-case handling. Systems behave less like a patchwork of approximations and more like reliable, consistent platforms that scale naturally as complexity grows.

SUMMARY

The Single Source of Truth principle brings clarity to software systems. Every piece of data must have one owner, definition, and authoritative home. Systems across all layers, like databases, services, frontend applications, and configuration management, must be designed to reference this single origin rather than duplicating or fragmenting it.

An SSOT reduces bugs, accelerates development, and strengthens operational resilience by eliminating duplication and enforcing clear ownership. It turns software systems into coherent, predictable platforms rather than collections of competing versions. In a world of growing system complexity, a single source of truth is an essential building block for systems that are scalable and trustworthy.

REFERENCES

M. Fowler, *Patterns of Enterprise Application Architecture*, Addison-Wesley Professional, 2003.

M-A. Sicilia, ed., *Handbook of Metadata, Semantics and Ontologies*, World Scientific Publishing Company, 2012.

B. Reselman, "Implementing a Single Source of Truth in an Enterprise Architecture," *Red Hat Blog*, 2021. https://www.redhat.com/en/blog/single-source-truth-architecture

S. Butterworth, "Introducing Entitlements: GitHub's Open Source Identity and Access Management Solution," *GitHub Blog*, 2022. https://github.blog/news-insights/product-news/introducing-entitlements-githubs-open-source-identity-and-access-management-solution/

29 • Message Ordering and Exactly Once Processing

"The nature of things is in the order of things." — Laozi, Tao Te Ching

INTRODUCTION

The Message Ordering and Exactly Once Processing principle ensures that message-driven systems process each message exactly once and in the correct sequence. In distributed environments where messages can arrive out of order, be delayed, or be delivered multiple times, maintaining strict order and preventing duplication is essential for preserving data integrity. Without these guarantees, workflows become unpredictable, and outcomes become unreliable across the entire system.

As applications increasingly rely on asynchronous messaging for scalability and responsiveness, enforcing guardrails becomes a critical design requirement. Systems must ensure that every message gets accounted for, processed only once, and moves through the pipeline in precisely the expected order to support reliable and consistent operations.

KEY CONCEPT

The core of this principle revolves around two distinct but deeply connected guarantees. First, strict ordering ensures that messages are processed in the exact sequence in which they were intended. When operations depend on the order of events, such as account updates, financial transactions, or state transitions, processing out of sequence can introduce subtle but serious inconsistencies. Second, exactly once semantics guarantee that each message is processed once and only once, no matter what network retries, broker failures, or client timeouts occur. Achieving this requires a combination of design strategies, including idempotency, unique message identifiers, and deduplication mechanisms.

Transaction coordination often plays a critical supporting role. Systems may leverage distributed transaction protocols or message brokers with transactional capabilities to ensure that message consumption and downstream operations either complete successfully together or not at all. Maintaining state, tracking sequence numbers, and embedding timestamps can help strengthen guarantees around ordering and uniqueness in systems where external factors can otherwise introduce disorder.

WHY IT MATTERS

Without guaranteed ordering, dependent actions may execute in the wrong sequence, causing irreversible corruption of business workflows. Inconsistent event ordering can trigger incorrect balances in financial systems, misaligned inventory levels in supply chains, or user-visible errors in collaborative applications.

Exactly once semantics protect against a different but equally damaging risk: duplicate processing. In distributed architectures, retries and network failures are common. Without a strategy to detect and prevent duplicate handling, the same message might update a balance twice, ship an order multiple times, or issue repeated notifications. Each duplication silently erodes user trust, increases operational overhead, and complicates system recovery.

Maintaining both ordering and exactly once delivery simplifies system behavior. Debugging becomes cleaner, as anomalies related to duplicates or out-of-order processing largely disappear. Business processes remain auditable and predictable, reinforcing user trust. In regulated industries like finance and healthcare, the ability to prove correct, consistent processing is essential for compliance and meeting SLAs.

IN PRACTICE

Implementing strict ordering and exactly once processing starts with careful architectural choices. Often, you begin by picking the right message broker. Tools like Apache Kafka, RabbitMQ, and AWS SQS (Simple Queue Service) each offer different levels of ordering and delivery guarantees. You also need to design your processing logic to be idempotent. Even if your infrastructure helps with deduplication, your application must be safe on its own. Make sure replaying a message never creates bad side effects. That way, retries from consumer crashes or timeouts won't corrupt your system state.

Use sequence numbers or timestamps in messages to add another layer of protection. With that metadata, you can detect stale or out-of-order messages and discard them, rebuilding the correct sequence even when the transport layer isn't perfect. Commit message consumption and business operations in a single atomic unit whenever possible. That prevents gaps where a message is acknowledged but the operation fails. If distributed transactions feel too heavy, lean on lightweight, idempotent designs and careful acknowledgment flows to protect consistency.

Finally, you also need to implement operational monitoring and auditability with comprehensive logging and anomaly detection. These tools alert teams when message flows deviate from expected patterns. Observability also ensures that when things inevitably go wrong, systems can detect, diagnose, and recover with minimal impact.

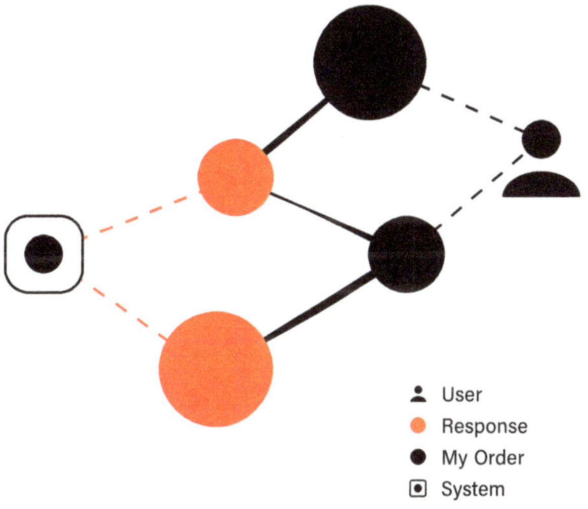

Figure 29 – Message Ordering & Exactly-One Processing

CASE STUDY

PayPal offers a clear demonstration of the importance of message ordering and exactly once processing at scale. Handling millions of financial transactions per day across global markets, PayPal must ensure that each transaction executes exactly once and in the precise order intended to avoid double-billing, missing payments, or regulatory violations.

To achieve this, PayPal deployed a messaging infrastructure built on Apache Kafka. Each transaction message carried a unique identifier and a sequence number, enabling strict tracking throughout the processing pipeline. Processing systems were designed with full idempotency, allowing safe retries without financial duplication. Kafka's transactional capabilities ensured that message consumption and downstream database updates occurred atomically, preventing any window where a transaction could be partially completed or inconsistently recorded.

Additionally, PayPal implemented distributed logs and real-time monitoring frameworks that continuously audited message flows. If anomalies were detected, compensatory actions could be taken immediately, restoring order without disrupting the customer experience. By investing in a robust approach to ordering and exactly once processing, PayPal significantly reduced transaction errors, improved system resilience, and reinforced customer trust. The design enabled the company to meet strict regulatory requirements while maintaining the scalability and responsiveness demanded by its global user base.

COMMON PITFALLS

Despite best intentions, many systems stumble when implementing message ordering and exactly once processing. Out-of-order delivery remains a persistent risk, particularly when relying on network transports or brokers that do not enforce strict sequencing. Even with ordered delivery, system failures can cause consumers to process messages in unintended orders if acknowledgments and retries are mishandled.

Duplicate messages are another frequent hazard. Distributed systems often use retries to improve reliability, but without idempotent consumers or deduplication logic, retries introduce subtle data corruption rather than solving problems. Crafting idempotent operations is itself challenging; not every business action is naturally repeatable without side effects, requiring careful design or creative fallback mechanisms.

Finally, striving for exactly once semantics can introduce significant complexity. Transactional messaging, sequence management, and deduplication all carry overhead. Balancing performance, reliability, and engineering effort demands pragmatic decisions about where full guarantees are necessary and where best-effort strategies may suffice without compromising business integrity.

SUCCESS INDICATORS

The system exhibits unmistakable characteristics when the Message Ordering and Exactly Once Processing principle is effectively applied. State transitions occur cleanly without duplicate actions or out-of-order updates. Even under stress, the system sustains high throughput because ordering and deduplication mechanisms are optimized and do not bottleneck performance.

Error rates related to message reprocessing, stale updates, or double processing decline, reducing operational firefighting and improving user experience. Clear audit trails confirm that every message was processed exactly once and in the intended order, enabling rapid troubleshooting and regulatory reporting. These behaviors signal a mature, resilient system capable of operating reliably even under the unpredictable realities of distributed networks.

SUMMARY

The Message Ordering and Exactly Once Processing principle is critical for building reliable, scalable messaging systems. By ensuring that each message is processed only once and in the correct sequence, systems protect data integrity, simplify error handling, and deliver consistent, trustworthy outcomes. Implementing this principle demands selecting capable middleware, designing robust idempotent operations, embedding reliable sequencing mechanisms, and continuously monitoring message flows. With good implementation, this principle transforms messaging infrastructure from a potential source of disorder into a foundation for dependable, predictable software systems.

REFERENCES

M. Kleppmann, *Designing Data-Intensive Applications: The Big Ideas Behind Reliable, Scalable, and Maintainable Systems*, O'Reilly Media, 2017.

Apache Software Foundation. (n.d.). *Apache Kafka documentation: Introduction to the platform.* https://kafka.apache.org/documentation/#intro_platform

M. Koppa, (2023, September 7). "Scaling Kafka to Support PayPal's Data Growth," *The PayPal Technology Blog*, 2023.

30 • Auto-Scaling

"To improve is to change; to be perfect is to change often." — Winston Churchill

INTRODUCTION

Applications rarely experience uniform demand. Some moments bring well-predicted load; others deliver spikes of demand. Without a system that adjusts to that variability, you either pay for unused infrastructure or lose performance when it matters most. The Auto-Scaling principle offers a better way forward by enabling systems to respond automatically to changing loads. It removes the guesswork, eliminates manual provisioning, and supports both cost-efficiency and resilience. Instead of choosing between stability and savings, you get both, on your terms and in real time.

KEY CONCEPT

Auto-scaling is the process of automatically increasing or decreasing system resources based on real-world demand. This elasticity is achieved by continuously monitoring metrics such as CPU usage, memory consumption, request rates, or queue lengths. When those indicators suggest that a service is under pressure, the system responds by adding capacity. When the demand drops, it scales back to conserve resources. Most implementations favor horizontal scaling, which means adding more service instances rather than increasing the power of a single one. This approach aligns better with fault-tolerant, distributed system design.

Policies guide every aspect of auto-scaling behavior. These policies define thresholds, limits, and cooldown periods, determining how quickly and how much the system should scale. A well-structured policy keeps the system nimble during spikes but prevents overreactions during temporary fluctuations. The result is a self-regulating environment that matches resources to need without constant human involvement.

WHY IT MATTERS

Auto-scaling solves a core tension in system design: how to prepare for traffic that changes without warning. Without it, teams either overprovision infrastructure, costing money, or underprovision it, which results in user-facing slowdowns or downtime. By dynamically managing resources, auto-scaling protects performance during surges while reclaiming costs during lulls. It allows systems to absorb large spikes in load without breaking and helps maintain consistent response times even when demand is unpredictable.

CASE STUDY

Airbnb's engineering team faced a familiar challenge: their demand patterns shifted dramatically by region, season, and global event. To handle this, they observed a blend of metrics. This included CPU utilization, request latency, and job queue depth. These signals gave a more complete picture of user activity and system load. Using AWS Auto Scaling groups alongside Kubernetes, they implemented policies that reflected real-world usage. The policies were reactive enough to respond to surges, but stable enough to avoid flapping. Cooldown windows and instance caps were regularly tuned based on traffic data and observability feedback. Logs captured every scaling event, making it easier to trace the root of instability and optimize rules.

Also, Airbnb made sure to scale back safely as demand dropped, avoiding waste while protecting in-flight bookings and sessions. This balance of responsiveness, restraint, and transparency turned auto-scaling from a reactive mechanism into a resilient strategy, freeing engineers from manual tuning and letting the platform flex naturally with user behavior.

The value of auto-scaling also extends to engineering operations. It removes the burden of manual resource tuning, reduces the need for reactive firefighting, and creates space for teams to focus on product delivery instead of capacity planning. When auto-scaling works well, it fades into the background. You don't notice it, but you benefit from its presence whenever the system stays responsive under stress or costs drop during quiet hours.

IN PRACTICE

Getting auto-scaling right starts with choosing metrics that reflect real demand and strain on your system. CPU and memory might be enough for compute-heavy workloads, but they often fall short on their own. For web apps, you want to watch request latency and throughput. If you're handling background jobs, queue size or wait times might give you better signals. No single metric tells the whole story. The best auto-scaling strategies look at several indicators and act only when the combined picture justifies it. You also need smart policies. Set thresholds high enough to filter out noise but low enough to react before performance dips. Cooldown periods help the system settle between changes. Define minimum and maximum limits so you don't scale too far in either direction. These rules aren't set-and-forget. You'll need to tune them regularly. What works today might lag tomorrow as traffic patterns shift or your app grows across regions.

Balancing the load is just as important. If traffic doesn't reach new instances quickly, scaling out won't help. Use load balancers, service meshes, or orchestration layers to route traffic evenly. Pay attention to cold-start times, too. If new instances come online slowly, they can't relieve pressure fast enough to matter. Remember to scale in as well as out. Many teams forget this and leave resources running long after demand drops. You need clear policies for when to shed capacity, and you should do it gradually to avoid cutting off active users or workloads.

Finally, build visibility into your scaling decisions. Your logs and metrics should show when you scaled, what triggered it, and how the system performed afterward. That transparency helps you improve policies, spot issues like flapping, and build guardrails around auto-scaling.

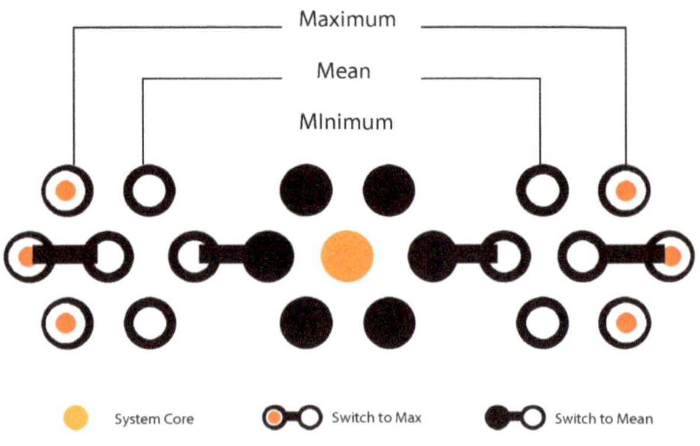

Figure 30 – Auto-Scaling

COMMON PITFALLS

Auto-scaling usually fails when the assumptions behind it are flawed. Poorly chosen metrics result in scaling at the wrong times. Misconfigured thresholds create instability. Slow startup times can also make scaling too late to help. Ignoring the need to scale down leads to costly infrastructure spend. When fallback rules don't exist or logs are missing, engineers are left blind when things go wrong, and without proper routing, added capacity doesn't help at all. Auto-scaling requires a full-system perspective, not just a toggle on a dashboard.

SUCCESS INDICATORS

You know auto-scaling is working when your system stays responsive even during unexpected bursts of demand. Users experience consistent performance whether they are using the system during peak hours or in an off-peak window. Engineers no longer scramble to adjust server counts. Resource graphs show a clear pattern of infrastructure expansion and contraction in sync with usage, not in anticipation or fear. Costs track with growth; when up- or down-scaling decisions are reviewed, they make sense.

SUMMARY

The Auto-Scaling principle enables modern systems to flex in real time, absorbing demand, protecting performance, and controlling costs. For high-scale environments, it's a baseline expectation for reliability and efficiency. Systems that scale automatically remove friction for users and teams alike. They weather spikes without stress, recover gracefully, and never use more than they need to.

REFERENCES

C. Pahl and P. Jamshidi, "Microservices: A Systematic Mapping Study," *Proceedings of the 6th International Conference on Cloud Computing and Services Science*, vols. 1 and 2, pp. 137–146, 2016.

S. Newman, *Building Microservices: Designing Fine-Grained Systems*, O'Reilly Media, 2015.

D. Morrison and E. Sheng, "Dynamic Kubernetes Cluster Scaling at Airbnb," *The Airbnb Tech Blog*, 2022.

31 • Multi-Tenancy

"We are more alike, my friends, than we are unalike." — Maya Angelou

INTRODUCTION

Multi-tenancy enables you to turn your product into a growth engine. In a traditional approach, each new customer for your products and services gets their own environment. This setup feels quick at first, but soon, for every new customer, you're cloning your infrastructure, chasing bugs across ten environments, and dreading every deployment. With multi-tenancy, instead of one-off deployments, you build a shared system where each customer and tenant feel like they're using their own private instance, even though everything runs on a single codebase. You deliver tailored experiences at scale, all while reducing complexity, streamlining operations, and cutting infrastructure costs.

This is the core pillar of modern SaaS (software as a service), where large and small service providers leverage multi-tenancy to deliver secure, scalable services to thousands of customers without slowing down development or reliability.

KEY CONCEPT

Multi-tenancy means running a single application that serves multiple distinct customers while keeping their data, configurations, and permissions fully isolated. Although all tenants share the same deployment, the system ensures that each one experiences it as if it were built just for them. Achieving this requires deliberate architectural decisions.

This starts with tenant isolation through strict access controls, tenant identifiers, or even separate database schemas to guarantee that no data or permissions ever leak between customers. At the infrastructure level, resources like compute, memory, and storage are shared, but they need to scale dynamically so that no single tenant dominates the system. There is still centralized deployment, so when you release a new feature or patch, all tenants benefit immediately. At the same time, flexibility remains essential. Tenants should be able to configure the product to fit their needs without forcing changes to the core codebase. When this all comes together, you reduce operational overhead, speed up onboarding, and avoid the long-term complexity of managing fragmented, tenant-specific infrastructure.

WHY IT MATTERS

A single-tenant mindset might feel manageable at first, but it quickly becomes a bottleneck as you grow. Maintaining separate environments for each customer creates technical debt in the form of duplicated infrastructure, slower release cycles, inconsistent user experiences, and added operational costs. You end up spending more time managing environments than improving the product itself. Multi-tenancy helps solve that. With a single, shared platform, onboarding becomes faster (taking minutes instead of days). Updates are deployed once and made available to every customer simultaneously, eliminating the need for tenant-specific rollouts. Resource usage becomes far more efficient, reducing overhead and minimizing cost. At the same time, growth remains secure because tenant data stays isolated, and resource consumption is sandboxed. Multi-tenancy gives you a foundation to scale with control and clarity.

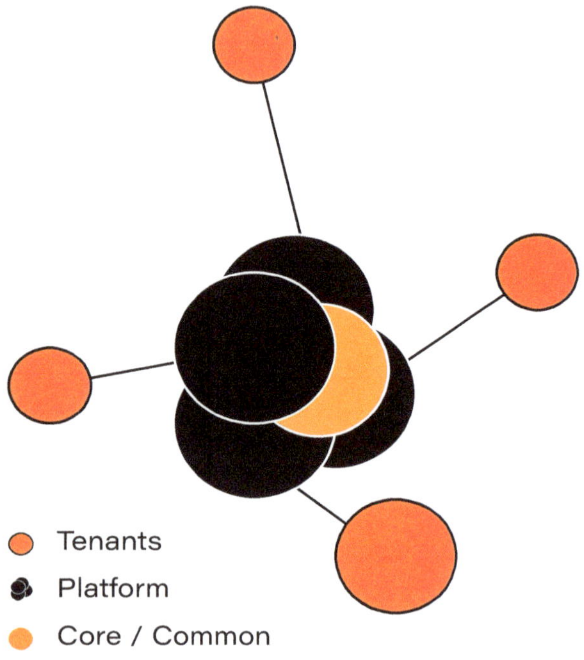

Figure 31 – Multi-Tenancy Principle

IN PRACTICE

Effective multi-tenancy starts with deliberate choices across data storage, compute, routing, configuration, and observability. You begin by thinking about how you partition data. Some systems use a shared database with a shared schema, tagging each row with a tenant ID and enforcing access controls in the application layer. This is efficient but risky if those controls fail. Others use separate schemas in the same database for stronger isolation, though that adds complexity. In some cases, especially with strict regulations or premium customers, you might choose completely separate databases, knowing they bring significant operational overhead.

You also need compute isolation. Tenants can share infrastructure underneath, but their workloads shouldn't bleed into each other. Using containers or lightweight virtual machines helps you keep processing environments separate, so one tenant's heavy batch job doesn't slow down another tenant's live dashboard. Auto-scaling ties in here, too. By watching usage patterns and scaling resources tied to a specific tenant, you can keep costs down and performance steady. Routing requests that identify the tenant early through subdomains, authentication tokens, or headers so every downstream service knows exactly who it's serving allows you to keep context across every part of the system.

Since customization requests are inevitable, you handle customization through feature flags and configuration, not tenant-specific forks. This lets tenants toggle features or tweak behavior without fragmenting your codebase. You build adaptive components that re-

CASE STUDY

As Shopify scaled to support hundreds of thousands of online stores, it adopted a multi-tenant architecture that balanced shared infrastructure with logical isolation. All merchants operated on the same application and database layers, with tenant IDs tagging each row and enforcing access controls across both app and data tiers. To prevent noisy neighbors, Shopify used container-based compute isolation and tenant-aware auto-scaling, ensuring one store's traffic spike didn't impact another. Routing layers injected the tenant context early, so downstream services like checkout and analytics always responded appropriately.

Customization was handled through configuration files and not through code forks. Merchants could tweak features and themes without fragmenting the platform. Observability was tenant-specific too, enabling the team to catch store-level issues before they escalated. By combining logical isolation, adaptive scaling, and centralized observability, Shopify turned multi-tenancy into a strategic enabler, allowing the platform to grow rapidly without compromising performance, security, or merchant flexibility.

spond to tenant-level settings, so the system stays flexible and maintainable without hardcoding exceptions.

Your observability also needs to be tenant-aware. Your metrics, logs, and alerts should show tenant-specific behavior. A spike in API latency for one customer shouldn't hide beneath smooth averages across everyone else. When you can isolate issues by tenant, you catch problems faster and stop them from spreading. When you design multi-tenancy this way, it becomes a scaling strategy that drives differentiation and sustainable growth as you operate and expand.

COMMON PITFALLS

Multi-tenancy can introduce more problems than it solves if not approached with discipline. One of the most common missteps is over-isolation. Teams sometimes fall into the trap of deploying separate environments for each tenant, which defeats the purpose of shared infrastructure and piles on operational overhead. On the other end of the spectrum, weak access controls pose a serious risk. A single missing filter or improperly scoped query can result in data bleeding between tenants, leading to trust-destroying security incidents. Performance degradation is another frequent issue. Without resource boundaries, a high-traffic tenant can monopolize compute and memory, slowing down the experience for everyone else.

Customization also becomes dangerous when it's hardcoded on a per-tenant basis. What begins as a quick fix soon becomes a tangled mess of forked logic that's hard to test, debug, and scale. Visibility compounds all of this. If you can't isolate metrics, logs, or errors by tenant, you're essentially flying blind. Debugging becomes guess-and-check, and performance tuning turns into a game of averages. Avoiding these pitfalls starts with setting clear architectural boundaries, keeping tenant logic configurable rather than fragmented, and designing observability as a first-class feature.

SUCCESS INDICATORS

A well-architected multi-tenant system feels effortless to scale. You add customers in minutes using scripts or APIs. Your teams deploy updates without worrying about compatibility across tenants. Users across the board experience fast, secure, stable systems, even when one customer has a usage spike.

You see improved team velocity because engineers aren't juggling ten environments. Logs and metrics are broken down by tenant, so you catch issues before they spread, and your infrastructure scales based on real usage. Everything runs from a single codebase, and new features hit the entire platform fast. That's how you know your multi-tenancy model works: your platform grows, your team moves faster, and your users stay happy.

SUMMARY

The Multi-Tenancy principle helps you serve many customers without multiplying your complexity. It transforms a single app into a flexible, secure, and scalable platform. One where tenants feel independent, even as they share the same infrastructure. Done right, multi-tenancy powers efficient growth and rapid innovation.

REFERENCES

S. Newman, *Building Microservices: Designing Fine-Grained Systems*, O'Reilly Media, 2015.

I. Ejeh, "What Is Multi-Tenancy and Why It Matters for B2B SaaS," *Clerk Blog*, 2025. https://clerk.com/blog/what-is-multi-tenancy-and-why-it-matters-for-B2B-SaaS

F. Weingarten, "Scaling Shopify's Multi-Tenant Architecture across Multiple Datacenters," *Proceedings of SREcon16 Europe (USENIX Association)*, 2016.

32 • The Hollywood and Tell, Don't Ask

"Give people responsibility, and they will surprise you." — Warren Bennis

INTRODUCTION

The Hollywood principle, often summarized as "Don't call us, we'll call you," describes a shift in how software is structured. Rather than having every component micromanage the flow of execution, systems following this principle control when and how individual parts are invoked. Components define what they can do, but do not dictate when those capabilities are activated. Instead, the system orchestrates interactions, calling components as needed.

Paired with the Tell, Don't Ask principle, this approach reinforces a powerful model of encapsulation and delegation. Tell, Don't Ask reminds us to empower objects to manage their own behavior instead of pulling out their data and making decisions externally. When combined with the Hollywood principle, the result is a system where components declare intent, wait to be activated, and handle their responsibilities internally. Together, these principles enable software designs that are cleaner, more resilient, and easier to extend as systems grow.

KEY CONCEPT

At the heart of the Hollywood principle lies a mindset shift: components define their capabilities but give up control over the execution flow. A service, handler, or module declares what it can do. After registration, the system decides when it will be called. Meanwhile, the Tell, Don't Ask principle strengthens this approach by ensuring that when components are activated, they own their behavior fully. Instead of passive data holders waiting for external logic to tell them what should happen, objects take responsibility for making their own decisions based on their internal state.

Together, these principles lead to designs where systems coordinate the big picture, and objects autonomously handle their domain-specific behaviors. The system manages timing and orchestration through lifecycle hooks, event-driven listeners, or service orchestrators, while individual components focus on clear, localized logic.

WHY IT MATTERS

Complex systems are often hard to change or scale because of how tightly and obscurely their parts are connected. When components control each other's flow, logic becomes entangled. When objects merely expose data but require external decision-making, responsibility becomes externalized. This makes systems harder to understand, debug, and extend.

Applying the Hollywood principle minimizes direct dependencies between components. Each part operates independently, responding to system orchestration rather than hardwired calls. Changes to one component do not extend unnecessarily through others, reducing regression risks and making changes safer. Applying the Tell, Don't Ask principle complements this by keeping logic and data encapsulated. Objects remain coherent, guarding their own behavior instead of exposing internal state for others to manipulate. Systems become more intuitive, as developers can get what an object does without needing to understand distant collaborators.

Together, these patterns significantly improve modularity, scalability, and testability. They also sharpen system clarity as developers can trace flows declaratively through configurations, routes, or event mappings, rather than deciphering scattered invocation chains embedded in code.

IN PRACTICE

Adopting the Hollywood and Tell, Don't Ask principles means changing how you build components and how they interact. Instead of creating tightly coupled calls between services, you register handlers, subscribe listeners, and define services that the system can activate when needed. You design your objects to own their behavior. Rather than exposing raw data through getters and pushing logic into external controllers, let each object receive instructions and act internally. This keeps business logic localized, protects encapsulation, and treats objects as active participants rather than passive data holders.

CASE STUDY

A good demonstration of the Hollywood and Tell, Don't Ask principles is in the architecture of Shopify's event-driven order processing system. Shopify's platform must handle millions of orders daily, each triggering a cascade of activities from payment processing to inventory updates to shipping fulfillment.

Rather than embedding a rigid sequence of service calls, Shopify's architecture embraces the Hollywood principle. Services register for domain events such as "Order Paid" or "Order Shipped" and respond autonomously when triggered. No service hardcodes knowledge of downstream workflows. The system itself orchestrates which components are activated based on events. At the same time, each service internally follows the Tell, Don't Ask principle. Payment services encapsulate validation and confirmation logic. Inventory services decide how to allocate stock. Shipping modules determine fulfillment logistics. External components do not micromanage these actions by retrieving internal data and deciding outcomes. Instead, each service receives commands and autonomously handles its responsibilities.

This combination results in a system that scales horizontally, adapts to evolving business requirements, and allows teams to innovate independently. New behaviors, such as promotional discount handling or fraud detection, are added by registering new listeners, without destabilizing existing workflows. By respecting the Hollywood and Tell, Don't Ask principles, Shopify turns high-volume, complex operations into manageable, modular flows.

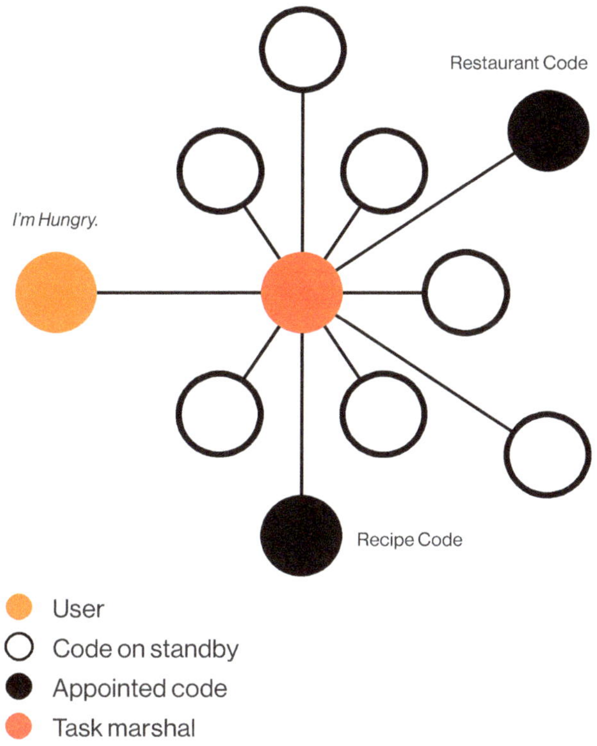

Figure 32 – Hollywood Principle

In event-driven systems, avoid chaining service calls. Instead, emit domain events like "order placed" or "user registered," then let listeners respond independently. This prevents tight coupling and makes it easier to add new behaviors without changing existing code. Use dependency injection so components get what they need without creating dependencies themselves. Orchestrators or middleware help coordinate complex flows while keeping responsibilities clean and separate.

Update your documentation practices, too. When components no longer call each other directly, you need to describe inputs and outputs clearly. Well-defined annotations, interface contracts, and event schemas give you visibility without sacrificing the autonomy these patterns support.

COMMON PITFALLS

While powerful, over-reliance on dynamic registration without clear orchestration can create hidden flaws that are difficult to trace. Systems must still maintain visible, declarative mappings of events to handlers to avoid becoming opaque. Overloading objects with too much behavior is also counterproductive. The goal of Tell, Don't Ask is not to turn objects into monoliths, but to localize related responsibilities cleanly. Objects must respect the Single Responsibility principle, keeping their tasks coherent and focused.

Finally, forcing Tell, Don't Ask, where simple reporting is sufficient, can add unnecessary indirection. Not every data retrieval needs to trigger behavior. Pragmatism is crucial to balance purity with practicality, especially in reporting and analytics domains.

SUCCESS INDICATORS

Systems that successfully implement the Hollywood and Tell, Don't Ask principles share several defining characteristics. Components feel lightweight, focused, and swappable. New features can be introduced by plugging in additional handlers or listeners, rather than rewriting existing logic. Code reviews become faster as the boundaries of responsibility are clear, and side effects are minimized. Objects expose clear actions rather than raw data, and business logic stays localized. Debugging workflows focuses on tracing event flows and orchestration, not figuring out hidden invocation chains. Systems scale naturally, as services can be deployed, versioned, and evolved independently behind clean, declarative boundaries.

Culturally, teams feel empowered rather than constrained. Developers understand how their components fit into the broader system without memorizing every interaction. As systems grow, complexity feels additive rather than explosive.

SUMMARY

The Hollywood principle, paired with Tell, Don't Ask, fosters architectures where autonomy, clarity, and scalability take center stage. These principles reduce coupling and build resilient, intuitive systems by shifting control from individual components to the system and encouraging objects to own their behavior.

Rather than orchestrating every detail, components declare what they can do and let the system call them when needed. Rather than exposing raw data for external decision-making, objects act decisively within their domain. This approach transforms codebases from chains of calls into robust compositions of cooperative, trustworthy parts. By adopting these principles, teams create software that grows gracefully, adapts easily, and remains manageable no matter how large or complex it becomes.

REFERENCES

E. Gamma, R. Helm, R. Johnson, and J. Vlissides, *Design Patterns: Elements of Reusable Object-Oriented Software*, Addison-Wesley Professional, 1994.

L. Bass, P. Clements, and R. Kazman, *Software Architecture in Practice* (3rd ed.), Addison-Wesley Professional, 2012.

B. Nguyen, "Using Server Sent Events to Simplify Real-time Streaming at Scale," *Shopify Engineering Blog*, 2022. https://shopify.engineering/server-sent-events-data-streaming

33 • The Principle of Least Astonishment (POLA)

"Don't make me think."— Steve Krug

INTRODUCTION

The Principle of Least Astonishment (POLA) is simple. Users should never feel surprised by the behavior of a system. When interacting with an interface, an API, or a piece of code, users build mental models based on their past experiences and familiar patterns. When software behavior violates those expectations, it creates frustration and errors.

The POLA applies to user interfaces and system behavior, API design, and internal code structure. Whether addressing a user clicking a button or a developer invoking a method, the principle insists that interactions must align closely with intuitive expectations. If users or developers find themselves thinking, "I didn't expect that to happen," the design likely needs to be reexamined. In a world of ever-growing system complexity, predictable behavior remains one of the most powerful tools for building trust and usability.

KEY CONCEPT

At its core, the Principle of Least Astonishment aims to minimize surprises by aligning system behavior with user expectations. The underlying concept is simple: when users interact with software, they should immediately understand what will happen next without requiring extensive documentation, special instructions, or trial-and-error learning.

Applying the POLA requires consistent attention to predictability across several dimensions. In user interfaces, design conventions must be honored. Buttons, menus, and interactions should behave as users expect based on common practice. A "Save" button should save, not delete; blue, underlined text should navigate, not trigger an unexpected side effect. In API design, method names must clearly reflect their behavior. A getUserProfile function should return user data, not alter or delete it. System behavior must remain uniform across modules and interactions. A keyboard shortcut that performs one action in one section of an application must not trigger a different, unrelated behavior elsewhere. Code structure must also respect logical expectations. Configurations should reside in predictable locations, not buried deep in unrelated files.

In short, the POLA demands that design choices match the mental models users bring with them, whether those users are navigating a screen or maintaining a codebase.

WHY IT MATTERS

Violating the Principle of Least Astonishment comes at a significant cost. Unpredictable behavior slows productivity, increases errors, and elevates the demand for documentation and support. For developers, misleading APIs and irregular code organization magnify onboarding time, introduce maintenance risks, and weaken team cohesion.

When the POLA is ignored, interfaces require extensive training instead of intuitive discovery. APIs are misused, generating subtle bugs that are difficult to track down. Cognitive friction accumulates as users must constantly second-guess what an action or method will actually do. Even minor inconsistencies compound over time, eroding trust and satisfaction.

Conversely, honoring the POLA results in improved experiences. Users operate software confidently without feeling lost or hesitant. Developers build and extend systems faster, needing fewer workarounds or safety nets. Interfaces behave predictably, reducing support overhead and accelerating feature adoption. Consistent, intuitive behavior in user experience, system reliability, or developer productivity yields tangible, lasting benefits.

IN PRACTICE

Implementing the Principle of Least Astonishment starts with respecting established conventions. In user interface design, you stick to standard patterns. Buttons, links, forms, and navigation elements should behave consistently, both within your application and in line with broader industry expectations. If you ever need to break from these norms, have a clear reason and document it well. Often, it's better not to break them at all.

In your APIs, make sure names match behavior exactly. If you write a function called *updateInvoice*, it should only update the invoice. It shouldn't archive it, delete it, or touch unrelated records. When a method does

CASE STUDY

GitHub provides a strong example of applying the Principle of Least Astonishment effectively. Early in its growth, GitHub faced user complaints about inconsistent behavior, particularly around repository deletion and user mentions. Deletion prompts varied across sections, sometimes lacking confirmation dialogs, while *@mentions* behaved differently in issues, pull requests, and comments.

In response, GitHub systematically applied the POLA. They standardized destructive actions with consistent, clearly marked red buttons and confirmation flows. They ensured that *@mention* behavior remained uniform across all interaction surfaces, providing the same autocomplete experience users had come to expect from similar platforms. They adopted familiar UX patterns, such as Twitter-like autocompletion and consistent navigation cues.

The result was a marked improvement in usability. New users navigated the platform with less hesitation. Error rates and user support tickets decreased. By aligning user interactions with consistent, intuitive models, GitHub reinforced trust, reduced friction, and strengthened its reputation as a platform that "just worked" the way users expected.

something unusual or performs multiple actions, be explicit in both its name and documentation. Basically, you don't rely on hidden assumptions.

Keep consistency across your application. Use the same keyboard shortcuts, button placements, and interaction flows everywhere. This lowers cognitive load so users can move smoothly from one part of the system to another. Organize your code where others expect to find it. Put configuration files, utility modules, and core services in clear, logical places. Don't tuck a database connection inside a random helper module. That surprises the next developer and makes maintenance harder.

When you do need to break from norms, communicate clearly. If a method both fetches and mutates data, don't hide that behind a simple retrieval name. Make its purpose obvious so you avoid confusion and keep the contract between the system and user honest.

COMMON PITFALLS

Neglecting the Principle of Least Astonishment often begins innocently. In an attempt to innovate or simplify, teams sometimes diverge from established patterns without considering the broader cognitive cost. A red button labeled "Submit" might seem harmless in isolation, but it can introduce hesitation into an otherwise smooth workflow. When a shortcut works differently in two parts of an application, users end up with added cognitive load. Hidden side effects in APIs are another common failure, creating subtle bugs. Poor documentation of non-standard behaviors compounds these problems. When unusual behavior is not explicitly signaled, users and developers run into surprises. Systems end up requiring increasing amounts of training and patching to function acceptably.

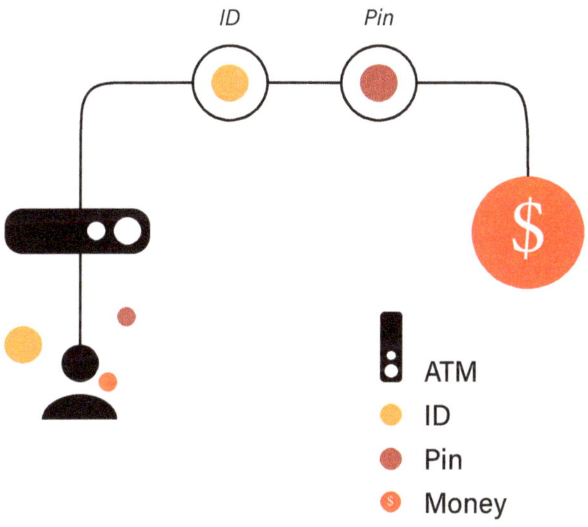

Figure 33 – Principle of Least Astonishment

SUCCESS INDICATORS

Systems built with the Principle of Least Astonishment in mind exhibit a distinct feeling of flow. Users navigate interfaces effortlessly, transferring skills and expectations from one part of the system to another without jarring surprises. APIs experience lower misuse rates because their behavior matches their names and signatures. Developers join projects and feel immediately at home within the codebase, locating files and understanding modules with minimal orientation.

Support teams field fewer tickets about misunderstood workflows or functions. Product teams ship features faster because each new addition extends familiar patterns rather than inventing unpredictable exceptions. Internal documentation shrinks, focusing not on explaining quirks but on enabling deeper capabilities. Over time, the predictability embedded by the POLA becomes a key competitive advantage, allowing systems to scale with ease.

SUMMARY

The Principle of Least Astonishment ensures that software behaves intuitively and consistently. By honoring established conventions, designing APIs with clear intent, maintaining uniformity across interactions, and structuring code logically, teams build systems that work without unwanted surprises.

Predictable interactions empower users to move faster and with greater trust. Logical APIs prevent accidental misuse and simplify development. When software "just works" exactly as users expect, it moves from merely functional to truly delightful. By embedding the POLA into every decision, teams create products that feel natural, systems that scale gracefully, and experiences that users want to return to again and again.

REFERENCES

J. Nielsen, "10 Usability Heuristics for User Interface Design," *NN/g*, 1994, updated 2004.

S. Krug, *Don't Make Me Think: A Common-Sense Approach to Web Usability*, 2nd ed., New Riders, 2005.

GitHub, "Design Principles," *GitHub Well-Architected*, retrieved on August 8, 2025 from https://wellarchitected.github.com/library/productivity/design-principles/ .

Apple, "Human Interface Guidelines," *Apple Developer*, retrieved on August 8, 2025 from https://developer.apple.com/design/human-interface-guidelines/.

34 · Exponential Backoff

"He that can have patience can have what he will."— Benjamin Franklin

INTRODUCTION

In distributed systems, failure is expected. Transient issues like network hiccups, overloaded servers, or short-lived timeouts can cause requests to fail unpredictably. Trying again is often the right move, but doing it immediately and repeatedly makes things worse. Systems under stress don't need a flood of retries. They need space.

The Exponential Backoff principle addresses this by pacing retry attempts with growing delays. Each time a retry fails, the wait gets longer. A bit of randomness is added to prevent synchronized spikes. This turns retrying from a brute-force reaction into a strategic recovery mechanism. You reduce strain, avoid compounding failure, and give the system time to bounce back.

KEY CONCEPT

Exponential backoff starts with a short delay between retry attempts and doubles it with each failure. A jitter factor adds randomness, preventing a retry storm. This pattern is used for errors that are likely to resolve on their own, like timeouts, service throttling, or server overloads. A typical sequence might begin with 200 milliseconds, then retry after 400, then 800, up to a cap. Once the max delay or max number of retries is hit, the system stops trying and either reports an error or triggers a fallback.

This strategy isn't for every failure. It's applied selectively to transient errors that might succeed on another attempt. Errors like 403 (unauthorized) or 400 (bad request) should fail fast without retrying. Backoff is a pressure valve. It turns hiccups into control by pacing retries so the system can heal while maintaining responsiveness.

WHY IT MATTERS

Retries seem harmless at first glance. But if a service is already failing, hammering it with retries only adds to the problem. Without pacing, retry storms can spiral into outages, bringing down systems that would have otherwise recovered. Backoff spreads the retry load and gives clients and services a fighting chance.

This principle protects shared infrastructure. APIs, queues, databases, and caches all benefit from reduced retry pressure during moments of instability. It also improves the user experience. When applied well, retry logic smooths over temporary glitches, making failures invisible. When a service takes too long to respond, a retry after a delay often succeeds, quietly fixing the issue without alerting the user. Backoff also supports graceful degradation. If retry attempts still fail after a few tries, the system can switch to a fallback, raise an alert, or return a clear message. It doesn't just keep trying forever. It knows when to stop.

IN PRACTICE

Implementing exponential backoff starts with setting sensible defaults. Usually, you pick a base delay, then double it with each retry. Set a cap so delays don't get out of hand. After a few retries (usually three to five), stop trying. For added protection, you can add randomness to your retry intervals. This prevents synchronized storms that can overwhelm a system. You can pick a random delay between zero and the current backoff value or apply a random delta to a fixed delay. Either way, spreading out retries helps smooth peak load.

Retry only when it makes sense. Use backoff for network timeouts, 5xx errors, or "service unavailable" responses. Don't retry on invalid inputs, expired credentials, or forbidden access. Log your retries and delays so you can trace problems later. Make sure retry metadata is available so you know how many attempts happened and why.

When you work with external APIs, respect their rate-limiting signals. If you get a 429 response with a "Retry-After" header, use it. Exponential backoff fits naturally here and makes you a better API client. Always tie backoff to user experience. Last, note that sometimes, the delay isn't worth it. Set limits or fallback strategies so you stop retrying when it no longer adds value.

CASE STUDY

Google Cloud Pub/Sub provides asynchronous messaging for event-driven systems. As with any large-scale messaging service, occasional delivery failures can happen due to transient network errors, overloaded consumers, or service throttling. Google's client libraries and delivery mechanisms implement exponential backoff with jitter to ensure reliable message delivery without overwhelming the system.

When a subscriber temporarily fails to acknowledge a message (e.g., due to a processing error or downstream dependency failure), the system waits, using a backoff strategy before redelivering. With each failed attempt, the delay increases exponentially, capped at a configurable maximum. Jitter ensures that multiple clients don't retry simultaneously, reducing network or service load spikes.

This approach is deeply embedded in how Pub/Sub handles reliability. It avoids cascading retries that can destabilize the system while still ensuring at-least-once delivery semantics. Combined with message deduplication and visibility into delivery attempts, Pub/Sub's use of exponential backoff creates a robust mechanism for processing at scale, even when subscribers are temporarily overwhelmed. Using exponential backoff, Google has served fewer message floods during failure conditions, more resilient subscriber behavior, and a smoother path to recovery under high or burst traffic.

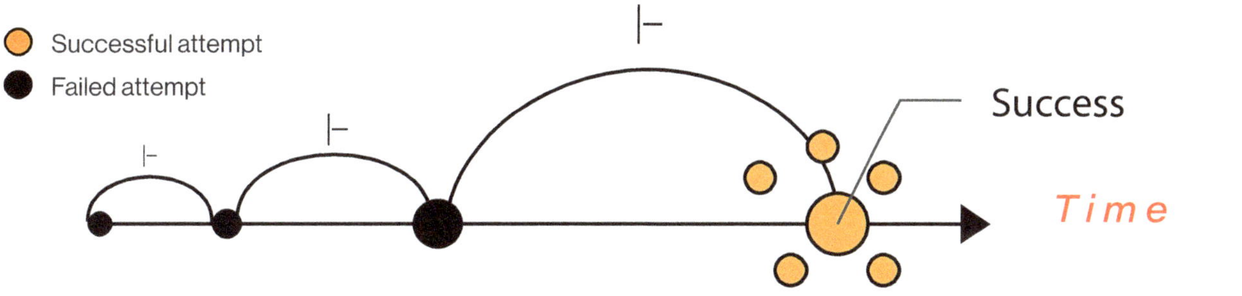

Figure 34 – Exponential Backoff

COMMON PITFALLS

Many teams implement retry logic but miss the nuance that makes it effective. Retrying without jitter causes synchronized spikes that can take systems down. Retrying everything, including permanent failures, adds noise without value. Skipping retry limits leads to zombie processes that never finish, and failing to log retries makes problems invisible until it's too late. Ignoring external retry signals (like HTTP 429 or "Retry After") is another common mistake. These headers exist for a reason, so account for them in how you handle the error.

Another trap is reacting too slowly. Starting with a considerable delay or applying too steep a growth factor can make the system unresponsive. Conversely, retrying too quickly results in a retry storm, so design your system to try again but with the proper guardrails.

SUCCESS INDICATORS

When exponential backoff is doing its job, things are quieter during failure. Transient issues resolve without incident. Load on dependent services decreases instead of spiking. Users experience fewer errors. Logs show retries happening at increasing intervals, which then stop when appropriate. Operators can see what failed, why it was retried, and what eventually succeeded.

Developers don't dread interacting with flaky services. They know the system will handle instability without large-scale failure, and when retries do fail, users get a clean fallback or error message, not a frozen screen or silent crash. In the background, systems stay responsive, traffic levels remain stable, and postmortems reflect graceful recovery, not runaway load.

SUMMARY

The Exponential Backoff principle is one of the most practical tools for building resilient software. It transforms retries from a liability into a recovery mechanism by introducing calculated delay and termination points. It makes distributed systems more forgiving, APIs more reliable, and users less likely to encounter frustrating failures. In complex systems, patience often differentiates between instability and graceful recovery.

REFERENCES

M. Brooker, "Timeouts, Retries, and Backoff with Jitter," *The Amazon Builders' Library*, 2019. https://aws.amazon.com/builders-library/timeouts-retries-and-backoff-with-jitter/

P. Murugan, "Exponential Backoff with Jitter: A Powerful Tool for Resilient Systems," *Presidio*, 2023. https://www.presidio.com/technical-blog/exponential-backoff-with-jitter-a-powerful-tool-for-resilient-systems/

Google Cloud, "Retry Requests," *Google Cloud Pub/Sub Documentation*, retrieved on August 8, 2025 from https://cloud.google.com/pubsub/docs/retry-requests.

35 · Adaptive Load Protection

"It is not the strongest of the species that survives, but the most adaptable to change."
—Charles Darwin.

INTRODUCTION

Distributed systems struggle to operate under growing pressure if traffic flow is not carefully regulated. Whether triggered by a sudden surge in demand, a degraded dependency, or an intermittent network glitch, unmanaged load transforms minor slowdowns into major collapses. The Adaptive Load Protection principle provides a framework for managing this volatility. It integrates three critical patterns, a) backpressure, b) circuit breakers, and c) rate limiting, into a cohesive defense system. Each plays a distinct role: backpressure regulates flow internally, circuit breakers isolate failures, and rate limiting shapes traffic at the edges. Together, they build resilient systems that operate predictably, even when conditions deteriorate unexpectedly.

KEY CONCEPT

The heart of adaptive load protection lies in coordinated, intelligent control of system flow. Backpressure serves as internal regulation, enabling components to signal when overwhelmed so upstream systems can slow production accordingly. This prevents queues from ballooning uncontrollably and keeps resource usage within safe bounds. Circuit breakers provide fault isolation. When a dependency repeatedly fails, the circuit breaker trips, cutting off requests and protecting the broader system from being dragged down. Instead of continuing to hammer a broken service, healthy parts of the system stay available while recovery takes place.

Rate limiting defines boundary control. By capping the number of incoming requests per client or across the system, rate limiting guards against sudden floods, whether from unintentional surges or malicious attacks. Adaptive feedback loops tie these mechanisms together. Systems must not simply react to overload; they must adjust behavior dynamically and recover gracefully. When flow control patterns work together, they avoid disaster and make failures manageable, expected, and non-catastrophic.

WHY IT MATTERS

Modern software faces constant, unpredictable stress. Peaks in usage, network disruptions, and service degradations are not rare events. They are routine challenges that every system must be built to withstand. Without flow control, failures can become unbounded. A slow dependency can clog downstream queues. Clients' unchecked retrying multiplies the load instead of alleviating it. Eventually, databases saturate, services brown out, and recovery becomes a costly, manual effort. When a system cannot handle its own pressure, even minor incidents can spiral into outages. Adaptive load protection changes this. Backpressure protects services from overwhelming themselves. Circuit breakers prevent bad actors from dragging down the entire application. Rate limiting shields the system's boundaries, making traffic manageable even when users or bots surge beyond normal thresholds.

These patterns are defensive, and they also improve user experience by avoiding sharp failures and enabling graceful degradation. They increase business continuity by containing failures within isolated domains rather than allowing platform-wide outages. For engineering teams, flow control reduces firefighting, accelerates recovery, and strengthens operational trust in the system's ability to heal without heroics.

IN PRACTICE

Applying the Adaptive Load Protection principle starts with backpressure. You need to design systems that expose their capacity so upstream components can adjust how much data they send. Use pull-based flow control where consumers set the pace. You can use queues to help here, acting as buffers between producers and consumers and giving you space to absorb sudden spikes.

Protect critical interfaces with circuit breakers. When you wrap calls to external or mission-critical services, you can trigger protective cutoffs after repeated timeouts or errors (see "The Exponential Backoff Principle"). Instead of flooding a failing service with more traffic, reroute, delay, or fail fast with fallback mechanisms. Fallback strategies matter. Make sure they're meaningful and don't depend on the same systems they bypass. Return cached results, default responses, or static pages so your system keeps working even when dynamic paths fail.

Use rate limiting as a perimeter defense. Build policies around user roles, API keys, or service tiers so you can control resource use. Token buckets and sliding windows help you flexibly manage throughput. Log and monitor every circuit breaker trip, backpressure event, throttle, and fallback. You need this visibility to tune thresholds, spot anomalies, and improve your defenses. Finally, test your load protection. Run synthetic loads, chaos tests, and failover drills so you know your system recovers smoothly when real stress hits.

CASE STUDY

Agoda, the global travel booking platform, tackled traffic surges by building an adaptive load-shedding system that kicks in when demand spikes. Instead of over-provisioning resources, they chose to dynamically adjust service thresholds at runtime, keeping things fast and responsive even when traffic gets heavy. Their system continuously monitors latency and capacity in real time, uses load testing tools like Gatling to find safe traffic limits, and relies on smart protections like timeouts, circuit breakers, and rate limiters. The result is a platform that stays up and performs smoothly under pressure, without burning through unnecessary infrastructure.

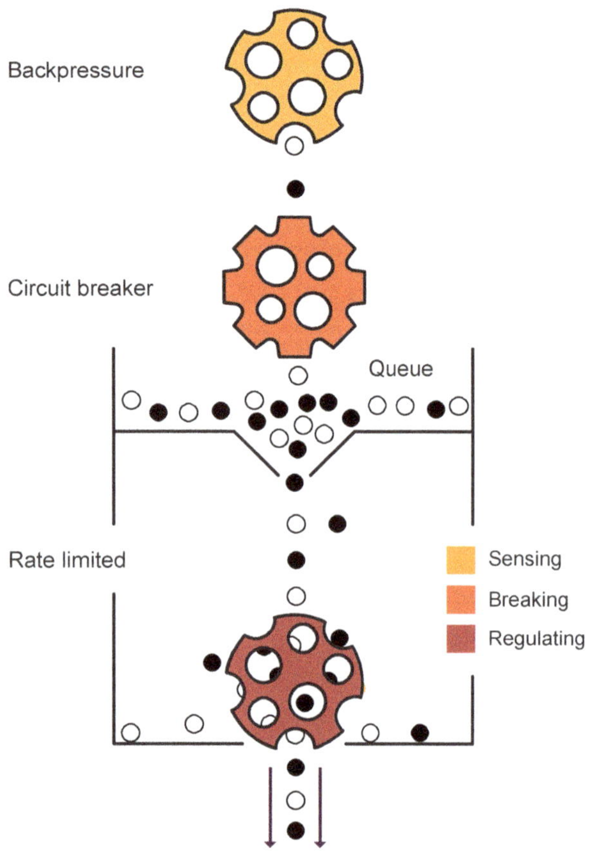

Figure 35 – Adaptive Load Protection

COMMON PITFALLS

Despite the clear benefits, adaptive load protection is often undermined by poor configuration or incomplete adoption. Overly aggressive throttling or conservative thresholds can stall legitimate traffic, sacrificing availability unnecessarily. Systems must be tuned to find the right balance between protection and throughput. Fallback strategies that are not adequately isolated from the primary system provide only an illusion of resilience. If the fallback path still depends on the failing backend, the user experience degrades like a hard failure.

Cooldown periods for circuit breakers must be adaptive because static time windows risk leaving services unnecessarily disconnected even after recovery. Dynamic probing, exponential backoff, and quick retries help systems reconnect efficiently. Partial implementation across a distributed system creates flow imbalances. If some services enforce backpressure but others do not, one section of the system may flood another, undoing the benefits of pressure regulation.

Finally, insufficient observability masks weaknesses. Without logs of pressure events, circuit trips, or throttle activations, engineering teams are blind to emerging risks. Tuning and capacity planning become harder without clear signals from the flow control layer.

SUCCESS INDICATORS

Systems that successfully implement adaptive load protection demonstrate a striking resilience under stress. Traffic surges are absorbed and regulated rather than cascading into failures. Critical dependencies fail gracefully, triggering fallback paths instead of outages. Circuit breakers trip and reset dynamically, isolating problems quickly and recovering efficiently.

Metrics show stable queue depths, controlled retry rates, and a sharp decline in user-visible errors. Observability tools provide clear, actionable insights into system pressure points and recovery behaviors. Teams spend less time reacting to incidents and more time proactively tuning thresholds and expanding capacity.

From a user's perspective, the product remains responsive even when internal services degrade. Internally, system health becomes a known, monitored quantity, not an unpredictable variable. As organizations scale, adaptive load protection becomes a key factor in maintaining stability and user trust even under unpredictable, extreme conditions.

SUMMARY

The Adaptive Load Protection principle arms modern systems with the defenses they need to thrive under unpredictable load and failure scenarios. By combining internal regulation through backpressure, failure isolation via circuit breakers, and external boundary control with rate limiting, systems can manage pressure intelligently and recover gracefully. These mechanisms enable reliability, scalability, and user trust. When configured thoughtfully, they allow systems to bend but not break.

REFERENCES

M. T. Nygard, *Release It!: Design and Deploy Production-Ready Software*, Pragmatic Bookshelf, 2007.

L. A. Barroso, J. Clidaras, and U. Hölzle, The Datacenter as a Computer: *An Introduction to the Design of Warehouse-Scale Machines* (2nd ed.), Morgan & Claypool, 2013.

J. Tiesinga, "How Agoda Handles Load Shedding in Private Cloud," *Agoda Engineering*, 2024. https://medium.com/agoda-engineering/load-shedding-private-cloud-first-81ddd5ab53ac

V DATA, THE LIFEBLOOD OF SYSTEMS

"Memory is the scribe of the soul." — Aristotle

Every system we build relies on one thing to bring it to life. It's not the services, or the APIs, or even the infrastructure. It's the data. Without data, a system is just an empty shell. You can wire every component perfectly, but without something flowing through it, it won't move, respond, or matter. Data is what makes a system real. It carries meaning, enables action, and gives software its lived experience.

Data can be static (or stored), but it is much more interesting when it flows through APIs and queues, across boundaries, into logs and caches. Like water, it can adapt to the shape of its container, but not without you leading it. If you design well, it moves cleanly. If you don't, it can't flow. It becomes stagnant, and no one likes stagnant water.

Data is also important because systems come and go, tools get replaced, and architectures shift, but the data outlasts them all. That's why every major migration, rebuild, or scaling effort begins with the same principle: protect the data, because if the data is lost, nothing else can be recovered.

As an engineer, you are responsible for data flow and stewardship. Sometimes your job is to keep data moving quickly. Sometimes it's to shape it through sharding, partitioning, or isolation. Sometimes it's to store it carefully, preserving history through snapshots and logs. Sometimes, it's simply to notice where the data is getting stuck, where access patterns are shifting, and where the structure needs to evolve.

The principles ahead, like Data Locality, Sharding, Polyglot Persistence, Event Sourcing, and Schema Evolution, are about that flow and stewardship. I hope reading them will help you manage how systems retain memory, make decisions, and adapt under pressure. When you treat data as something alive, something that flows, you will build systems that can grow with it.

36 • Data Locality

"The nearer the bone, the sweeter the meat." — Old English proverb

INTRODUCTION

In distributed systems and modern computing architectures, the distance between data and computation is a central determinant of performance and scalability. The Data Locality principle is simple: the closer your data is to the processing that needs it, the faster, more efficient, and more resilient your system becomes.

At every level, from CPU caches to global cloud infrastructure, reducing the number of hops between data and code minimizes latency and improves system stability. Data locality transforms architectures from slow-moving systems into responsive, high-throughput platforms that can grow and adapt under real-world conditions.

KEY CONCEPT

Data locality focuses on the physical or logical proximity between where data is stored and where it is processed. When computation happens near the data it needs, systems avoid costly network transfers and reduce the risks introduced by distributed dependencies.

In high-performance computing, data locality principles govern everything from cache hierarchies inside processors to task-scheduling strategies in distributed clusters. For example, frameworks like Hadoop and Spark prioritize executing tasks on nodes that already hold the relevant blocks of data. In web-scale applications, co-locating backend services with their data stores within the same availability zone or even on the same machine achieves similar gains.

Data locality is not a single design decision, but a mindset woven throughout system architecture. It touches on storage layout, network topology, task scheduling, and caching strategies. Every time a system accesses data, a key question to ask is this: Is the access happening as close to the computation as possible? When systems are designed with this proximity in mind, they deliver lower latency, better throughput, and stronger fault tolerance. When locality is taken for granted, it can lead to performance penalties, scalability issues, and reliability risks.

WHY IT MATTERS

Every remote data access carries a tax. Moving data across machines, racks, or regions introduces latency, increases the probability of communication failures, and increases operational costs, especially in bandwidth and energy usage. In large-scale systems, these costs are continuous, multiplying every time a request traverses the network unnecessarily.

Ignoring data locality leads to slow responses, overloaded networks, and compute resources that sit idle while waiting for data to arrive. Batch processing jobs can drag on for hours because tasks repeatedly fetch remote blocks. Web applications load slowly because every user action triggers cross-zone database queries. Systems brown out during traffic spikes because the system is constantly waiting for distant data.

By designing for data locality, you can mitigate these risks. Systems become faster because processing happens close to where data resides, minimizing round trips and network dependency. They become more resilient because local access avoids many of the transient failures that plague distributed networks. They become more scalable because the bottlenecks caused by centralized data access gradually disappear. In environments where milliseconds matter and resilience under load is non-negotiable, data locality is an important consideration in your system design.

IN PRACTICE

Applying data locality starts by looking closely at how you partition, store, and access data. Whether you're working with relational tables, document stores, or event streams, you need to divide datasets into shards or partitions that match the way your application actually uses them. Next, schedule computations where the data already lives. If you're using platforms like Spark, let the job planner assign tasks based on data placement to cut down on shuffling and network transfer. In service-based systems, keep your application servers and databases in the same physical or virtual zone. That proximity reduces latency and makes your system more reliable.

Use caching to push locality even further. Keep frequently accessed data close to where it's needed. That can mean CPU caches, in-memory stores like Redis, or edge networks that serve users from nearby locations. For read-heavy workloads, replicate

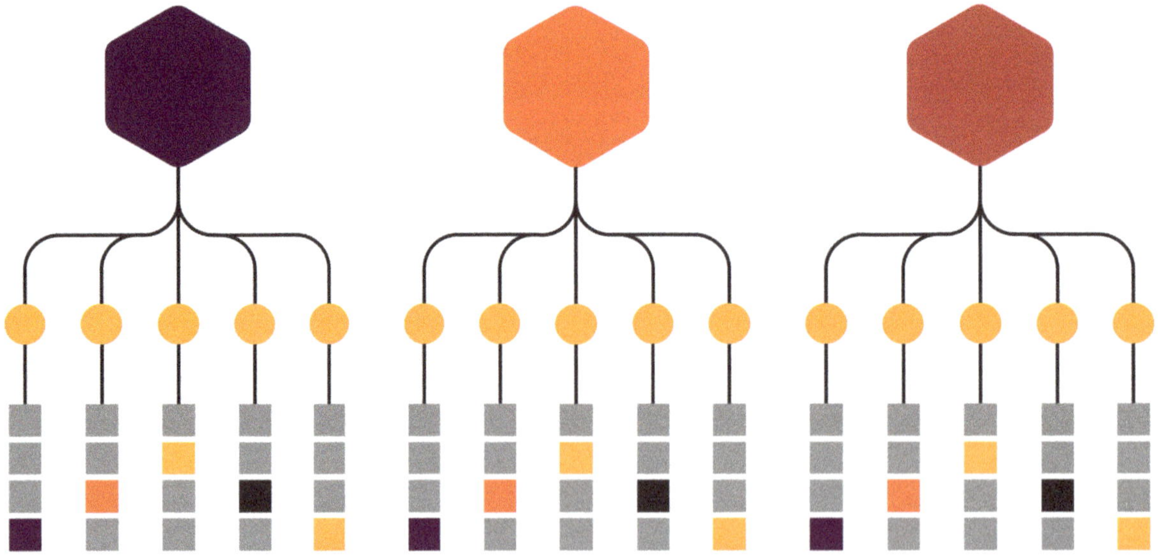

Figure 36 – Data Locality Principle

CASE STUDY

As DoorDash, a food ordering and delivery service, scaled, its microservices struggled under heavy read traffic and inconsistent caching. Different teams had implemented their own caching patterns, leading to multiple remote calls per request and poor reliability. Each user request traversed a deep stack of network calls, and data often sat far from where it was needed. The team set out to improve data locality and reduce the layers between compute and storage.

To address this, DoorDash built a multi-layer caching system that brought frequently accessed data closer to the application. The first layer held request-local data in memory, preventing duplicate computations during the same execution. A second layer used a process-wide in-memory cache, built with Caffeine, to store hot data across requests. The third layer retained Redis (in-memory data structure store) as a shared fallback. This structure allowed most read operations to be satisfied in-process, with only a small fraction of requests reaching the network. When Redis was used, the result was backfilled into local caches for the next time. The caching interface was standardized, making it easy to adopt across all services. Features like "time to live" (TTL) management and background freshness checks helped teams implement the system safely and consistently.

The results were immediate. End-to-end latency dropped as more requests were served from memory. The steady-state cache hit rate reached 78 percent, meaning nearly four out of five reads avoided external calls entirely. Throughput increased without adding infrastructure, as CPU cycles went to serving responses rather than waiting for data. Redis and database traffic declined, improving system resilience. If Redis became unavailable, local caches continued to serve most requests.

DoorDash's caching strategy exemplifies both data locality and stack flattening. By aligning storage with compute, services responded faster and scaled more efficiently. It shows that when hot data lives close to where it is used, systems also become simpler and more robust.

data across zones or regions so you can respond to users locally. Just be careful with replication. If you overdo it, you might run into consistency issues or unnecessary duplication.

Keep an eye on how your data is accessed. Hotspots can form when certain nodes get overloaded with popular data. Design your system to detect and rebalance those loads so locality continues to work in your favor, not against it.

COMMON PITFALLS

Despite its clear advantages, achieving effective data locality requires careful, ongoing attention. One common mistake is assuming that initial data placement is sufficient. Over time, data access patterns change. Hotspotting, workload shifts, and evolving usage models can create skewed distributions that erode locality benefits. Without regular monitoring and rebalancing, systems gradually slip back into expensive cross-node communication patterns.

Another risk is over-replicating data in an attempt to improve access times. While replication can enhance locality, it introduces coordination overhead and potential consistency challenges. In system design, strike a balance between improving access and maintaining coherence. Similarly, if job planners or application servers do not prioritize data proximity when dispatching tasks, the advantages of careful data placement are wasted. Systems must be designed to both store data wisely and to access it intelligently.

Ultimately, maintaining a locality requires vigilance. Your work is not done with one-time improvement, and you will have to make continuous architectural commitment to proximity, efficiency, and responsiveness.

SUCCESS INDICATORS

When data locality is successfully embedded in a system's design, the benefits are tangible and sustained. Request latencies decrease because services no longer wait for remote data fetches. Throughput improves because CPU cycles are spent processing data, not waiting for it. Internal network traffic drops significantly, freeing up bandwidth for critical coordination tasks rather than bulk data transfer.

Job completion times shrink as more computations occur directly where the data resides. User-facing responses get better due to edge caching and regional replication. Systems tolerate spikes and disruptions more gracefully because fewer operations depend on long-distance communication links. Operationally, teams observe a clearer mapping between resource usage and system behavior. Logs reflect faster task durations, timeouts and disconnections are reduced, and scaling operations become more predictable because new capacity can process data locally rather than competing for access across the cluster. Over time, systems designed for locality exhibit reliability and high performance as default.

SUMMARY

The Data Locality principle is a key part of modern system design. By keeping data close to the code that needs it, systems achieve higher performance and scalability. Designing for locality demands attention to data partitioning, task scheduling, caching strategies, and continuous rebalancing. It requires seeing data movement not as inevitable but as a cost to be minimized whenever possible. Systems that embrace data locality are better equipped to serve users with speed as they grow.

REFERENCES

S. Usman, R. Mehmood, I. Katib, and A. Albeshri, "Data Locality in High-Performance Computing, Big Data, and Converged Systems: An Analysis of the Cutting Edge and a Future System Architecture," *Electronics*, vol. 12, no. 1, pp. 53–72, 2023.

P. J. Denning, "The Locality Principle," *Communications of the ACM*, vol. 48, no. 7, pp. 19–24, 2005.

L. Neiman and J. Fan, "How DoorDash Standardized and Improved Microservices Caching," *DoorDash Blog*, 2023. https://careersatdoordash.com/blog/how-doordash-standardized-and-improved-microservices-caching/

37 • Schema Evolution

"The art of progress is to preserve order amid change and to preserve change amid order."
— Alfred North Whitehead

INTRODUCTION

Database schemas must grow and adapt alongside the systems they support. As applications introduce new features the underlying data structures must evolve without causing disruption. The Schema Evolution principle guides this process by emphasizing backward-compatible changes, ensuring that updates enhance functionality without introducing instability. Schema evolution enables organizations to release new features rapidly and reduce risks of regressions or service interruptions.

KEY CONCEPT

The Schema Evolution principle rests on the foundation of backward compatibility. Changes to the database should allow existing applications and services to continue functioning as before, even as new capabilities are introduced. Additive modifications like introducing new columns with default values or creating supplementary tables protect against unintended breakages. This allows consumers of the database to adapt at their own pace, and systems remain resilient even as underlying structures shift. In mature environments, schema evolution is not a one-time event but an ongoing process that safeguards continuity while supporting growth.

WHY IT MATTERS

Changing database schemas is one of the higher-risk activities in software development. When schema modifications break compatibility with existing systems, users face outages, data corruption, or broken functionality. In production environments, even minor schema mistakes can lead to failures that take hours or days to resolve.

The Schema Evolution principle addresses these risks by advocating changes that are invisible to dependent systems until they are ready to adapt. By embracing backward compatibility, organizations maintain continuous uptime, allowing users to interact with applications seamlessly, even during major backend upgrades. Agile development depends on the ability to evolve quickly without destabilizing what already works. Without a consistent schema evolution strategy, feature rollouts slow down, and deployment cycles take longer to resolve. When database changes become as predictable and recoverable as application deployments, teams can move faster without sacrificing reliability.

IN PRACTICE

Schema evolution is real engineering work. That means you treat it as you would treat a critical code change by documenting changes clearly, analyzing their impact across services, and always having a rollback plan ready. You start by thinking about compatibility and favoring changes that extend functionality without breaking what already works. When you add new fields, use sensible defaults so older versions of your system don't fail. If you're building new features, consider adding new tables instead of rewriting existing ones. This protects current workflows and avoids unexpected side effects.

Manage schema changes through versioned migrations so every change is tracked, tested, and auditable. Instead of scattered SQL scripts, let your migrations run in a controlled, repeatable way. With versioning in place, you reduce the risk of errors and make rollbacks cleaner and more reliable. For gradual rollouts, use feature toggles. This lets you support both the old and new schema during the transition. You avoid big-bang deployments and instead shift things over safely, step by step. Just like releasing code, back all of this with strong staging environments, realistic tests, and clear observability. That way, your changes only reach production after you've seen them work under pressure. When you treat schema evolution with care, you make change less risky and progress easier to sustain.

COMMON PITFALLS

Destructive schema changes are a common source of failure. Dropping or altering columns without a proper deprecation path can break systems that still depend on that structure, sometimes in ways that don't surface until production. It's easy to overlook background jobs, or external consumers that quietly rely on the existing schema.

Just as risky is skipping rollback planning. A simple migration error can become a full-blown incident if there's no clear, tested way to undo it. Schema evolution should always be treated as reversible by default, not as a fallback.

CASE STUDY

Airbnb's booking platform is a good use case of disciplined schema evolution. As the company expanded its offerings with features like dynamic pricing, enhanced reviews, and new payment options, the underlying booking database required significant changes. Rather than disrupting existing services or forcing immediate code rewrites, Airbnb's engineering teams adopted a strategy of non-destructive, version-controlled migrations.

New columns and tables were introduced gradually. Existing data structures remained intact, allowing legacy services to function without modification while newer features leveraged the expanded schema. Migration scripts were automated and tested extensively in staging environments before reaching production. Clear rollback plans accompanied every deployment, ensuring that any issue could be rapidly reversed without service disruption.

The result was a system that evolved seamlessly alongside business growth. New capabilities reached users quickly. Legacy functionality remained stable. Development velocity increased because schema evolution became a routine, predictable part of Airbnb's continuous delivery pipeline.

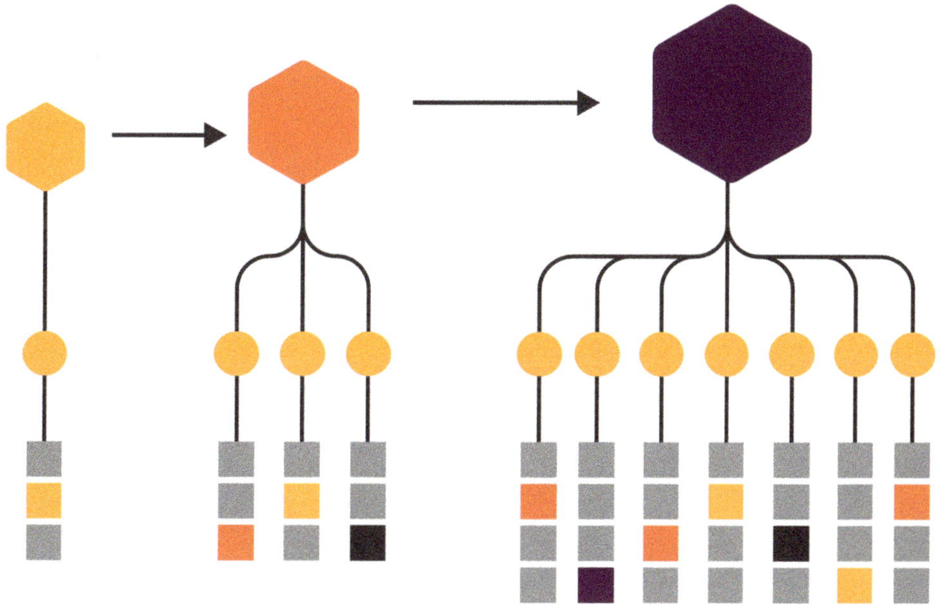

Figure 37 – Schema Evolution

SUCCESS INDICATORS

When the Schema Evolution principle is applied successfully, schema upgrades occur without requiring service downtime or maintenance windows. Legacy and new features operate side-by-side without regression or conflict. Developers and teams release new features faster because database changes are no longer a source of anxiety or delay. Rollouts become smoother, with feature toggles enabling controlled, incremental adoption rather than risky all-at-once switches. Migration incidents decrease, and when issues do arise, they are contained quickly through clear rollback strategies. Over time, the process of evolving the schema becomes as mature and reliable as the evolving application code itself.

SUMMARY

The Schema Evolution principle emphasizes backward compatibility, non-destructive change, and structured migration processes. It enables organizations to evolve their databases without sacrificing stability or user trust. It empowers teams to build new features quickly, deploy upgrades safely, and maintain continuous service availability even during significant transitions.

REFERENCES

P. Sadalage and S. Ambler, *Refactoring Databases: Evolutionary Database Design*, Addison-Wesley Professional, 2006.

H. Hagen, "Version Control Your Database on AWS Using Flyway," *AWS Blog*, 2023. https://www.tecracer.com/blog/2023/03/version-control-your-database-on-aws-using-flyway.html

S. Belefqih, Z. Ahmed, and M. Berquedich, "Schema Extraction in NoSQL Systems: A Systematic Literature Review," *Recent Advances in Computer Science and Communications*, 17(8), 2023.

M. Kleppmann, Designing Data-Intensive Applications: *The Big Ideas Behind Reliable, Scalable, and Maintainable Systems*, O'Reilly Media, 2017.

38 • Sharding

"Divide et impera." (Divide and rule) — Latin proverb

INTRODUCTION

As systems grow, scaling a single database vertically yields diminishing returns. The Sharding principle unlocks horizontal scalability by splitting data across multiple databases. Instead of building a towering vertical monolith, Sharding distributes data intelligently, keeping systems fast and scalable as they expand. Infrastructure grows organically alongside data volumes without forcing teams to re-architect applications or overload a central database. Companies operating at massive scale rely on sharding to handle billions of transactions without sacrificing speed or reliability.

Sharding also strengthens resilience. By isolating failures to individual shards, systems minimize blast radii, simplify recovery efforts, and maintain service continuity. Once implemented, sharding becomes invisible to users and seamless to engineers, laying the groundwork for architectures that scale naturally and withstand change.

KEY CONCEPT

Sharding revolves around the horizontal partitioning of data across independent nodes. Rather than placing the full dataset in a single storage system, sharding divides it into smaller, focused partitions, each hosted separately. Distributed storage across multiple shards enables linear scalability. As traffic and data volumes rise, additional shards can be added incrementally, expanding system capacity without disturbing core application logic. Sharding requires intelligent query routing to ensure that operations are directed efficiently to the appropriate shard, preventing cross-shard dependencies that add latency and complexity.

WHY IT MATTERS

Without sharding, scaling a database often means scaling vertically by adding more memory, more storage, and more compute power to a single machine. While initially effective, this strategy eventually reaches hard limits where further upgrades become impractical, prohibitively expensive, or technically impossible.

Sharding provides an alternative that aligns infrastructure growth with data growth. As the dataset expands, new shards absorb the additional load without degrading system-wide performance. Query execution remains fast because operations only touch relevant portions of the data, avoiding the long scans and heavy locks that plague monolithic storage systems. Reliability also improves because sharding contains failures in isolated partitions rather than allowing them to propagate across the system. If one shard becomes unavailable, the rest continue serving traffic, limiting disruption and supporting graceful degradation.

Systems scale horizontally, and it becomes a routine matter to add shards rather than overhauling architecture. This scaling model aligns better with cloud-native environments, where elasticity and operational flexibility are paramount. Operational efficiency also increases. Smaller databases are easier to monitor, maintain, and back up. Teams can update or migrate individual shards with minimal impact on the broader system, reducing downtime and operational risk.

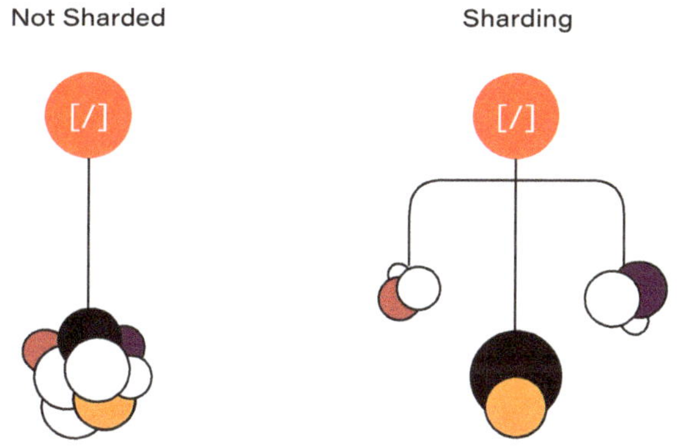

Figure 38 – Sharding

IN PRACTICE

Effective sharding starts with choosing the right partitioning strategy and selecting a stable sharding key. For the partitioning strategy, you want to match your sharding approach to the behavior of your application. Use hash-based sharding when access is random and even distribution matters. For time-series data, range-based sharding works well because it follows ordered keys like timestamps. Geo-based sharding reduces latency by keeping data close to the user. If your partitioning rules may change over time, directory-based sharding gives you flexibility through a mapping layer between records and shards.

After choosing a strategy, make sure the key stays consistent as your system grows. Route queries directly to the correct shard to avoid unnecessary hops. Toward that, you want a key such as a user ID, geographic region, or hashed value that distributes data evenly and matches your access patterns. A poor key causes hotspots and uneven load, which defeats the purpose of sharding.

CASE STUDY

Figma, the collaborative design tool, relies heavily on sharding to support its rapid user growth and global reach. As millions of users design and edit files in real time, Figma ensures performance by splitting data across shards and partitioning by file ID and user organization. This means that when you open a design file, your session talks only to the shard responsible for that file, not a giant monolithic backend. The team invested early in selecting stable sharding keys and building a routing layer that keeps queries scoped and efficient. Their approach allows them to scale storage and processing horizontally, maintain fast response times, and isolate failures to individual shards. Instead of struggling with a massive, centralized database, Figma made scaling feel seamless so designers around the world can collaborate smoothly without ever noticing the complex data architecture working behind the scenes.

Before going live, treat each shard as an independent unit. Apply encryption, access control, and backup policies at the shard level. Once in production, monitor request volume, usage patterns, and storage growth per shard. Be ready to rebalance as traffic shifts or datasets expand. When shards fill up, you will have to support live migration, splitting, or merging without downtime. These operations are possible with modern tooling, but only if you build for them early. Sharding works best when you anticipate scale and design with the future in mind.

COMMON PITFALLS

While sharding addresses key scaling challenges, poor execution creates its own set of risks. Choosing the wrong sharding key can concentrate traffic on a few nodes, creating hotspots that degrade performance and stability. Even balanced datasets can slow down over time if access patterns shift, and rebalancing is not in place. Cross-shard queries add complexity and cost, so try to avoid this by minimizing multi-shard transactions through denormalization or enabling architectural changes that reduce joins.

As the number of shards grows, so does the operational burden. Without automation for deployment, monitoring, backups, and failover, shard sprawl can overwhelm teams and increase the chance of failure. However, waiting too long to implement sharding makes the problem worse. Retrofitting a loaded monolith into a distributed setup under pressure is costly and risk-prone. It is better to plan for sharding early, while the system is still flexible enough to handle it.

SUCCESS INDICATORS

When the Sharding principle is applied successfully, query performance remains stable even as data volumes and user counts grow because operations touch only a manageable subset of the total dataset. Latency remains low across normal and peak loads alike. Infrastructure scales horizontally. Adding new capacity involves introducing new shards rather than overhauling core systems. Deployment operations become more modular, with shards upgraded or maintained independently, reducing system-wide risks during changes.

Failures become isolated events because an issue in one shard affects only a narrow slice of the user base, allowing graceful degradation rather than complete outages. Recovery from shard-level incidents becomes fast and predictable. Developer productivity accelerates. Teams working on separate shards or domains of data operate more independently. Changes can be tested and deployed with reduced coordination overhead. Observability improves as logs, metrics, and alerting become shard-aware, making issues easier to detect and resolve.

SUMMARY

The Sharding principle lays the foundation for systems that scale predictably and adapt easily to changing demands. By partitioning data horizontally, sharding removes the inherent bottlenecks of monolithic databases and distributes load intelligently across independent nodes. It allows systems to remain fast and flexible even as they handle more data and complexity. Rather than waiting until scale forces desperate action, sharding enables teams to build systems ready for success from the very beginning.

REFERENCES

A. Lakshman and P. Malik, "Cassandra: A Decentralized Structured Storage System," *ACM SIGOPS Operating Systems Review*, vol. 44, no. 2, pp. 35–40, 2010.

A. Payong, "Database Sharding: Strategies for Seamless Scaling and Performance Optimization," Redgate, *Simple Talk*, 2024.

S. Steele, "How Figma's Databases Team Lived to Tell the Scale," *Shortcut*, Figma's editorial newsletter, March 14, 2024.

39 • Decentralized and Polyglot Persistence

"The good carpenter does not use only one tool." — Confucius, Analects 13.28

INTRODUCTION

The principle of Decentralized and Polyglot Persistence is about two ideas: database per service and polyglot persistence. Database per service isolates each service's data store, while polyglot persistence aligns the database choice with each service's data access patterns. When services own their data and use the right storage engine (relational, NoSQL, graph, or time-series), they becomes easier to scale, easier to maintain, and better equipped to evolve independently.

KEY CONCEPT

The Decentralized and Polyglot Persistence principle relies on two complementary practices that reinforce each other. Database per service insists that every microservice owns its database outright, with no direct data sharing across services. Communication occurs strictly through APIs, events, or asynchronous messages, preserving clear ownership boundaries and isolating failure domains.

Polyglot persistence complements this independence by selecting the most appropriate database technology for each service's needs. Structured transactional workloads benefit from relational databases, while flexible, high-volume datasets thrive in NoSQL environments. Time-series databases efficiently manage metrics and event logs, while graph databases model complex relationships that relational schemas struggle to capture.

Together, these practices create architectures where data storage strategies align directly with service behavior, unlocking better performance, greater fault isolation, and more sustainable scaling. The system becomes a collection of specialized, self-sufficient units.

WHY IT MATTERS

Tightly coupled, one-size-fits-all database architectures place artificial constraints on growing systems. As data volumes increase and service complexity deepens, shared databases can turn into bottlenecks. Decentralizing persistence mitigates these risks. By giving each service its own database, failures become local events rather than system-wide incidents. Teams gain the freedom to evolve service data models without fear of destabilizing other parts of the system. Upgrades and schema changes proceed at the speed of individual services, not the slowest ones.

Choosing the right database technology for each service adds to these benefits. Workloads no longer compromise to fit an ill-suited relational schema when a document store or graph database would serve them better. Systems perform faster, queries become simpler, and storage scales more naturally with usage patterns. Operational flexibility also improves. Services can be deployed and scaled independently. Teams are free to innovate, experiment, and specialize without entangling their work with unrelated systems. Over time, the organization's ability to adopt new technologies and deliver value to users increases substantially.

IN PRACTICE

Designing for data independence and specialization means giving each microservice full ownership of its database. You don't share schemas, tables, or allow backdoor queries. Service boundaries extend all the way to the data layer. Communication between services flows through APIs or event streams, not direct database access.

When you adopt polyglot persistence, let the workload shape your database choices. Use relational databases when you need strong transactions and structured relationships. Choose NoSQL when you're dealing with flexible schemas or heavy write loads. Time-series databases work best for metrics or timestamped events. If your domain centers on relationships, such as social graphs or recommendations, graph databases offer a natural fit.

To preserve independence while still supporting eventual consistency, keep services in sync through events, not cross-database writes. When data changes inside one service, publish it. Let other services react as needed. As you add more technologies, you'll need to invest in automation and observability to avoid drowning in complexity. That investment will help you monitor each database, back it up independently, manage access, and perform many other operational tasks without missing a beat.

COMMON PITFALLS

Although decentralized and specialized data architectures offer strong advantages, they introduce new forms of complexity that require careful management. Without clear discipline, isolated databases can lead to uncontrolled data duplication. When redundancy is not synchronized intentionally, it creates inconsistency and reliability issues across the system. A common mistake is reaching across service boundaries to query foreign databases. This breaks isolation and increases the risk of cascading failures. Atomic operations across services also become harder. Traditional multi-record transactions rarely work across boundar-

CASE STUDY

At Vilnius Gediminas Technical University (based in Lithuania and among the top 2.1% of universities in the world[7]), a team set out to modernize a legacy mainframe system that had grown too rigid and complex over time. They approached it by breaking the legacy system into a set of microservices, each with its own database, tailored to its specific needs. Instead of forcing every service to use the same kind of storage, they matched each one with the right tool for the job. This approach allowed them to reduce dependencies between services and gave each team more control over how their data was managed. The payoff was better data quality, improved consistency, and a more resilient system overall. By decentralizing data ownership and choosing storage strategies purposefully, they showed how even a tightly bound mainframe could be turned into a modern, scalable architecture.

7 Based on QS World University Rankings

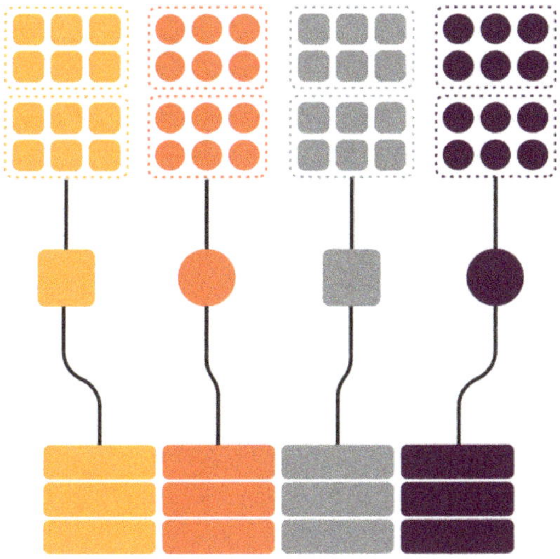

Figure 39 – Decentralized and Polyglot Persistence

ies, so teams must rely on patterns like eventual consistency and compensating transactions to preserve correctness without sacrificing separation.

As more database technologies enter the mix, integration complexity increases. Without strong tooling, clear documentation, and effective onboarding, teams struggle to navigate a maze of formats, protocols, and operational expectations. This adds friction and raises operational costs. Each new database comes with its own maintenance overhead and security posture. Organizations that succeed in this space standardize and automate wherever possible and build strong platform teams to manage the sprawl.

SUCCESS INDICATORS

Systems that apply decentralized and polyglot persistence correctly show signs of architectural maturity. Services scale independently, with no contention over shared storage resources. Query performance improves consistently because each database is optimized for the specific workloads it serves.

Developer velocity accelerates, and teams modify service data models confidently without broad coordination. Releases become faster and safer, and innovation proceeds without risk of unintended side effects from changes elsewhere. New services come online faster, each supported by a storage engine chosen deliberately for its domain. Incidents become smaller and easier to manage. Failures are contained within individual services, limiting their impact on the overall system. Recovery operations focus narrowly rather than triggering full-platform interventions. Operational metrics like uptime improve as blast radii shrink. Over time, systems designed with this principle become easier to scale and better equipped to adapt as needs and technologies evolve.

SUMMARY

The principle of Decentralized and Polyglot Persistence provides a roadmap for building distributed systems that are resilient, performant, and adaptable. Assigning each service its own database and selecting it based on real-world data patterns aligns infrastructure with application behavior, strengthening system boundaries and accelerating growth. While this approach demands greater operational sophistication, it delivers significant rewards in scalability and development agility. Growth and change feel natural rather than painful.

REFERENCES

E. Evans, *Domain-Driven Design: Tackling Complexity in the Heart of Software*. Addison-Wesley Professional, 2003.

S. Newman, *Building Microservices: Designing Fine-Grained Systems*, O'Reilly Media, 2015.

T. Garrett, "Polyglot Persistence Architectures: When to Use Multiple Database Types," *Dev3lop*, April 25, 2025.

J. Kazanavičius, D. Mažeika, and D. Kalibatienė, "An Approach to Migrate a Monolith Database into Multi-Model Polyglot Persistence Based on Microservice Architecture: A Case Study for Mainframe Database," *Applied Sciences*, vol. 12, no. 12, p. 6189, June 2022, doi: 10.3390/app12126189.

40 · Event Sourcing and Snapshots

"The farther backward you can look, the farther forward you are likely to see."
— Winston Churchill

INTRODUCTION

The Event Sourcing and Snapshot principles work together to capture a system's current state and become the custodian of the system's history. Event sourcing captures every change as an immutable event, preserving the full evolution of a system over time. Snapshotting complements this by periodically saving the current state, ensuring that recovery from failure remains fast and efficient.

Together, these principles offer fault tolerance and observability. By preserving the full timeline of events and strategically capturing checkpoints along the way, systems become easier to debug and recover. This makes recovery a well-oiled and routine operation.

KEY CONCEPT

Event sourcing reshapes how systems think about data persistence. Rather than overwriting state with every change, systems append discrete, immutable events that record what happened, when, and why. The complete sequence of events becomes the system's true source of truth. The current state is no longer stored directly but reconstructed by replaying this sequence.

Snapshots serve as fast recovery anchors. They capture the complete system state at a specific point in time, allowing recovery to start from the latest snapshot rather than from the origin of the event log. This allows systems to balance the historical depth of event sourcing with the operational need for a quick, reliable startup. Combined, these practices ensure that every change is remembered, and every recovery is fast without sacrificing performance or historical integrity.

WHY IT MATTERS

Recording only the latest state discards valuable information about how the system reached that point. Debugging becomes hard, and recovering from failures forces ad hoc patches rather than trusted, verified transitions. Event sourcing resolves these gaps by treating history as a first-class citizen. A complete, immutable event log enables full system reconstruction, transparent auditing, and time-travel debugging. Systems gain the ability to replay every decision, every action, and every consequence, leading to greater trust and control.

However, raw event logs alone can become unwieldy. Recovery can slow to unacceptable speeds as the volume of events grows. Without careful management, you end up with historical fidelity but can't really use it effectively. Snapshotting ensures that the system

CASE STUDY

Eventbrite, the global event management platform, adopted event sourcing and snapshotting to modernize its core ticketing and payment systems. As their platform grew, traditional relational models struggled to handle disputes, audits, and system failures efficiently.

To solve this, Eventbrite began persisting ticket purchases, cancellations, and refunds as immutable events in a dedicated event store. They introduced snapshots after every few hundred events per entity to speed up recovery and reduce the cost of reconstructing the state. This approach dramatically improved system resilience and recovery times. Instead of replaying thousands of historical events, services could load a recent snapshot and replay only the newest changes. It also enhanced auditability, customer support resolution, and business insights by providing a complete historical record without impacting production performance. While managing schema evolution and idempotency added complexity, the transition enabled Eventbrite to scale reliably, meet compliance requirements, and deliver a faster, more trustworthy experience for both users and developers.

recovery process remains swift even as history grows. By capturing the full state periodically, snapshots allow systems to load the most recent checkpoint and replay only the newest events, drastically reducing downtime during failure recovery.

Together, event sourcing and snapshots improve resilience, simplify compliance reporting, support safer deployments, and provide better business insights through historical trend analysis.

IN PRACTICE

Applying event sourcing and snapshots means modeling every state change as an explicit event. You treat events as durable, descriptive records that capture what actually happened. You store them in an event log designed for immutable, append-only writes with tools like Kafka, EventStoreDB, or specialized persistence frameworks. You take snapshots at defined points, say after a set number of events or after a certain time interval. When you store them, you store each snapshot in a versioned, reliable repository so you can guard against corruption and track schema evolution over time.

As you build, pay special attention to idempotency. Replaying events must always lead to the same state. Validate your snapshots regularly to catch silent corruption early. When schemas change, version both your events and your snapshots so past data remains usable and trustworthy. Once in effect, when your system starts up, recovery becomes a hybrid process. You load the most recent snapshot, then replay the events that came after it. This shortens recovery time without losing the full history that event sourcing provides.

COMMON PITFALLS

While event sourcing and snapshotting offer clear benefits, letting event logs grow unchecked without regular snapshots creates long and costly recovery times. Taking snapshots too infrequently also defeats the purpose of fast restoration. If a snapshot becomes corrupted and no one notices, the entire recovery process can fail when it's needed most, so make sure snapshots are validated and stored redundantly. These checks during normal operation are what make recovery possible when things go wrong. Schema

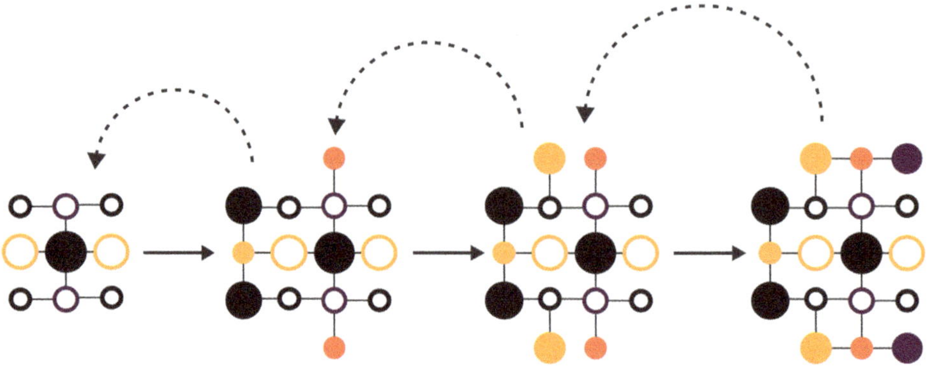

Figure 40 – Event Sourcing and Snapshots

evolution and versioning mistakes can also break old snapshots and events if backward compatibility isn't planned from the start. That leads to painful migrations and recovery paths.

Just as critical is designing idempotent event handlers. Systems must behave the same whether an event is processed once or replayed many times. Without that, recovery introduces subtle, unpredictable bugs. In event-sourced systems, details like event modeling, snapshot strategy, and replay behavior are key milestones on the path to better resiliency and recovery.

SUCCESS INDICATORS

When event sourcing and snapshotting are integrated successfully, their effects permeate the system's behavior and operational culture. Recovery from failures becomes rapid and predictable, with systems loading the latest snapshot and replaying only a manageable volume of events. Downtime shrinks, even under adverse conditions. Auditability improves effortlessly, and teams no longer scramble to piece together system histories from partial records. Instead, they possess a full timeline of every decision and every action, verifiable and immutable.

Debugging grows faster and more reliably. Developers can reproduce historical scenarios by replaying event streams, making even subtle issues visible and reproducible. Business insights and historical trends become accessible through the analysis of event streams, enabling better strategic planning, customer behavior analysis, and anomaly detection.

SUMMARY

The Event Sourcing and Snapshot principles form a powerful foundation for building resilient, scalable, and auditable systems. Event sourcing captures every change, preserving the full historical narrative. Snapshotting enhances operational efficiency, ensuring recovery remains swift even as history grows. These principles deliver systems that do not forget their past and are quick to recover.

REFERENCES

M. Fowler, "Event Sourcing," *martinFowler.com* (blog), 2005. https://martinfowler.com/eaaDev/EventSourcing.html

V. Vernon, *Implementing Domain-Driven Design*, Addison-Wesley Professional, 2013.

P. Helland, "Immutability Changes Everything," *Communications of the ACM*, 59(1), 64–70, 2015, https://doi.org/10.1145/2844112.

41 • Read-Heavy vs. Write-Heavy Optimization

"To each according to its kind." — Plato, Republic, Book IV, 443c

INTRODUCTION

Modern data systems exhibit different workload patterns, some dominated by reads, others by writes. The Read-Heavy vs. Write-Heavy Optimization principle emphasizes the need to tailor system design to the dominant traffic pattern. By aligning caching, storage, and processing strategies with the workload's true nature, organizations can significantly improve performance, reduce latency, and optimize resource usage.

Recognizing whether a system is primarily read-heavy or write-heavy is a foundational design decision that shapes scalability, user experience, and operational efficiency. Systems that match their infrastructure to their load behave predictably under pressure and evolve gracefully as demand grows.

KEY CONCEPT

Read-heavy systems benefit from designs that prioritize quick retrieval and distribution. Techniques such as in-memory caching, read replicas, and content delivery networks minimize query latency and database strain by moving data closer to users and applications. Write-heavy systems demand a different approach. Their architectures prioritize rapid, reliable recording of incoming data. Strategies like using write-optimized storage engines, batching write operations, sharding datasets, and employing asynchronous write processing enable these systems to maintain high throughput without bottlenecks or data loss.

Crucially, read-heavy and write-heavy strategies must balance performance with consistency and fault tolerance. The system's requirements must drive the specific techniques chosen.

WHY IT MATTERS

Optimization according to workload matters because it transforms raw capacity into usable performance. In read-heavy systems, caching accelerates response times and offloads work from core databases, allowing more users to be served with fewer resources. In write-heavy systems, efficient write paths preserve system responsiveness even as transaction volumes climb.

By designing for expected access patterns, teams avoid wasting CPU, memory, and I/O bandwidth on unnecessary operations. This improves user experience with faster page loads, instant updates, and consistent service availability, driving user trust and satisfaction. Whether browsing a product catalog or completing a purchase, users notice applications that respond quickly and reliably. In the end, this principle allows systems to grow without re-architecting at every inflection point.

IN PRACTICE

For read-heavy applications, you start by cutting down on repeated database queries. Use in-memory caches like Redis or Memcached to keep data close to where it's needed. You set up read replicas in multiple regions, so users get faster responses no matter where they are. For static content, let a content delivery network handle the heavy lifting. That way, users get assets from the edge, not your core systems.

For write-heavy systems, choose storage engines built for fast ingestion. NoSQL databases like DynamoDB or relational engines using log-structured merge trees give you a strong foundation. Where possible, batch your writes and process them asynchronously to reduce per-transaction cost and absorb bursts more smoothly. If you don't need strict consistency, eventual models can improve performance without hurting the user experience.

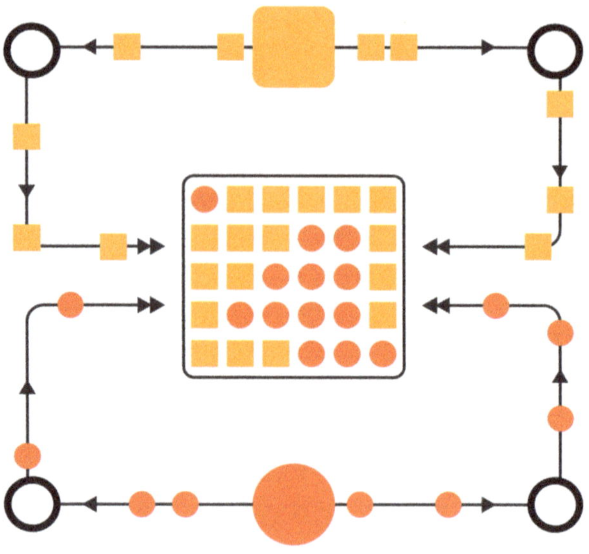

Figure 41 – Read-Heavy vs Write-Heavy Optimization

Once in production, continue to watch how the system behaves over time. A read-heavy workload today might shift tomorrow. To stay on track, keep profiling your read/write ratios, latency, cache hit rates, and write throughput. This way, you will make sure your optimizations match the system as it actually runs.

CASE STUDY

Twitter (X) offers a real-world example of optimizing for distinct read-heavy and write-heavy workloads. As the platform scaled, engineers identified two patterns: user timelines were read-heavy, while tweets and interactions like retweets and likes were write-heavy. To optimize for reads, Twitter adopted a fan-out-on-write model, pushing new tweets directly into followers' timelines at the time of posting. This made the timeline read extremely fast and efficient. For write-heavy operations, Twitter developed Manhattan, a distributed key-value store designed to handle massive write throughput with flexible consistency guarantees. By separating strategies for fan-out for fast reads and scalable storage for writes, Twitter maintained responsiveness and reliability as it grew to billions of daily operations across a global user base.

COMMON PITFALLS

Misjudging the dominant workload pattern is one of the most common mistakes in system optimization. Over-investing in caching for a write-heavy system leads to stale data, invalidation storms, and missed expectations. Underestimating the need for write scalability results in transaction queues, bottlenecks, and, ultimately, system outages. Static designs present another risk; workloads are not fixed forever. Systems optimized for one pattern must remain flexible enough to adapt when usage patterns evolve. Failing to monitor and adjust in response to changing traffic can erase early performance gains. Successful optimization requires continuous measurement, thoughtful trade-offs, and a readiness to revisit assumptions as systems and users evolve.

SUCCESS INDICATORS

Systems designed around workload-aware optimization display good signs of health and agility. In read-heavy systems, cache hit rates climb, page loads accelerate, and database load stabilizes at sustainable levels. Users notice the difference through faster, smoother experiences. In write-heavy systems, sustained high-throughput writes occur without backlogs or degraded latency. Queues remain shallow, write success rates stay high, and the system absorbs spikes in traffic without manual intervention.

Across both types of workloads, performance under load remains consistent. User experience remains responsive during high-traffic events. Monitoring dashboards show stable resource utilization. Release cycles become smoother because scaling concerns are anticipated, not improvised.

SUMMARY

The Read-Heavy vs. Write-Heavy Optimization principle recognizes that not all workloads are created equal. Systems that tailor their caching, storage, and processing strategies to the dominant traffic pattern achieve better performance and scalability. Whether caching aggressively for reads or engineering fast, resilient write paths, the key is to align system behavior with real-world demands.

REFERENCES

M. Kleppmann, *Designing Data-Intensive Applications: The Big Ideas Behind Reliable, Scalable, and Maintainable Systems*, O'Reilly Media, 2017.

B. Schwartz, P. Zaitsev, and V. Tkachenko, *High-Performance MySQL: Optimization, Backups, and Replication*, 3rd ed., O'Reilly Media, 2012.

H. Tadiparthi, H. Patel, and R. Ponugumati, "Scale Read and Write Workloads with Amazon Redshift," *AWS Blogs*, 2022. https://aws.amazon.com/blogs/big-data/scale-read-and-write-workloads-with-amazon-redshift/

Twitter Engineering, "Manhattan, Our Real-time, Multi-tenant Distributed Database for Twitter Scale," *X Engineering* (blog), 2014.

42 · Data Backup and Migration Strategy

"The general who wins the battle makes many calculations in his temple before the battle is fought." — Sun Tzu, The Art of War

INTRODUCTION

Whether powering cloud platforms, enterprise systems, or everyday applications, data integrity and availability determine operational stability. Still, many organizations treat backup and migration as afterthoughts. The Data Backup and Migration Strategy principle instead calls for a proactive, disciplined approach to keep the data safe. Without it, businesses risk catastrophic loss, extended downtime, and regulatory violations. A structured strategy ensures data remains safe and recoverable, providing the resilience needed to thrive through change.

KEY CONCEPT

A data backup and migration strategy is about ensuring critical data can be restored quickly and securely. Effective strategies blend backup techniques, recovery objectives, and migration processes into a coherent operational plan. For example, full backups create complete restore points but consume significant time and storage. Incremental and differential backups capture only changes, improving efficiency but requiring coordination during recovery. Snapshots offer quick rollback capabilities at the system or database level. Continuous data protection captures changes in near real time, minimizing loss between backups.

Both backup and migration strategies depend on a clear understanding of recovery time objectives (RTOs) and recovery point objectives (RPOs), ensuring the chosen strategy matches business risk tolerance and performance needs.

WHY IT MATTERS

A strong backup and migration strategy ensures data is stored and protected. Secure and protected data ensures that services can recover after an outage and that customer data remains safe and compliant even during large-scale migrations. Data loss is not a theoretical risk. Hardware fails, human error happens, services malfunction, and cyber threats are real. You only hear about these things happening to some other organization or company until it happens to you. Without reliable backup and recovery processes, minor incidents can grow into major crises, and unrecoverable systems mean disrupted operations, loss of customer trust, regulatory fines, and reputational damage that is harder to restore.

Similarly, poorly planned migration and transitions between platforms can corrupt data, introduce downtime, and violate compliance requirements. The cost of mistakes can multiply quickly, especially when systems operate across hybrid or multi-cloud environments.

IN PRACTICE

To build an effective backup strategy, start by defining clear policies. You need to decide what data requires protection, how often it should be backed up, and how long you need to keep it. Let those decisions reflect your business needs, compliance requirements, and operational risks. Once the policies are in place, automate the process. Automate scheduling, deduplication, monitoring, and alerting so backups become part of your daily operations, not an error-prone manual task. In your automation, make sure you're not just backing up data but also validating it. Run restore drills regularly. If you skip this step, you're trusting backups that might fail when you need them most.

For migration, before migrating data, take time to analyze your system's dependencies, data structures, and security model. Choose your migration method based on how much downtime and risk you can tolerate. Whether you go with a cold, hot, or phased approach, make sure synchronization keeps the data consistent as it moves. Throughout this process, security is not optional. You have to encrypt backups in transit and at rest. Lock down access and log every action, just as you would in production. During migration, validate the data and prepare rollback plans so you can recover from corruption or unexpected failure.

Finally, make these practices routine. Fold backup validation and migration checks into your development cycle, deployment process, and incident response drills. Recovery should never be a last-minute scramble. It should be something you've practiced and can execute with self-assurance.

CASE STUDY

In 2020, 3M committed to migrating nearly all enterprise workloads to AWS. The company operates in 70 countries and relies on hundreds of critical functions, including 11,000 servers, with approximately 1,200 servers for its SAP environment. Migration was needed to support global operations without significant downtime. Working with AWS, 3M executed the migration in planned waves over 18 months. Using AWS Professional Services, the team automated lift-and-shift transitions and replicated data continuously. Even the company's largest enterprise resource planning (ERP) system , spanning hundreds of terabytes, was migrated with under 20 hours of downtime.

By prioritizing both data integrity and efficiency, 3M finished ahead of schedule, met strict recovery objectives, and kept business operations running throughout (even during the COVID pandemic). By investing in automation, careful sequencing, and cloud-native operations, 3M modernized its infrastructure at a global scale without disruption.

COMMON PITFALLS

Failures in backup and migration strategies often stem from preventable mistakes. Undefined recovery goals can leave systems vulnerable when disaster strikes. Without clear RTOs and RPOs, organizations may find that their backups are too slow or too stale to be useful. Outdated or incomplete backups can create a false sense of security until a restore is urgently needed and impossible to perform.

Manual processes such as human-triggered backups or migrations should not be over-relied on; they are error-prone and easily forgotten under stress, undermining recovery efforts when precision matters most. Security oversights, such as backups stored without encryption or access controls, become attractive targets for attackers, turning protection into a vulnerability. During migration, skipping dependency mapping, ignoring performance considerations, or failing to simulate transitions often results in longer outages and degraded user experiences. These pitfalls are not inevitable. With thoughtful planning, automation, rigorous testing, and clear ownership, organizations can build robust data protection frameworks that stand the test of time.

SUCCESS INDICATORS

Organizations that implement this principle successfully experience smoother recovery from incidents and faster system migrations. After unplanned outages, services are restored within defined RTOs, and data loss is kept within agreed-upon RPOs. Routine recovery drills are uneventful, with backup integrity consistently validated over time. Compliance audits

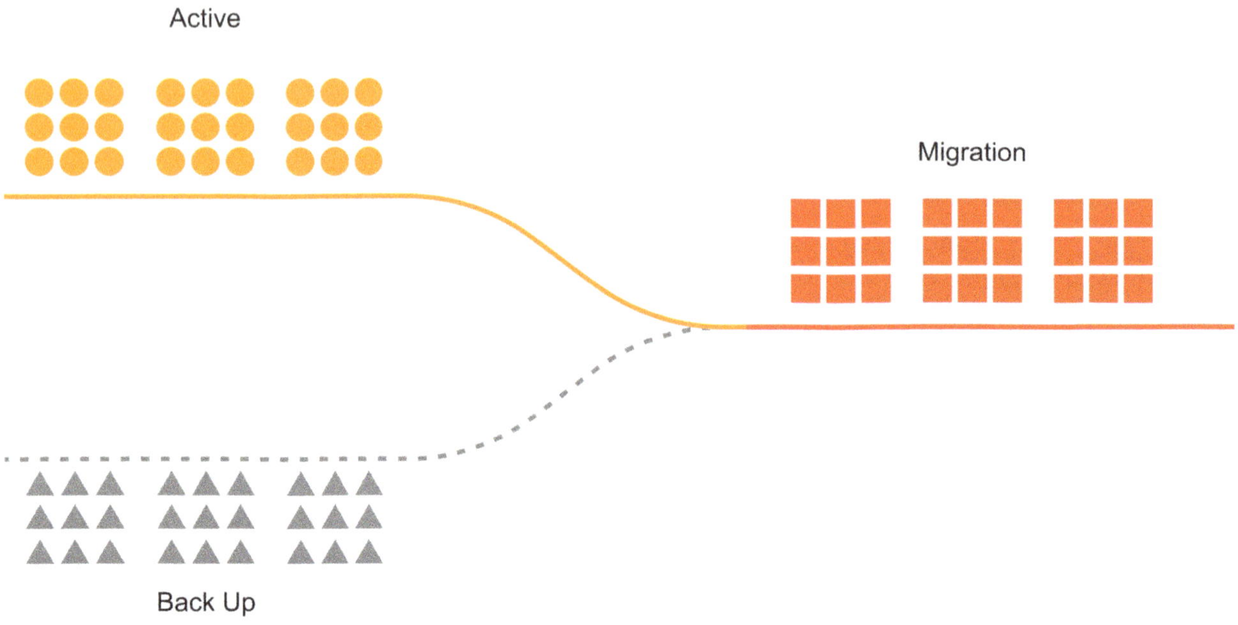

Figure 42 – Data Backup and Migration Strategy

pass without a hitch, as backup retention, encryption, and recovery practices are demonstrably aligned with regulatory standards. Migration efforts become structured and predictable, minimizing user impact and operational disruption.

From a cultural perspective, backup and recovery shift from being treated as burdens to becoming core competencies. Engineering and operations teams trust the process because it is tested and automated. When failures occur, responses are coordinated and decisive. Long-term, this operational maturity translates into greater agility, new platforms are adopted more easily, and incident response times improve.

SUMMARY

The Data Backup and Migration Strategy principle combines automated backups with thoughtful, tested migration processes. This principle helps organizations safeguard their most critical assets against disruption. Protecting data is foundational to user trust, regulatory compliance, and long-term sustainable growth. A reliable backup and migration strategy can change risk into strength and enables growth for the business.

REFERENCES

M. Swanson, P. Bowen, A. W. Phillips, D. Gallup, and D. Lynes, *Contingency Planning Guide for Federal Information Systems*, National Institute of Standards and Technology (NIST), NIST Special Publication 800-34 Rev. 1, 2010.

M. Fischer et al., "AWS Well-Architected Framework: Reliability Pillar," *Amazon Web Services*, 2024.

Amazon Web Services, Inc., "Migrating Critical ERP Workloads to AWS Using SAP on AWS with 3M Company" [case study], retrieved July 4, 2025, from the AWS website. https://aws.amazon.com/solutions/case-studies/3m-migrating-critical-erp-workloads/

VI THE COVENANT OF CONFIDENCE

"Honor is purchased by the deeds we do." — Christopher Marlowe

The word confidence traces back to the Latin confidentia, from confidere: to have full trust. In our work, confidence has to be built deliberately, through the work we ship and the habits we keep. At the center of that work are two covenants.

The first is an internal covenant, the silent contract you make with yourself about what you consider acceptable. It's about the bar you are willing to meet (or raise) and the bar you will not lower. It is the agreement between your ambition and your craftsmanship: "*I will not ship work I would not stand behind. I will not lower the bar because no one is looking.*" The second is an external covenant. The promises you make to everyone who trusts your work. To your customers, who assume the system will simply work. To your colleagues, who build on your designs without rechecking every assumption. To your product managers, who stand in front of users and say: "*You can trust us*," and to everyone who expects reliability, security, and performance from your systems.

The stakes of these covenants are real. As systems become more automated and code more easily generated, trust doesn't get simpler. It becomes more vital. Earning this trust and confidence requires deliberate practice. In deliberate practice, you prove your intent to meet these covenants by putting in effort where it matters. For example, you write behavior-driven tests to show intent. You use mutation and risk-based tests to prove that your checks are meaningful. You load-test to see how the system bends. You test for accessibility to make sure everyone can use what you built. You validate contracts so that when things change, they don't silently break something else. You honor the older versions and commitments of the past, even while you push forward.

The principles ahead, risk-based testing, behavior-driven development, end-to-end flows, scalability, accessibility, and compliance, are technical best practices and good foundations to achieve that. Through them and others, find a way to show respect for your work, customers, and the covenant of confidence. They will help you prove your work before it goes live. You will sleep better knowing that it will carry weight when it's in production.

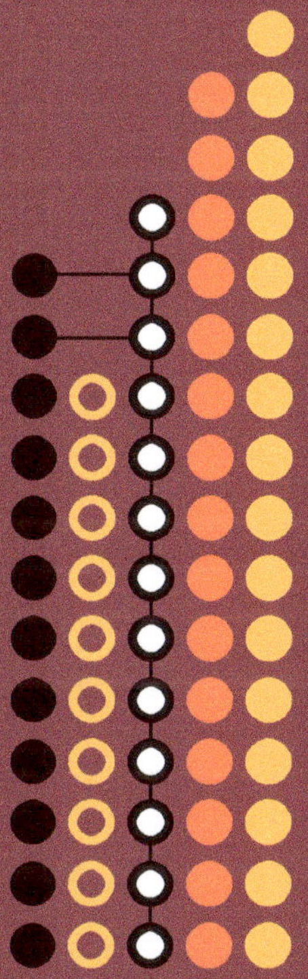

43 • Shift-Left and Test Pyramid

"Well begun is half done." — Aristotle, Nicomachean Ethics, Book I

INTRODUCTION

The Shift-Left and Test Pyramid principle brings together testing early in the development process and layering tests strategically to achieve both speed and reliability. Shift-left testing ensures that validation begins from the first design conversations, while the test pyramid offers a blueprint for balancing fast, focused tests with broader, more expensive validations. Combined, these principles produce higher-quality software, faster feedback loops, and fewer surprises near release.

KEY CONCEPT

The Shift-Left and Test Pyramid principle emphasizes two interconnected ideas. First, it urges you to embed testing into every phase of the development lifecycle, starting from requirements and design. Instead of waiting until the code is complete, you validate assumptions, designs, and early implementations through automated checks and static analysis. Early involvement of QA in planning and story refinement further tightens the quality in the process.

This mindset aligns closely with the principle of defect containment, which calls for the strategic practice of catching and resolving issues as closely as possible to their point of introduction. Techniques like structured code reviews, design walkthroughs, and early unit testing act as guardrails, preventing small problems from becoming costly downstream failures.

Second, it guides you to layer your tests intentionally. Most tests should be unit-level: fast, isolated, and abundant. A smaller set of integration tests validates that components interact correctly. At the top, a limited number of end-to-end or UI tests simulate real user flows to catch system-wide issues. Structuring your suite this way ensures high speed and high reliability without elongated testing cycles. Together, through these actions, quality is engineered and not inspected at the end.

WHY IT MATTERS

Without early testing, defects creep deep into systems, making them harder and more expensive to find and fix. Without structured layering, test suites become rigid and unreliable, delaying feedback and eroding trust in test suites. Embracing the Shift-Left and Test Pyramid principle addresses these problems.

When you test early, you detect defects while they are still cheap to fix. You avoid costly rework and late-stage surprises. When you structure tests thoughtfully, you achieve faster feedback at every level, allowing teams to move quickly without sacrificing quality. These practices also foster stronger collaboration between developers, testers, and product teams, reinforcing a culture of shared responsibility for reliability and user satisfaction.

IN PRACTICE

You start applying this principle with planning. You bring quality assurance into sprint planning, technical design, and story grooming from the beginning. Align on clear acceptance criteria so you can design automated tests up front. As a developer, write unit tests alongside your application code. Treat failing tests as real blockers, not cleanup work for later, and structure your test suite with care. Focus on unit tests to verify logic and edge cases precisely. Use integration tests to check that modules talk to each other correctly, especially across APIs and critical business flows. Reserve end-to-end tests for the most essential user journeys, like checkout or account recovery. These help you catch system-wide issues without overloading your pipeline.

Tie testing into your CI pipeline. Every commit should run automated unit, integration, and key UI tests. Failures should stop merges immediately, so broken code never slips through unnoticed. As your system grows, keep refining your test pyramid. Review your test suite regularly. Remove redundant or inflexible tests and replace full environment dependencies with mocks when they are sufficient. Speed matters, so run tests in parallel where you can. Treat your test infrastructure like production by monitoring it for reliability and maintaining it as you would a live system.

Culturally, jointly figure out a way to share the responsibility. You, your testers, and your product managers

CASE STUDY

At the scale of billions of daily queries, Google Search cannot afford downtime or degraded quality. To manage this complexity, Google applied a strict interpretation of shift-left testing and the test pyramid.

From the earliest stages of feature development, Google engineers work closely with test engineers to design robust, automatable acceptance criteria. Each new feature includes unit tests that validate logic and input handling, integration tests that ensure APIs perform reliably across services, and a small number of end-to-end tests that model real user searches across a global infrastructure. Testing is embedded into every commit via continuous integration pipelines. Unit tests provide immediate feedback within minutes. Integration and UI tests run in parallel, ensuring failures are detected within the same development cycle. Defect tracking and test metrics are collected automatically, and the maintenance of the test suite is treated as a top engineering priority.

By maintaining a strong base of unit tests, a solid mid-layer of integration tests, and a slim top layer of UI validation, Google consistently achieves rapid release cycles while preserving the quality and reliability of its search results. This strategy minimizes regression risks, keeps development velocity high, and allows rapid recovery if any defect does escape. Google's disciplined application of early testing and structured layering demonstrates how these principles enable scale without sacrificing trust.

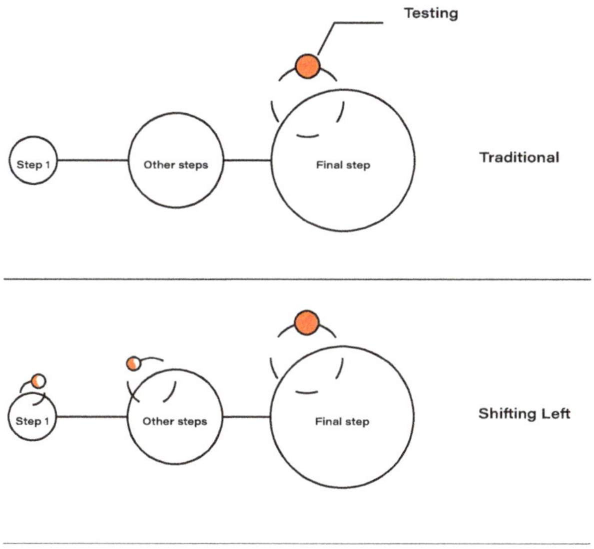

Figure 43 – Shift-Left Testing

should all play a role in defining, automating, and maintaining tests. Shifting quality left only works when ownership moves left, too.

COMMON PITFALLS

Organizations adopting these principles often falter by overweighting end-to-end tests, leading to slow, flaky pipelines that frustrate developers and delay releases. Others involve QA too late, treating testing as a phase after development instead of a parallel, ongoing activity. Some teams create brittle unit tests focused on implementation details rather than behavior, making them liabilities during refactoring. Others neglect integration tests altogether, assuming strong units guarantee strong systems. This is a dangerous and costly mistake. Even a well-structured test suite degrades over time: orphaned tests, redundant checks, and slow execution slowly erode the benefits. Teams must actively measure and prune their tests to preserve agility.

SUCCESS INDICATORS

When the Shift-Left and Test Pyramid principle is properly applied, teams move faster with greater assertiveness. Commit-to-deploy cycles shrink because failures are caught early, and repairs are lightweight. Test pipelines stay fast and reliable thanks to strong unit and integration foundations. Production incidents decrease because systems are validated thoroughly before deployment. Developers, testers, and product managers collaborate naturally around quality rather than working in isolated silos. Over time, this approach creates a culture of ownership, accountability, and trust. A solid foundation emerges that fosters high-performance engineering organizations at scale.

SUMMARY

The Shift-Left and Test Pyramid principle teaches you to embed testing early and layer it wisely by validating assumptions before code is written and structuring your test suite for fast, reliable feedback. You build higher-quality systems with less friction. Applied correctly, these practices speed delivery, improve stability, and shift the conversation from reactive bug-fixing to proactive quality engineering.

REFERENCES

M. Fowler, "The Practical Test Pyramid," *martinFowler.com* (blog), 2018. https://martinfowler.com/articles/practical-test-pyramid.html

M. Kleppmann, *Designing Data-Intensive Applications: The Big Ideas Behind Reliable, Scalable, and Maintainable Systems*, O'Reilly Media, 2017.

P. Gupta, M. Ivey, and J. Penix, "Testing at the Speed and Scale of Google," *Google Testing Blog*, 2011. https://testing.googleblog.com/2011/06/testing-at-speed-and-scale-of-google.html

P. Norman, "Sensenmann: Code Deletion at Scale," *Google Testing Blog*, April 28, 2023. https://testing.googleblog.com/2023/04/sensenmann-code-deletion-at-scale.html

44 · Unified and Layered Testing Strategy

"Quality is not an act; it is a habit." — Aristotle

INTRODUCTION

The Unified and Layered Testing Strategy principle reminds you that building quality software is not about checking a few boxes right before release. It's about weaving testing into every phase of the development and deployment cycle. Regression testing, sanity checks, and end-to-end validation must all work together and be integrated into your CI/CD pipelines. Each type of testing plays a distinct role: regression tests safeguard what already works, sanity tests quickly catch obvious issues, and end-to-end tests verify full workflows from a user's perspective. Together, they ensure that both new and existing functionality is protected against regression and unexpected side effects. This layered approach transforms testing from a bottleneck into a powerful enabler of confident, continuous delivery.

KEY CONCEPT

Unified and layered testing is about designing a holistic test suite that validates software quality across different levels of abstraction. Regression testing ensures previously working features remain stable as new changes are introduced. Sanity testing verifies that critical functions still behave as expected after builds or deployments without the overhead of a full regression cycle. End-to-end testing confirms that the system behaves correctly from the user's perspective, traversing all integrated components. Integrating all three layers into the CI/CD process provides fast feedback loops for small changes and robust validation for full workflows. Structuring your testing this way minimizes blind spots, maximizes coverage, and speeds up the delivery of reliable software.

WHY IT MATTERS

When you skip structured testing, the risks of issues go up at every level of your system. Without regression tests, old bugs can come back. Without sanity tests, obvious breakages slip past unnoticed. Without end-to-end tests, you miss the bigger picture of how users experience your product. Disconnected testing efforts slow teams down and erode user trust over time. A unified strategy ensures that your testing reflects how your system actually operates, from the smallest logic units to the most significant business flows. It allows you to ship faster without increasing risk and maintain a clean test suite for future growth.

IN PRACTICE

You build a unified and layered testing strategy by embedding testing early and treating it as part of the system design. Start with a solid foundation of automated regression tests that cover your critical workflows and edge cases. Set up fast sanity checks that run with every build and deployment. These should catch obvious failures right away before the system moves any further.

For end-to-end tests, simulate real user journeys that touch the core value paths but avoid bloating your suite with redundant or flaky flows. Your CI pipeline should run each type of test at the right stage. Let sanity checks gate early merges while using regression tests on feature branches. Run end-to-end tests before release so you know the system works from the user's point of view.

Track what the tests tell you. Look at flakiness, failure rates, and time-to-detect metrics. Use that feedback to tune the strategy, refine your tooling, and strengthen the reliability of your pipeline. When testing is layered thoughtfully and runs continuously, it protects both speed and stability.

COMMON PITFALLS

Overloading the test suite with flaky or slow end-to-end tests can paralyze your pipelines. Many teams confuse quantity with quality, writing hundreds of UI-driven tests that are hard to maintain, slow to run, and prone to false positives. Another common failure is neglecting sanity tests entirely, assuming that full regression suites will catch everything. Without fast gates, obvious issues sneak into mainline branches and waste engineering hours on later debugging. Some teams fall into the trap of outdated regression suites where tests no longer reflect current functionality. They stop trusting the tests, and when the tests lose credibility, so does your deployment process. A less visible mistake is ignoring integration between test layers. Treating regression, sanity, and end-to-end tests as disconnected activities delays detection and creates blind spots between what the unit tests check and what the users experience. Skipping test result analysis also weakens your system. When teams only look at pass/fail status without investigating patterns of failure, recurring regressions, and flaky tests keep showing up.

CASE STUDY

As Jira scaled, Atlassian's reliance on slow, flaky end-to-end Selenium tests created major release bottlenecks. To fix this, they restructured their testing approach around a unified, layered model: fast unit tests formed the base, integration tests validated service boundaries, and only a small set of critical workflows were covered by end-to-end tests.

They embedded all test layers into their CI/CD pipelines, enforcing strict checks at every stage. No pull request could merge without passing unit and integration tests, and production releases required successful end-to-end validations. Observability improvements allowed the team to trace and fix issues within the right test layer quickly. This shift cut build times by 35%, reduced flaky tests by 60%, and quadrupled deployment frequency. By layering tests properly and integrating them tightly with CI/CD, Atlassian turned testing from a bottleneck into a speed advantage.

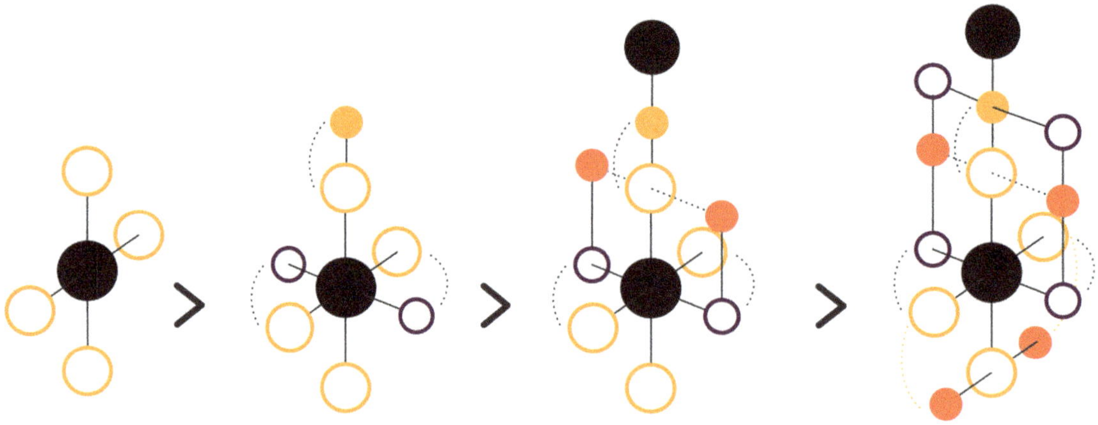

Figure 44 – Unified and Layered Testing Strategy

SUCCESS INDICATORS

When your testing strategy is unified and layered correctly, you will notice a visible increase in delivery velocity. Regression test suites run automatically on every merge request, and failures highlight issues that are easy to trace and fix. Sanity checks catch breaking changes early in the build pipeline, preventing obvious errors from progressing downstream. End-to-end tests validate the most critical user flows with minimal flakiness, ensuring that you simulate real-world usage patterns. You experience fewer production incidents caused by simple mistakes slipping through. Deployment cycles become faster and less stressful because automated tests filter out risky changes before they reach users. Engineering morale improves because teams trust the test results and no longer fear last-minute surprises at release time. Quality metrics such as defect escape rates and mean time to recovery trend downward consistently. The user experience improves steadily because fewer bugs, regressions, and usability issues slip into production.

SUMMARY

The Unified and Layered Testing Strategy principle teaches you that quality is not a box you check at the end. It's a system you build from the ground up, combining fast sanity tests, deep regression coverage, and real-world end-to-end validations. Each layer reinforces the others inside your CI/CD pipelines. By designing and executing tests strategically across layers, you catch issues earlier, ship features faster, and maintain user trust longer. This principle transforms testing from a late-stage obstacle into a continuous foundation of product excellence.

REFERENCES

J. Humble and D. Farley, *Continuous Delivery: Reliable Software Releases Through Build, Test, and Deployment Automation*, Addison-Wesley Professional, 2010.

G. Kim, J. Humble, P. Debois, and J. Willis, *The DevOps Handbook: How to Create World-Class Agility*, Reliability, and Security in Technology Organizations, IT Revolution Press, 2016.

A. Hristov, "How Automated Testing Enables DevOps," Atlassian, retrieved on August 13, 2025 from https://www.atlassian.com/devops/devops-tools/test-automation.

45 • Defensive Testing

"Praemonitus praemunitus." (Forewarned is forearmed.) — Latin prover

INTRODUCTION

The Defensive Testing principle encourages teams to assume failure is inevitable and to proactively validate how their systems respond. Instead of verifying only ideal scenarios, defensive testing explores adverse conditions, error paths, and system resilience. Modern systems operate in unpredictable environments. Network interruptions, invalid user inputs, backend failures, and resource exhaustion are all routine challenges. Defensive testing addresses these realities by designing tests that simulate failures, validate error-handling behavior, and expose vulnerabilities before they reach production.

KEY CONCEPT

The core idea behind defensive testing is simple. Expect things to go wrong. Systems must be validated for correct behavior and for their ability to survive and recover when facing adverse conditions. Testing strategies include simulating service outages, injecting faulty or malformed inputs, and creating resource constraints. These tests validate whether error-handling routines activate properly, whether fallback mechanisms preserve functionality, and whether recovery paths maintain user experience without cascading failures. Defensive testing also emphasizes integrating defensive programming practices directly into the development cycle. Automated tests need to confirm robust input validation, structured exception handling, and circuit breakers tripping as expected. In resilient systems, defensive testing is continuous and systemic, not an afterthought.

WHY IT MATTERS

Systems that work perfectly in the lab but fail under real-world stresses are more common than you would think. Without defensive testing, unexpected conditions and system vulnerabilities are unknown. Embracing this principle transforms failure from an emergency into an anticipated event. Defensive testing improves overall system resilience, catching hidden defects that only appear during failures or edge cases. It builds user trust by ensuring graceful degradation rather than sudden crashes. It also reduces the cost of defects by detecting them early, when fixes are faster, cheaper, and less disruptive. Organizations that invest in defensive testing move faster and deliver software that works better in the face of failures.

IN PRACTICE

When you practice defensive testing, you start by simulating failure early and often. Design tests that reflect real-world issues such as delayed or dropped packets, database outages, malformed API requests, or resource exhaustion. You use tools like Chaos

Monkey, Toxiproxy, or your own scripts to automate and scale these tests so they become part of your regular workflow.

You embed these tests into your CI pipeline. Every commit and deployment should go through a failure simulation. Tie them closely to observability so you are also making sure the telemetry is clear, accurate, and useful when things go wrong. Treat defensive testing as a process that evolves. As your system grows, new threats will appear. Update your test suite to reflect those changes. Use incident reports to spot blind spots and expand your test coverage based on what actually happens in production. When you validate early and treat failure as a normal condition, your system becomes more resilient.

CASE STUDY

In sectors like finance and healthcare, organizations are making fault injection and chaos testing part of standard operations to improve uptime and drive system-level resilience. Infosys embedded fault injection for one of their clients' CI/CD pipelines using Gremlin and custom load-testing tools. By running simulated component failures and disaster recovery drills alongside performance tests, the team lifted system availability to nearly 99.99 percent. The time to detect real production failures dropped from several hours to under 15 minutes, with automated alerts replacing slow human detection. Similarly, National Australia Bank took the approach further by deploying Chaos Monkey directly in production. The tool randomly terminated infrastructure components to ensure that autoscaling and failover worked as expected. Before implementing chaos testing, the bank's engineers were repeatedly called at night for false alarms and avoidable failures. After introducing these practices, noisy alerts disappeared, and high-severity incidents became rare. According to engineers at NAB, resilience in production became measurable and manageable only after they actively tested it.

In healthcare, Main Line Health took chaos testing beyond software. In 2023, the team began running live downtime drills inside clinics, where IT systems were pulled offline without advance notice. Clinical staff practiced fallback procedures using paper records and manual check-ins, with the goal of maintaining care standards even during unexpected IT disruptions. The approach worked. During real outages, the hospital system reported significantly reduced care delays and smoother transitions to backup workflows. Their program earned a 2024 CSO Award for minimizing patient impact during system failures.

These organizations report clear results. One bank achieved near-perfect uptime and sub-fifteen-minute detection times. Another eliminated around-the-clock on-call pages. A health system avoided patient care disruptions and earned national recognition for resilience. Each one moved from theory to practice by regularly injecting faults and measuring outcomes. They treated failure as a testable condition rather than a hypothetical risk. The outcome was a measurable increase in availability, faster recovery times, and fewer critical incidents, all without waiting for an actual outage to learn where the system would break.

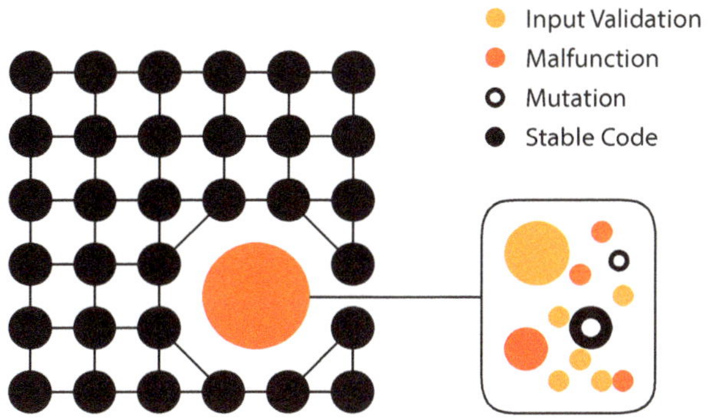

Figure 45 – Defensive Testing

COMMON PITFALLS

Teams often simulate only common failure modes while ignoring rare but catastrophic edge cases. Overlooking silent failures like delayed retries, partial writes, or corrupted in-flight data can leave dangerous blind spots. Another common mistake is underestimating the complexity of orchestrated failures. Testing single-component failure is important but insufficient; real-world outages often involve cascading effects. Defensive tests must model multi-point failure conditions to truly validate system resilience. Finally, teams sometimes introduce defensive testing without automating it, relying on manual chaos simulations or sporadic disaster drills. Without automation and continuous validation, feedback loops remain too slow to keep up with evolving systems.

SUCCESS INDICATORS

When the Defensive Testing principle is applied thoroughly, systems respond to failures with predictability. Service degradation is controlled, user-visible impact is minimized, and recoverability metrics such as the mean time to recovery improve steadily. Over time, production incidents decrease in severity and duration. Deployment pipelines catch failure-handling regressions automatically without waiting for user reports. Development teams move with greater agility, knowing that even when things go wrong, they can handle it. Organizations adopting this principle develop a culture that sees failure as a condition to be expected and mastered.

SUMMARY

The Defensive Testing principle transforms failure from a disruptive force into a manageable, even routine, event. By proactively testing how systems behave under stress, simulating a wide range of failure conditions, and validating error recovery mechanisms continuously, organizations build software that survives the unexpected. In a world where change and disruption are constants, defensive testing helps maintain trust and competitive advantage.

REFERENCES

B. Beyer, C. Jones, J. Petoff, and N. Murphy, *Site Reliability Engineering: How Google Runs Production Systems*, O'Reilly Media, 2016.

"Principles of Chaos Engineering," 2017, last updated 2019, principlesofchaos.org. https://principlesofchaos.org/

Ali Basiri, Niosha Behnam, Ruud de Rooij, Lorin Hochstein, Luke Kosewski, Justin Reynolds, Casey Rosenthal, "Chaos Engineering", *IEEE Software*, vol.33, no. 3, pp. 3541, MayJune 2016, DOI: 10.1109/MS.2016.60

B. Violino, "Main Line Health Deploys Chaos Engineering to Bolster Healthcare Resilience," *CSO*, 2024. https://www.csoonline.com/article/3490060/main-line-health-deploys-chaos-engineering-to-bolster-healthcare-resilience.html

46 • Behavior-Driven Development (BDD)

"The beginning of wisdom is the definition of terms." — Socrates

INTRODUCTION

Software succeeds when teams communicate clearly about what it must do. The Behavior-Driven Development (BDD) principle brings clarity to that communication by using plain language to describe expected system behavior. Instead of writing tests that only developers can understand, BDD frames tests as conversations between business, QA, and engineering. By adopting a familiar "Given-When-Then" structure, BDD transforms requirements into executable stories that guide development and ensure that systems meet both technical and business expectations.

KEY CONCEPT

Behavior-driven development bridges the gap between requirements and implementation by promoting natural language specifications. Teams describe user interactions and system responses using short, structured statements that everyone can understand. The core of BDD involves collaborating across disciplines to define behavior early, writing tests that reflect those shared expectations, and ensuring that those tests remain living executable documentation.

BDD focuses on what the system should do, not how it is built. It steers teams toward thinking about user behavior, business rules, and edge cases from the start. By aligning on behavior before writing code, BDD reduces ambiguity, increases shared understanding, and builds quality into the software lifecycle.

WHY IT MATTERS

Software projects often run into issues because of misaligned expectations. When requirements are unclear or hidden behind technical jargon, teams build what they think is needed rather than what is truly needed.

By introducing a shared language, BDD ensures that developers, testers, and business stakeholders all operate from a common understanding. Requirements become visible and verifiable. Edge cases are discussed earlier. Misunderstandings are caught before they become defects. As the project evolves, the living documentation of BDD tests ensures that the team's knowledge stays current, reducing onboarding time and protecting against silent regressions. Testing becomes a continuous conversation to sharpen the entire development process.

IN PRACTICE

Implementing BDD starts with collaboration. During refinement sessions or workshops, developers, QA engineers, and product owners come together to describe user scenarios in natural language. Instead of technical specifications, teams craft Given–When–Then stories that describe initial conditions, user actions, and expected outcomes.

These scenarios are then automated using frameworks such as Cucumber, SpecFlow, or Behave, ensuring that each piece of behavior is continually verified as part of the CI/CD pipeline. Regular reviews ensure that scenarios evolve with the system, keeping the living documentation accurate and relevant. As BDD matures within an organization, the process becomes second nature. Requirements, development, and validation converge into a unified, streamlined workflow that accelerates delivery without sacrificing quality.

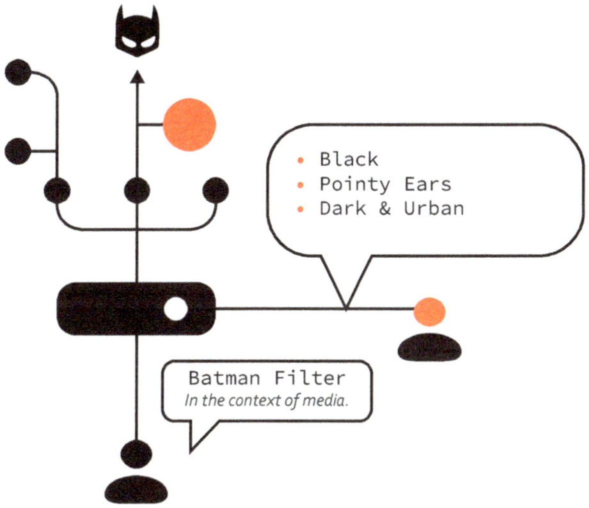

Figure 46 – Behavior-Driven Development (BDD) Principle

CASE STUDY

Nationwide, one of the largest financial institutions in the United Kingdom, adopted behavior-driven development to improve collaboration across its development teams and business units. Prior to BDD, projects often suffered from requirements misinterpretation, leading to costly rework late in the release cycle.

Nationwide introduced BDD workshops at the start of every new feature, bringing together developers, QA engineers, and business analysts to co-create scenarios using the–Then format. These scenarios were automated using SpecFlow and became part of their deployment pipelines. By shifting the conversation about behavior earlier in the process, teams identified ambiguities faster, validated assumptions before implementation, and significantly reduced the volume of last-minute defect triage.

As a result, Nationwide reduced defect rates by over 30 percent across critical projects. Teams reported smoother handoffs between business and technical stakeholders, while time-to-market for new features improved without compromising compliance or stability. The living documentation provided by the BDD tests also simplified audit trails, an important benefit in a highly regulated industry.

COMMON PITFALLS

Teams new to BDD sometimes fall into the trap of writing scenarios that are overly detailed or focused on technical implementation rather than business behavior. When scenarios describe how the system works instead of what it should do, they lose the communicative power that BDD is meant to provide. Another common issue is fragmented adoption, where only part of the team writes behavior-driven tests while the rest continue using traditional approaches. This disconnect undermines the value of shared understanding and slows feedback loops. Successful BDD requires full-team commitment and discipline in maintaining clear, concise, business-focused scenarios.

Finally, organizations sometimes mistake BDD tools for BDD practice. True BDD is about using structured conversations to shape development from the beginning.

SUCCESS INDICATORS

When BDD is working, everyone on the team can read the scenarios and immediately understand what the system is supposed to do. Test suites evolve naturally alongside the codebase, reflecting both the current functionality and the business intent behind it. Fewer defects escape to production, especially defects caused by misunderstandings or missed edge cases.

Teams move faster because they spend less time clarifying vague requirements and more time building the right solutions the first time. New team members ramp up quickly because the living documentation tells the story of the system in plain language. Stakeholders outside of engineering can easily validate system behavior without needing to ask for help. When these outcomes appear consistently, BDD has matured from a process into a mindset across the organization.

SUMMARY

The Behavior-Driven Development principle turns requirements into conversations and tests into living documentation. By aligning teams through plain-language scenarios and using those scenarios to drive development, BDD improves clarity, strengthens collaboration, and builds quality into software from the start. It creates systems that behave as users expect, documents that remain accurate over time, and teams that share a common vision of success. In fast-moving, complex environments, BDD provides a powerful foundation for cross-team collaboration and customer-focused testing.

REFERENCES

D. North, "Introducing BDD," *Dan North & Associates, Ltd.*, 2006. https://dannorth.net/blog/introducing-bdd/

J. F. Smart, *BDD in Action: Behavior-Driven Development for the Whole Software Lifecycle*, Manning Publications, 2014.

Planview, "Nationwide Building Society Taps Planview Solution to Underpin Agile Transformation Initiative," *Planview*, retrieved on August 10, 2025 from https://www.planview.com/resources/case-study/nationwide-building-society-planview-transformation/.

47 • Efficient Test Design

"There is nothing quite so useless as doing with great efficiency something that should not be done at all." — Peter Drucker

INTRODUCTION

The Efficient Test Design principle unifies equivalence partitioning and boundary value analysis into a disciplined approach for creating targeted, effective test cases. Rather than attempting to test every possible input exhaustively, this principle emphasizes designing tests that cover logical groups of input data and focus attention on their critical boundaries. The goal is to maximize coverage with minimal redundancy, ensuring that both typical and extreme scenarios are addressed without burdening the development and testing cycle with unnecessary overhead.

KEY CONCEPT

Equivalence partitioning simplifies test design by dividing input data into distinct partitions where every member is expected to behave similarly. Instead of testing every possible value, testers select a representative value from each partition, reducing the number of necessary test cases while maintaining trust in the system's correctness. Boundary value analysis complements this strategy by focusing on the edges of each partition, where defects like off-by-one errors are most likely to emerge. Testing minimums, maximums, and points just inside and just outside valid ranges captures errors that average-case testing often misses. Together, these approaches balance efficiency with rigor, streamlining test suites without compromising the detection of critical flaws.

WHY IT MATTERS

Exhaustive testing is impractical for all but the simplest systems. Without an intelligent approach, test teams either drown under unmanageable test suites or leave dangerous gaps in coverage. The combination of equivalence partitioning and boundary value analysis offers a solution by achieving high trust with fewer tests. This disciplined method improves efficiency by focusing on meaningful variations, enhances defect detection by targeting where systems are most vulnerable, and ensures that testing remains sustainable as systems grow. It also promotes predictability, making it easier to model and anticipate system behavior across a wide range of inputs.

IN PRACTICE

You start implementing this principle by carefully mapping the input domain. Identify all the relevant inputs and define their valid and invalid ranges. Make sure the partitions you create reflect real behavior patterns, not just theoretical categories or organizational boundaries. Once you have the partitions, choose one clear, representative value from each group. Then focus on the edges. Test the minimum and maximum allowed values, along with values just outside those limits.

Use automation to run these tests efficiently. Frameworks like JUnit, PyTest, or NUnit make integration into your CI pipeline easy so these checks run as part of every development cycle. Keep your test suite lean. As requirements change, adjust your partitions and boundaries without adding unnecessary cases. The goal is to validate whether your system handles real inputs, edge cases, and outliers with predictability. When you apply this approach consistently, you find the issues that matter before users do.

CASE STUDY

As part of a broader quality assessment, Mataram, a public university in Indonesia, conducted formal black-box testing on its Academic Information System (SIA UNRAM), a platform used by students, faculty, and administrators to manage academic records. The system had been in use for some time, but previous testing had been limited in scope. Users had reported missing functionality and inconsistent behavior, prompting the university's IT team to adopt a more rigorous testing approach. To improve both efficiency and effectiveness, the team centered its test design around equivalence partitioning and boundary value analysis.

The testers began by identifying core modules and user roles across the system. Input conditions were grouped into logical partitions, with representative values selected from each. Boundary analysis was applied to test edge conditions with minimums, maximums, and just-outside limits. This method allowed the team to cover key scenarios without creating an unmanageable number of test cases. Four user roles were tested, including students, lecturers, and administrative operators at both the department and faculty levels. Inputs such as date fields, text length, and allowed characters were evaluated using a combination of equivalence classes and boundary limits.

With efficient test design, they came up with targeted test scenarios, of which about 75 percent of the test cases passed, while nearly a quarter exposed functional failures. Team uncovered that defects concentrated in areas that were either more complex or less frequently used. These findings showed that equivalence partitioning and boundary value analysis can find issues in corner cases and infrequently exercised paths. The university's IT department reviewed the findings, and rather than running thousands of tests or relying on random input, the testers achieved targeted coverage with fewer, better-designed scenarios. The testing strategy yielded strong validation outcomes, providing a clear map of where and why the system was failing.

Mataram University's experience illustrates that efficient test design using equivalence partitioning and boundary analysis can raise software quality without inflating test volume. By applying these foundational techniques, the team delivered measurable improvements and strengthened confidence in a critical academic system.

COMMON PITFALLS

Many teams either under-partition or over-partition the input domain. Incomplete partitioning risks missing entire classes of behavior, while overly granular partitioning defeats the goal of efficiency and leads to bloated test suites. Ignoring boundary values is another frequent mistake, allowing critical edge-case bugs to slip through testing undetected. Some organizations also fail to maintain their equivalence classes and boundary tests as software evolves, resulting in stale tests that no longer reflect system realities. To succeed, teams must find the right balance: partitions and boundaries must be representative, and test cases must evolve with the system itself.

Figure 47 – Efficient Test Design

SUCCESS INDICATORS

The impact of the Efficient Test Design principle becomes visible across several dimensions. Test suites shrink in size without losing effectiveness, allowing faster execution and tighter feedback loops. Early defect discovery improves, especially for common pitfalls like input validation errors and off-by-one mistakes. Defect detection rates climb because test cases target both the typical and the extreme. As a result, system quality improves and testing overhead drops. Teams experience shorter testing cycles, enabling more frequent and lower-risk releases.

SUMMARY

The Efficient Test Design principle transforms how teams approach testing by uniting equivalence partitioning and boundary value analysis into a streamlined, powerful strategy. Instead of chasing exhaustive coverage, teams identify meaningful input partitions and reinforce them with precise boundary tests. This discipline delivers comprehensive coverage with fewer cases, catching critical defects early and sustaining velocity as systems grow.

REFERENCES

G. J. Myers, C. Sandler, and T. Badgett, *The Art of Software Testing*, 3rd ed., Wiley, 2011.

C. Kaner, J. Bach, and B. Pettichord, *Lessons Learned in Software Testing: A Context-Driven Approach*, Wiley, 2001.

P. A. D. A. Santi, R. Afwani, M. A. Albar, S.E. Anjarwani, and A.Z. Mardiansyah, Black Box Testing with Equivalence Partitioning and Boundary Value Analysis Methods (Study Case: Academic Information System of Mataram University)" [conference paper]. In *Proceedings of the First Mandalika International Multi-Conference on Science and Engineering 2022 (MIMSE 2022)*, pp. 207–219, Atlantis Press, 2002.

48 • Risk-Based Testing

"It is better to be roughly right than precisely wrong." — John Maynard Keynes

INTRODUCTION

Testing every feature equally might seem responsible, but it spreads your attention too thin. The Risk-Based Testing principle helps you flip that mindset. Not all bugs are equally painful, and not every line of code deserves equal scrutiny. You prioritize testing around the areas where failure actually matters, like business-critical flows, legal obligations, and security boundaries. This principle pairs naturally with the Code Coverage Is Not Quality principle. Vanity metrics like coverage percentages show you where code was touched, not where risk lives. Both challenge the assumption that more tests automatically mean better quality. Instead, they push you to ask more thoughtful questions. What's the worst that could break? Where would a failure cost the most? How do you design tests to catch that early? That shift from quantity to consequence is what makes this principle a foundation for software that works well.

KEY CONCEPT

Risk-based testing starts with a simple observation that your system has uneven risk. Payment systems carry more liability than static help pages. Login logic is more critical than a settings screen. Testing with that in mind means adjusting your effort accordingly. You assess each area of the system by how likely it is to fail and how much damage that failure would cause. That assessment sharpens your testing priorities, and that approach is much better than a one-size-fits-all metric like line coverage.

Risk-based testing also asks you to test better. A line of code that runs during a test isn't the same as a line that's validated. If your assertions are shallow, your tests don't mean much. Real coverage is behavioral. It proves outcomes, detects regressions, and protects the flow on which users depend. When you start writing tests that match the system's most sensitive points with the system's most meaningful behaviors, you stop testing for numbers and start testing for safety.

WHY IT MATTERS

Risk-based testing forces teams to map where failure hurts most and put their best testing effort there. Instead of spreading effort evenly across the whole system, you apply it where it earns trust. You also create space to ignore the noise. Not every function needs complete test scaffolding. Not every warning in a coverage report needs a fix. You stop reacting to numbers and start responding to risk. When this principle is working, your testing stops being a checklist and starts becoming a protective layer around what actually matters.

CASE STUDY

GBST, a global financial software provider in Australia, struggled with long test cycles and slow releases caused by overly exhaustive test coverage across its systems. To improve efficiency without sacrificing quality, the company adopted a focused testing strategy centered on business risk. Instead of aiming for complete coverage, GBST prioritized automation around its most critical workflows. This included targeting areas with the highest potential impact if broken, such as transaction processing and client reporting. This shift allowed them to streamline regression efforts and build a lean, risk-aligned test suite. Within six months, GBST reduced the time and effort needed for core test execution by 80%, cut production defects in key flows, and accelerated delivery timelines. By putting the most important behaviors at the center of their testing, the team achieved both greater confidence and faster release velocity.

IN PRACTICE

You put risk-based testing into action by starting early. Before you write a line of code, map out where failure is most likely and most costly. You use past incidents, complex architecture maps, business-critical flows, or intricate user paths to shape your plan. From there, apply testing as a gradient. High-risk areas get deeper attention. You write more tests, simulate edge cases, validate behavior, and build automated safeguards. Lower-risk areas get lightweight coverage, so you avoid overinvesting where it's not needed. Treat coverage reports as signals, not goals. If you see gaps in code that don't matter much, you leave them. If there's a gap in a high-risk path, you take it seriously. When bugs slip through, you treat them as feedback. Feed those cases into your risk model so the next round of testing is smarter.

This makes your test strategy adaptive. You focus your effort where it counts, and you let that focus evolve. Even your testing process gets tested and improved over time.

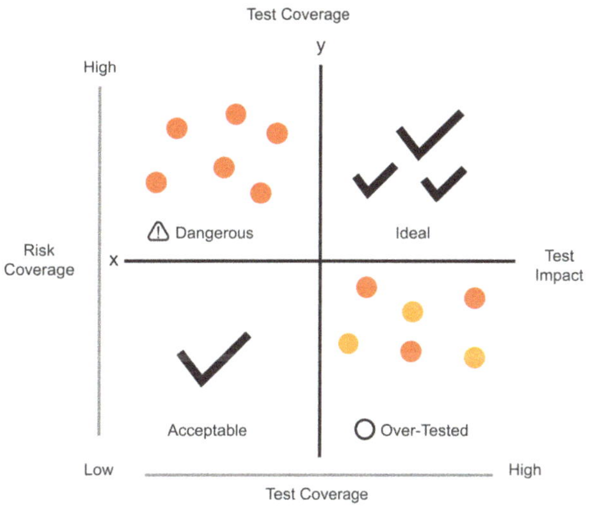

Figure 48 – Risk Based Testing

COMMON PITFALLS

Most failures of this principle come from confusing activity with value. It's easy to think that because your team is writing a lot of tests, you're doing well. However, if those tests don't match business logic or risk, they're just noise. You also see problems when risk assumptions go stale. What used to be a low-risk component might evolve into something mission-critical, and unless your testing evolves with it, you're carrying that hidden risk.

Another trap is isolating testing decisions to QA. Developers and product owners bring essential context about what's changing and why. If they're not involved in prioritizing what to test, you end up protecting the wrong things. The goal is to make testing smarter, which requires a complete picture of the system and its usage.

SUCCESS INDICATORS

When you apply risk-based testing consistently, your system starts to feel calmer. High-risk areas become more stable, and bugs that used to sneak into production now get caught during development. During reviews, instead of asking whether tests were written, you start asking whether they're protecting the right behaviors. You still use metrics like coverage, but only as a compass, and when your team discusses quality, they talk in terms of risk, value, and user experience.

SUMMARY

Risk-based testing helps you move beyond surface-level coverage and toward real software confidence. It moves focus toward where your system can break, how bad that would be, and designing tests that keep that from happening. When you test with purpose, you don't need a wall of green to feel safe. You know your system is protected because the things that matter most are being watched most closely.

REFERENCES

P. Ammann and J. Offutt, *Introduction to Software Testing*, Cambridge University Press, 2008.

M. Pezzè and M. Young, *Software Testing and Analysis: Process, Principles, and Techniques*, Wiley, 2007.

Tricentis. (n.d.). *GBST accelerates testing by 90% with model-based test automation.* https://www.tricentis.com/case-studies/gbst-accelerates-testing

G. Kim, J. Humble, P. Debois, and J. Willis, *The DevOps Handbook: How to Create World-Class Agility, Reliability, and Security in Technology Organizations*, IT Revolution Press, 2016.

J. Bach, "How to Investigate Intermittent Problems," *Satisfice*, 2005. https://www.satisfice.com/blog/archives/34

49 • Defect Clustering

"For many phenomena, 80% of consequences stem from 20% of the causes."
— Vilfredo Pareto

INTRODUCTION

Not all parts of your codebase are created equal. Some modules, no matter how often you refactor or test them, seem to collect bugs at a much higher rate than others. The Defect Clustering principle helps you recognize and respond to this reality. Rather than distributing testing effort evenly across every part of your system, it encourages you to focus on the small fraction of code that causes the majority of failures.

This idea builds on the Pareto principle (the 80/20 rule). Roughly 80 percent of software defects tend to come from just 20 percent of the code. That concentration isn't a liability. It's a strategic advantage. If you can identify the parts of your system where defects tend to cluster, you can direct your testing and review efforts precisely where they'll make the most significant impact.

KEY CONCEPT

Defect clustering is based on the observation that software defects tend to be unevenly distributed. A relatively small portion of your codebase is responsible for a large share of your failures. Instead of seeing this as bad luck, this principle encourages you to treat it as actionable insight. By identifying the specific components or services that frequently show up in bug reports or post-mortems, you can focus your attention where it matters most. That might mean assigning more reviewers, designing deeper test cases, or rethinking the structure of code that repeatedly breaks.

WHY IT MATTERS

When teams try to give every module the same level of attention, they end up spreading themselves too thin. In reality, you likely have a few well-known pain points in your system: maybe a complex billing service, an overloaded API handler, or an integration with an external vendor that behaves unpredictably. These areas are the ones that break most often, cause the biggest incidents, and eat up the most developer time. By focusing on them, you catch more meaningful bugs, reduce the risk of critical failures, and avoid wasting time on parts of the system that rarely cause problems.

You also give your team a clearer sense of what to prioritize. QA, product managers, and engineers can align on what needs the most attention and why. Test cycles become faster because they're not cluttered with checks that aren't yielding value. This shift improves system reliability and conviction in the testing process.

IN PRACTICE

You apply the Defect Clustering principle by first studying the history of your system. Review past incidents, bug reports, and hotfixes. Look for patterns. Which components keep showing up? These could be modules with high-severity failures, services that break under load, or features with constant churn. Code that changes often tends to be more error-prone. Parts of the system that are overly complex or lack ownership become magnets for defects because no one is truly watching them. Once you spot those hotspots, layer in supporting data.

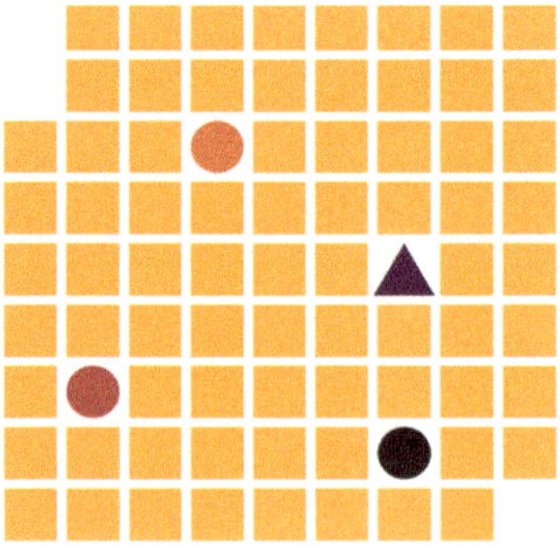

Figure 49 – Defect Clustering

CASE STUDY

In the early 2000s, Microsoft launched its Trustworthy Computing initiative to improve the reliability of its flagship products. As part of this effort, the company analyzed millions of crash reports submitted by users of Windows and Office. The data showed a sharply uneven distribution of defects. A small number of bugs were responsible for most of the observed crashes. Roughly twenty percent of the defects caused eighty percent of the errors, and one percent of the bugs accounted for nearly half of all failures. These findings aligned precisely with the defect clustering principle; the majority of stability problems originated from a concentrated set of modules.

Microsoft used this insight to shift its development and testing priorities. Instead of treating all defects equally, the engineering teams focused on the modules generating the highest crash volume. Error-reporting infrastructure was expanded to route crash data directly to the relevant product teams. Developers received minidump reports that pinpointed failure sources and error codes. Bug triage was informed by impact, and resources were directed toward stabilizing the top one percent of failure-prone code, where the returns were highest.

The results were measurable. Windows XP's first service pack addressed twenty percent of all known defects, most of them concentrated in high-crash areas. Office XP's second service pack removed more than half of the documented application errors. Visual Studio .NET's beta build eliminated seventy-four percent of reported bugs before launch. These improvements were a consequence of a focused effort to identify and fix the most disruptive components. Not all code is equally error-prone, and not all bugs are equally costly. When development and QA teams focus their attention on defect clusters, they reduce risk and improve reliability faster than with generalized testing. Microsoft showed that defect clustering can lead to significantly more stable software. This pattern holds across products and industries, making defect clustering one of the most practical and proven strategies in real-world software engineering.

Once you know where problems cluster, adjust your workflow. Focus deeper testing on high-risk areas. Explore more edge cases, vary your test data, and simulate less obvious failure conditions. During code reviews, give extra scrutiny to risky parts of the system. You can also trigger automated tests when sensitive files change, so those updates never go unchecked.

Keep in mind, these hotspots won't stay static. A refactor might stabilize one part of the system, while a new feature starts creating its own wave of issues. That's why feedback matters. You have to feed incident reports, test failures, and release quality data back into your risk map. Once ready, you share that map with engineering, QA, and product teams so everyone stays focused on the right areas.

COMMON PITFALLS

Defect clustering is most effective when it's applied with nuance. One common mistake is assuming that low-risk areas require no testing at all. Just because a module hasn't caused trouble before doesn't mean it never will. Lightweight regression testing and smoke tests should still be in place to catch regressions system-wide.

Another pitfall is relying too heavily on metrics like code churn or complexity without considering the context behind them. These indicators are useful, but they can mislead if not paired with actual defect history and team insight. Some teams also fall into the trap of overcorrecting, concentrating too much on one area while neglecting the rest. Testing should remain adaptable, with attention shifting based on the system's evolution. Finally, defect clustering fails when feedback loops break down. When incidents and outages aren't informing future testing strategies, the value of clustering fades, and testing gets decoupled from data-driven prioritization.

SUCCESS INDICATORS

When the Defect Clustering principle is working, you'll notice fewer surprises and smoother test cycles. The modules that once caused issues become more reliable. Critical bugs drop in frequency because your team is catching them earlier. Testing becomes more efficient because you're aiming your efforts where they matter most. QA and developers stop debating what to cover and start building consensus around shared risk. Your coverage feels deliberate, and your team moves faster, with fewer setbacks and more clarity.

SUMMARY

The Defect Clustering principle helps you target the areas of your system where problems are most likely to appear. Instead of trying to test everything with equal weight, you test the parts that pose the greatest risk. That precision lets you ship faster, catch critical bugs earlier, and reduce the time spent fixing what could have been prevented. Every system has its weak spots; this principle gives you a way to find them early and strengthen them.

REFERENCES

T. J. Ostrand, E.J. Weyuker, and R.M. Bell, "Predicting the Location and Number of Faults in Large Software Systems," *IEEE Transactions on Software Engineering*, 31(4), 340–355, 2005.

N. Nagappan and T. Ball, "Use of Relative Code Churn Measures to Predict System Defect Density," in *Proceedings of the 27th International Conference on Software Engineering* (pp. 284–292), 2005.

M. Pezzè and M. Young, *Software Testing and Analysis: Process, Principles, and Techniques*, Wiley, 2007.

P. Rooney, "Microsoft's CEO: 80-20 Rule Applies to Bugs, Not Just Features," *CRN*; retrieved July 5, 2025, from CRN website. https://www.crn.com/news/security/18821726/microsofts-ceo-80-20-rule-applies-to-bugs-not-just-features

50 • Code Coverage Is Not Quality

"A map is not the territory." — Alfred Korzybski

INTRODUCTION

You can hit ninety-five percent code coverage and still miss bugs and issues that take your system down. That's the reality behind the Code Coverage Is Not Quality principle. Coverage tools tell you what lines of code were executed during a test run, but they can't tell you whether the system was truly tested. It's a comforting number, but that doesn't mean your tests are doing anything useful. This principle reminds you that test quality isn't about volume. A test that checks a box isn't the same as a test that prevents a failure.

KEY CONCEPT

When you rely on coverage percentages to measure testing effectiveness, you start optimizing for the wrong outcome. You begin writing tests to make numbers go up, not to verify that the software works in meaningful ways. That kind of testing touches code without proving it behaves as expected. It might execute a function, walk through a branch, or mock an interaction, but if it never checks an assertion or verifies a critical business rule, it doesn't matter. What gives a test value isn't whether it runs a line of code. It's whether it would fail if that line were wrong.

WHY IT MATTERS

Relying on code coverage as your primary quality indicator optimizes the team for the metrics and not the end result. A high number of tests may suggest your system is well-tested, but if your test suite isn't asserting the right things or validating failure conditions, you've built a shield with holes in it. That leads to a culture where testing is treated as box-checking rather than risk reduction. You also waste time and energy. Teams chasing full coverage often spend hours writing tests for trivial code like getters, constructors, or logging statements just to satisfy a metric. Meanwhile, core business logic goes untested. In worst-case scenarios, coverage becomes a weapon: test suites grow but with weak, shallow tests that only exist to satisfy process gates. Issues escape, even though the dashboard shows all green.

When you shift the goal away from "how many lines were executed" and toward "what matters most to protect," you end up with cleaner tests and better coverage in each release.

IN PRACTICE

Meaningful testing starts with identifying what matters most in your system. Your goal is to build tests around flows like checkout, login, pricing, or data syncing. It also means challenging your tests to prove themselves. Instead of chasing broad coverage across the codebase, you focus your tests on what matters most. Ask what must work when a customer checks out. What happens if inventory runs out? What if a payment token is invalid? These are the moments that carry risk or build trust. That is where your tests should go first.

You stop writing tests that only check for presence or response codes. Start verifying output, tracking state transitions, simulating failures, and confirming side effects. Your tests should move from passive checks to active validation. If your code changes, your tests should change too. A test that never fails may not be doing real work. It might just be noise. Instead, use tools that expose weaknesses that coverage metrics can't show. For example, mutation testing flips logic in your code on purpose. If your tests still pass, that means something important is missing. When you apply this kind of pressure, you stop treating coverage as the goal and start using it as a signal.

COMMON PITFALLS

While applying the Code Coverage Is Not Quality principle, there is a risk of testing code that carries no business risk and missing out on critical validations. A helper that formats strings or a class that holds configuration data doesn't need elaborate tests. However, a price calculator or token validation function does. Getting this part right is hard and requires cross-team collaboration across the product manager, developers, and quality team. Without that, the team stops trusting the test suite because when tests pass, no one's reassured, and the team ends up falling back to the full coverage fallacy.

SUCCESS INDICATORS

You'll know this principle is working when your team trusts the test suite again. When someone introduces a bug, a test fails immediately, and when a test fails, it tells you something useful. When that happens, you fix the code, not the test. When your CI pipeline passes, you deploy with poise, knowing that critical workflows

CASE STUDY

Atlassian's Jira team noticed that despite achieving high test coverage percentages, critical issues still slipped into production. This prompted a shift in strategy. Instead of measuring quality through numbers, they began aligning their tests with risk. They prioritized testing core flows like issue creation, permission changes, and reporting logic because these areas were most likely to impact users or cause cascading failures. Mutation testing was introduced to validate test strength. When a test passed even after logic was altered, it was flagged as ineffective and either improved or removed.

Instead of chasing 100% coverage, Atlassian targeted the 20% of logic where 80% of the risk lived. Test reviews also changed. Instead of celebrating new tests for increasing coverage, reviewers asked whether the test meaningfully reduced risk. Did it catch regressions? Did it validate edge cases? Did it break when the code did? This focus led to fewer noisy failures, more meaningful signals during development, and a test suite that adapted to the product.

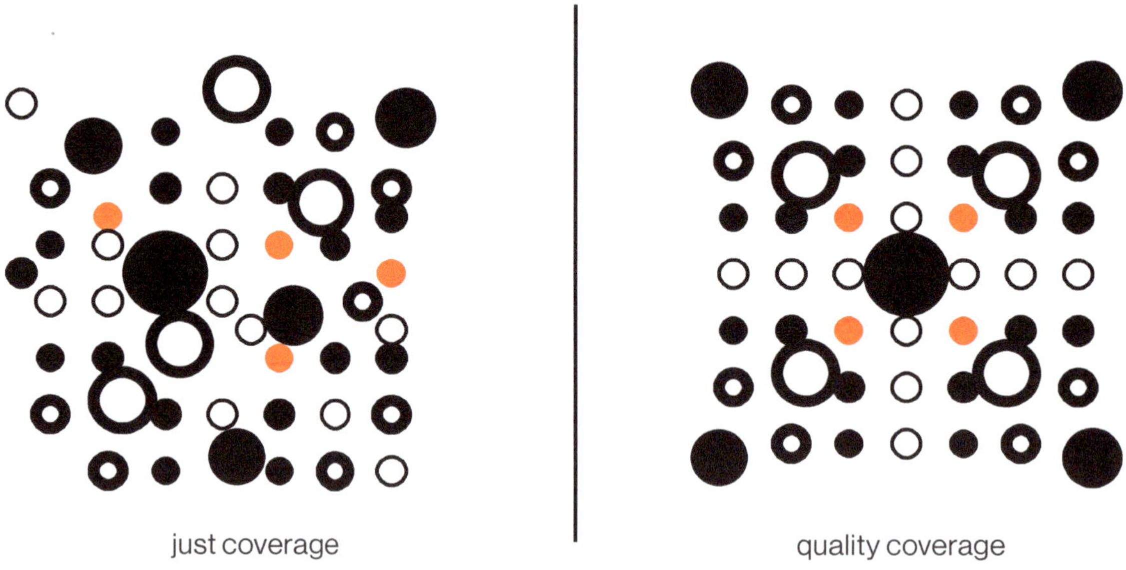

Figure 50 – Code Coverage Is Not Quality

are guarded and edge cases are validated. Stakeholders stop worrying about regression. They see it in the data. You also stop talking about raw coverage numbers. Instead, you review test gaps, mutation scores, and failure patterns. Your team starts having better conversations about quality. You discuss what's tested, what's risky, and what needs improvement.

SUMMARY

The Code Coverage Is Not Quality principle reminds you that numbers can deceive. A line of code that gets executed isn't the same as a line of code that's verified. Quality comes from intent, not volume. When you write tests that protect your product's logic, you build a suite that earns its keep.

REFERENCES

M. Seemann, "Code Coverage Is a Useless Target Measure," ploeh blog, 2015. https://blog.ploeh.dk/2015/11/16/code-coverage-is-a-useless-target-measure/

M. Hilton, J. Bell, and D. Marinov, "A Large-scale Study of Test Coverage Evolution," in Proceedings of the 2018 33rd ACM/IEEE International Conference on Automated Software Engineering, pp. 53–63, 2018. https://doi.org/10.1145/3238147.3238183

S. Pittet, "What Is Code Coverage?" Atlassian, retrieved on August 10, 2025 from https://www.atlassian.com/continuous-delivery/software-testing/code-coverage.

51 • Test Data Management

"Practice does not make perfect. Only perfect practice makes perfect."
— Vince Lombardi

INTRODUCTION

In modern development, testing against dummy data is not enough. The Test Data Management principle stresses the importance of using realistic, production-like data to validate system behavior under conditions that truly reflect how the software will operate in the real world. Properly managed test data bridges the gap between simulated testing and production experience, helping teams catch critical defects early, tune performance accurately, and meet compliance requirements without exposing sensitive information.

KEY CONCEPT

At the heart of this principle lies the practice of replicating production data complexity while maintaining control and security. Realistic test data should mimic production in structure, volume, and variability, revealing how systems behave under authentic conditions. Techniques like data masking anonymize sensitive fields while preserving vital characteristics. Synthetic data generation complements this by creating realistic datasets where direct copying is impractical. Test environments must stay synchronized with production evolution, ensuring that test cases remain relevant and that tests continue to expose meaningful risks. Successful implementation transforms test data into a living asset that enables continuous validation, performance tuning, and risk reduction.

WHY IT MATTERS

Systems relying on simplistic or outdated test data fail to reproduce production anomalies. Realistic data ensures that performance bottlenecks, edge-case logic errors, and integration mismatches surface during development, not after release, preventing costly late-stage surprises. Beyond technical benefits, controlled test data environments preserve privacy, enabling teams to comply with regulatory standards, such as the EU's General Data Protection Regulation (GDPR) or the US's Health Insurance Portability and Accountability Act (HIPAA), without sacrificing realistic scenarios.

IN PRACTICE

You operationalize this principle by starting with your production data. Study its structure, distribution patterns, and edge cases. This helps you understand what the real system looks like. From there, apply strat-

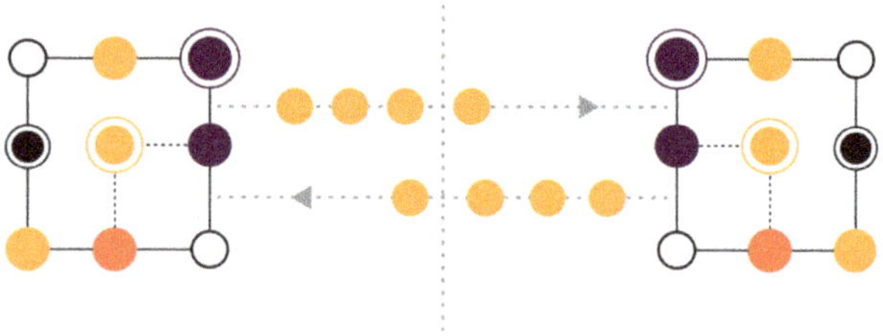

Figure 51 – Test Data Management

egies like data masking to anonymize sensitive fields or generate synthetic datasets that mimic key behaviors and edge conditions. Use test data management tools to automate your environment refreshes. Make sure they maintain referential integrity and check the quality of the test data continuously. Build high-fidelity environments that mirror production. Match schema versions, data volumes, and user behavior patterns as closely as possible.

To keep test data in sync with production, use structured synchronization processes so that your test environments evolve in parallel. That way, you reduce drift and keep your tests grounded, even as the system changes.

COMMON PITFALLS

Despite best intentions, teams often stumble by relying on stale or overly simplified data that hides real-world complexity. When datasets are over-sanitized, critical edge cases get scrubbed out, and it creates blind spots that weaken test coverage. Without strong data governance, test environments can deviate from production, leading to missed defects. Mishandling sensitive data adds even greater risk. Without proper anonymization, teams expose the organization to compliance violations, legal consequences, and a loss of customer trust. Effective test data management requires more than tooling. It takes technical precision paired with operational discipline to keep environments safe and useful.

CASE STUDY

Mizuho Securities, an investment bank and one of Japan's leading financial institutions, faced major delays in software testing due to slow, manual test data provisioning and outdated masking practices. Preparing production-like environments required dedicated database teams and took days or even weeks, leading to misaligned test cycles and missed edge-case validation. To address this, Mizuho adopted a DevOps-enabled test data platform that combined automated data masking with on-demand data virtualization. This shift allowed teams to spin up secure, production-like datasets in hours, fully anonymized to meet Japan's strict financial data regulations. The test data platform and initiative cut test data provisioning time by 90%, reduced operational costs by over $700,000 annually, and enabled more realistic, frequent testing. By aligning test environments with real-world conditions while preserving compliance, Mizuho improved software quality, reduced late-stage defects, and accelerated delivery across its development pipeline.

SUCCESS INDICATORS

Systems tested with realistic data exhibit greater reliability and fewer surprises post-deployment. Defects tied to data anomalies, integration mismatches, or boundary conditions decrease significantly. Performance tuning becomes precise because it is based on actual workload patterns rather than theoretical assumptions. Compliance audits validate that testing processes respect data protection standards. Engineering teams gain value in the predictive power of their tests, enabling them to release software faster without sacrificing quality.

SUMMARY

The Test Data Management principle transforms testing from an isolated exercise into a realistic rehearsal for production. By prioritizing controlled, production-like datasets, organizations expose critical risks earlier and protect sensitive information without compromising test accuracy.

REFERENCES

Gopinath, R., Alipour, M. A., Ahmed, I., Jensen, C., & Groce, A. (April 2014). *An empirical comparison of mutant selection approaches* (Technical Report, School of Engineering and Computer Science, Oregon State University).

J. Humble and D. Farley, *Continuous Delivery: Reliable Software Releases Through Build, Test, and Deployment Automation*, Addison-Wesley Professional, 2010.

Perforce Software. (n.d.). *Mizuho Securities: Managing risk with a secure, centralized development platform.* https://www.perforce.com/customers/case-studies/pdx/mizuho-securities

52 · State and Data Integrity Testing

"Character is revealed in action." — Aristotle

INTRODUCTION

This principle combines two critical practices: state transition testing and data integrity validation. State transition testing ensures that a system behaves correctly as it moves from one state to another. Data integrity testing ensures that information remains accurate and consistent as it moves across databases and APIs. Together, they provide a complete lens for validating dynamic system behavior, revealing issues that static snapshots cannot detect. Traditional static testing focuses on what the system looks like at rest. The State and Data Integrity Testing principle focuses on what happens in motion.

KEY CONCEPT

Modern applications thrive on transitions. Users move through multi-step workflows, background services update status fields, and APIs push data through a web of systems. Capturing and validating these transitions is essential for system reliability.

State transition tests this reliability by modeling every possible system state and clearly defining the valid transitions between them. State transition testing verifies the correctness of the movement itself, including edge cases like retries, failures, and rollbacks, on top of checking that a system reaches a target state. Validating only end states risks overlooking subtle but dangerous errors introduced during the path from one state to another. Data integrity testing follows similar information across its entire lifecycle. Verifying that data remains intact across boundaries and services is critical for user trust and operational stability.

WHY IT MATTERS

Quite often, real-world failures are not static flaws; they are transition failures. A status change misses a critical step, a background job overwrites something, or a network hiccup corrupts an in-flight payload. Without explicit transition and data integrity tests, these issues escape unnoticed into production.

Testing state transitions and data flows ensures that applications behave predictably under dynamic conditions. It also accelerates the detection of regressions, revealing inconsistencies during transformations before they accumulate into bigger failures. Beyond operational stability, this approach directly improves user experience. In regulated industries, organizations can demonstrate compliance more easily through a verified history of state transitions and clean data handoffs.

IN PRACTICE

You apply the State and Data Integrity Testing principle by mapping out every possible system state. Use diagrams to chart transitions, including retries, timeouts, and failure paths. These diagrams give you a blueprint for writing test cases that cover real scenarios. Next, you embed state testing at both the unit and workflow levels. Integration and system tests simulate real-world flows like canceling a task mid-process, recovering from an error state, or dealing with partial updates during a network delay.

For data integrity, you follow critical data from entry to exit. Use reconciliation jobs, snapshot comparisons, and hashing to detect inconsistencies across services. In distributed systems, attach checksums to payloads and verify them at every step. This helps you catch data corruption the moment it happens.

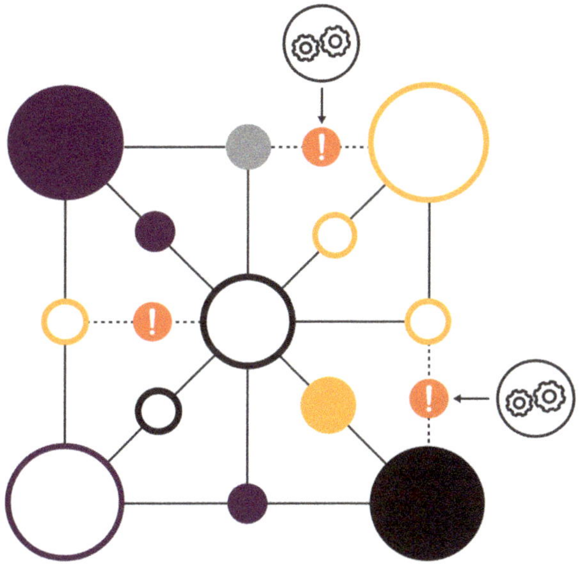

Figure 52 – State and Data Integrity Testing

CASE STUDY

In the finance and banking sector, precision is paramount. When JPMorgan Chase Co. faced rising duplicate transaction errors within its internal banking workflows, it noted that while traditional test coverage confirmed end states, it missed subtle errors occurring during retries and asynchronous handoffs.

To address this, the engineering teams adopted automated state transition testing across payment and compliance systems. Every financial workflow, such as transaction initiation, authorization, settlement, and post-settlement reporting, was mapped with explicit state models. Transition tests validated success paths and error recoveries. In parallel, the teams implemented hash-based validation between upstream and downstream data streams. At each processing hop, transaction records were hashed and compared to detect any silent drift or corruption across microservices and APIs.

The results were transformative. Transaction reconciliation errors dropped by over 50%. Recovery from service failures became faster and more predictable. With full historical traceability of every financial state transition, audit teams reported growing trust in compliance reporting. Developers, armed with real-time feedback on transition failures and data drift, reduced regression rates and accelerated safe deployments. JPMorgan Chase's experience shows that validating motion and endpoints builds financial-grade system reliability.

To automate these tests, run them on every commit, after deployment, and on a production schedule. Use observability tools to detect transition failures, data drift, and recovery issues as they happen. Test edge cases too. Simulate retries, double submissions, stale states, and partial failures so your system can handle the messiness of real usage.

COMMON PITFALLS

Even with good intentions, teams fall into predictable traps. Missing undocumented states, such as retries, timeouts, or stale session expirations, are frequent mistakes that can leave dangerous blind spots. Focusing only on the happy path hides issues where real users and systems often operate. For example, relying purely on schema validation ignores the possibility of corrupted values or missing fields within "valid" structures. In distributed systems, assuming that eventual consistency will "just work" without explicit checks often leads to silent data divergence. Avoiding these pitfalls requires a mindset of structured modeling, automation first, and a deep respect for the messy realities of real-world systems.

SUCCESS INDICATORS

When the State and Data Integrity Testing principle is applied well, system transitions become routine. Features like retriable uploads, transaction rollbacks, or session expirations work smoothly without introducing bugs. Data flows cleanly across services, APIs, and layers without silent corruption. Engineering teams catch regressions early. User incidents tied to broken states or missing data decrease significantly. Compliance audits show full traceability of how, when, and why data and state changes occurred. CI/CD pipelines run faster and more confidently because failures are caught before they reach production. In short, your software moves reliably.

SUMMARY

The State and Data Integrity Testing principle recognizes that most failures occur during movement, not at rest. By rigorously modeling transitions, validating data across its journey, and simulating edge conditions, teams can build systems that are resilient, auditable, and trustworthy.

REFERENCES

T. Y. Chen and S. C. Mak, "A Survey on State-Based Testing: Techniques and Issues," *IEEE Transactions on Software Engineering*, vol. 23, no. 8, pp. 512–525, 1997.

C. Batini and M. Scannapieco, *Data Quality: Concepts, Methodologies and Techniques*, Springer, 2006.

IEEE, "IEEE Standard for Software and System Test Documentation," in *IEEE Std 829-2008*, 2008. https://standards.ieee.org/standard/829-2008.html

53 • Golden Master Testing

"The mirror is the perfect judge: it never speaks, but it shows." — Chinese proverb

INTRODUCTION

When you're working in a large or legacy system, writing precise, assertion-based tests isn't always practical. The behavior might be too complex to describe up front. The output might be too big or structured to validate easily, but that doesn't mean you have to test mindlessly. Golden master testing gives you a powerful safety net. You capture the system's output when it's correct, treat it as the "golden" version, and compare all future runs against it. If the behavior changes, you'll see it line by line, byte by byte. It's a way to preserve working behavior even when you don't fully understand or want to define it yet. Instead of asserting what the output should be in abstract terms, you preserve what the output actually was when it worked and use that as your ongoing source of truth.

KEY CONCEPT

Golden master testing isn't about abstract theory. It's a practical method grounded in observed behavior. You run the system with known, stable inputs, capture the resulting output, and treat that result as the gold standard for all future comparisons. This output might be JSON, HTML, logs, reports, or screen renderings, basically anything structured and consistent enough to validate. Once a baseline is established, future test runs with the same inputs generate new outputs that are automatically compared using diff tools. If those outputs differ, the test fails and prompts a review. Your team then inspects the changes to determine whether they're expected or accidental. Only update golden masters after a deliberate review confirms the change is valid and intentional.

This technique is especially helpful when the system produces outputs that are too broad or unpredictable to assert manually, such as those from report generators, rendering engines, or complex data pipelines. For instance, if you're testing a legacy billing system that outputs large CSV files, writing assertions for each field can be brittle and exhausting. Instead, you capture a trusted CSV once, and from then on, every change to the code is verified by comparing new outputs against that baseline. If any values, structure, or formatting shifts unexpectedly, the test will fail and alert you before the change reaches production. Golden master tests preserve not what you predict but what you've already proven to work.

WHY IT MATTERS

Golden master testing shines in situations where traditional assertion-based testing falls short. It allows you to catch regressions without writing custom test cases for every output, making it especially effective for large or complex systems. When you're refactoring or migrating code, golden master tests act as a guardrail, alerting you to any unexpected behavioral shifts, even subtle ones. In legacy systems where original intent may no longer be documented, these tests help preserve working knowledge by capturing a snapshot of what "correct" looked like. They also improve collaboration by providing clear output diffs that show exactly what changed, helping teams align more easily during code reviews.

By focusing on actual behavior instead of just structure, golden master testing saves time and reduces reliance on brittle tests. It transforms your system's output into a durable, inspectable artifact that evolves only when you want it to. The result is safer code changes, more confident refactoring, and smoother day-to-day maintenance.

IN PRACTICE

Golden master testing works best when your outputs are structured, consistent, and stable. Start by picking outputs that only change when behavior changes. Think of JSON responses, HTML pages, or generated reports. Run the system with representative inputs and manually check that the results are correct. Once you are confident in the output, save it. That becomes your golden master.

When you are ready, clean the data before comparing. Strip out anything non-deterministic, like timestamps, Universally Unique Identifiers (UUIDs), or environment-specific paths. Then, automate the comparison using diff tools, structural validators, or visual regression tools. Make sure this runs in your CI

CASE STUDY

Codurance, a boutique software consultancy, was engaged by a client to modernize a legacy system that lacked automated tests. The system was characterized by a sprawling codebase with deeply intertwined logic and a heavy reliance on database operations, making traditional unit testing approaches impractical.

To address this challenge, Codurance implemented golden master testing. They began by executing the existing system with known inputs and capturing the resulting outputs, which included database states and generated files. These outputs served as the "golden masters." Subsequent test runs involved feeding the same inputs into the system and comparing the new outputs against the golden masters. Any discrepancies signaled potential regressions, prompting further investigation.

This approach enabled Codurance to refactor and enhance the legacy system confidently, ensuring that existing functionalities remained intact. By capturing and comparing outputs, they could detect unintended changes early in the development process, facilitating safer and more efficient modernization efforts.

pipeline, so you catch unexpected changes early. When a golden master does change, you treat it like a code change. Make the diff visible in the pull request. Everyone on the team should understand what changed and why before accepting the update. This turns your tests into a living record of how the system behaves. It gives you a clear baseline and makes it easier to evolve the system without guessing what you might break.

COMMON PITFALLS

Golden master tests are a powerful tool, but they are not a silver bullet. When applied without care, they can introduce new risks instead of preventing them. One common pitfall is starting with a bad baseline. If the original output used to create the golden master is incorrect or incomplete, you've locked in flawed behavior that future tests will defend. This can lead to a false sense of safety. Another issue is applying golden master testing to scenarios where simpler, assertion-based testing would suffice. For straightforward logic, golden masters tend to overcomplicate what could be verified with a few clear checks.

Unnormalized or noisy data can also undermine test reliability. If your outputs contain timestamps, UUIDs, or other variable content, you risk frequent false positives that erode trust in the suite. Golden master tests should never be updated blindly. Automatically accepting changes without review undermines the entire purpose of golden master testing. Like any form of testing, golden masters require upkeep. If they fall behind the current behavior of the system, they no longer provide value and can become a source of uncertainty or delay. This principle only works when supported by clean baselines, thoughtful review, and consistent maintenance.

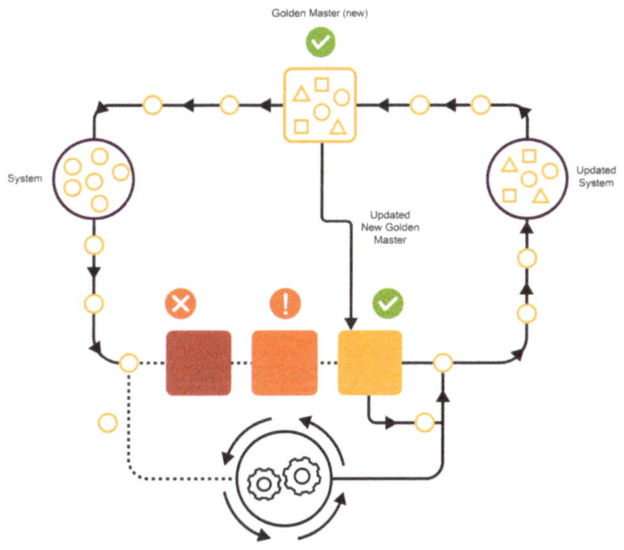

Figure 53 – Golden Master Testing

SUCCESS INDICATORS

You'll feel golden master testing working when refactors stop feeling risky. Developers update legacy logic and trust that subtle breakages won't sneak past them. Debugging becomes faster because you can see what changed in full detail. Even if no one wrote a test for a particular behavior, you'll catch it when it shifts. Pull requests include output diffs as part of the review. Over time, this builds a shared understanding of the system's actual behavior, leading to fewer regressions and a culture of inspecting what matters.

SUMMARY

The Golden Master Testing principle helps you protect the real-world behavior of your system by capturing known-good outputs and monitoring for change. It's especially powerful when working in complex or legacy systems, where expectations are unclear, but correctness is critical. It can't replace unit tests or specs, but it can record what works, make changes visible, and keep evolution intentional.

REFERENCES

G. Meszaros, *xUnit Test Patterns: Refactoring Test code*, Addison-Wesley, 2007.

S. Davies, "How to Test Legacy Software (That Was Not Designed to Be Tested) When Modernising," *Codurance*, 2022. https://codurance.com/publications/how-to-test-legacy-software-when-modernising

M. Pearl, "Setting Up the Golden Master Using ApprovalTests.Net," *Mark Pearl on Software*, 2015. https://blog.markpearl.co.za/Setting-Up-The-Golden-Master

M. Feathers, *Working Effectively with Legacy Code*, Prentice Hall, 2004.

54 · Isolation and Contract Testing

"The best contract is the one you never have to enforce." — Anonymous legal maxim

INTRODUCTION

Stable systems require stable foundations. When external services, databases, or APIs introduce unpredictability in your systems during testing, the Isolation and Contract Testing principle addresses it by replacing real-world dependencies with controlled substitutes and establishing explicit agreements about how services interact. Isolation ensures that your tests focus squarely on your own logic. Contracts guarantee that interactions between systems remain reliable, even as those systems evolve independently. Together, these practices create tests that are faster, more trustworthy, and better aligned with reality.

KEY CONCEPT

This principle operates on two complementary ideas: isolating dependencies during testing and formalizing service expectations through contracts. Dependency isolation involves substituting real services with mocks or stubs. By mocking expected behavior, these stand-ins eliminate external variables and provide a clean environment to verify system behavior that you own. Contract testing strengthens this by defining the exact formats, responses, and error behaviors expected between services. These contracts act as living agreements, continuously validated through automation. The combination of isolation and contracts ensures that tests are focused and remain valid even as external systems grow or change behind the scenes.

WHY IT MATTERS

Testing against live external systems introduces unpredictability, slow feedback loops, and false negatives. A network timeout, third-party rate limit, or schema change outside your control can derail a test suite and mislead developers into chasing problems that are not their own. Isolating dependencies removes this noise, allowing failures to point clearly at your own code. Without contract testing, even small undocumented changes in APIs or services can cause issues that testing could have prevented. When isolation and contracts are applied together, tests become faster, and integrations become safer. These practices improve release velocity while reducing the risk of late-stage integration failures.

IN PRACTICE

You start by identifying every external dependency your system relies on. This includes APIs, databases, message queues, and media assets. In your unit and integration tests, replace those dependencies with mocks or stubs that simulate expected behavior. Run tests against these controlled responses so they are consistent and isolated from external failures.

Alongside your mocks, define contracts. These describe the structure of requests and responses, including status codes and error formats. Make contract validation part of your CI pipeline. If someone breaks the contract, the build should fail. That protects the system from hidden assumptions and misaligned changes.

As your services evolve, treat contract changes with care. Use versioning strategies that maintain compatibility and avoid breaking consumers. The goal is to catch problems early and to make your system easier to change without disrupting the teams around you. When contracts are clear and enforced, your tests stay focused, and your boundaries stay strong.

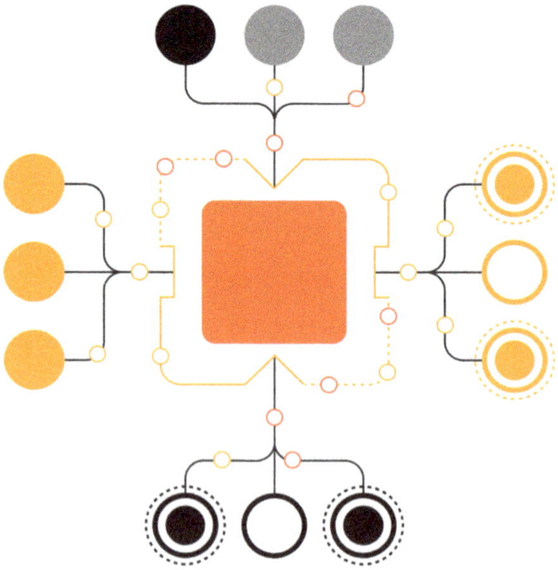

Figure 54 – Isolation and Contract Testing

CASE STUDY

Zalando, a leading European online fashion retailer, manages a complex architecture of microservices that power everything from product catalogs to payment processing. Early in their transition to microservices, Zalando teams experienced frequent failures during cross-service deployments. Changes made by one team often unintentionally broke other teams' services because there was no formalized expectation about API behaviors.

To address this, Zalando adopted consumer-driven contract testing using Pact. Each service team documented its API contracts based on real consumer needs, ensuring that providers validated against consumer expectations before deploying. Mocks based on these contracts replaced live dependencies in unit and integration tests, reducing reliance on unstable external systems during development and CI pipelines.

Over twelve months, this shift reduced cross-team integration defects by over 50%. Services became more autonomous, with fewer breaking changes reaching production. Developers also reported a higher sense of ownership and trust, as contracts provided a clear, shared understanding of how systems were supposed to interact. As Zalando's architecture continued to evolve, Contract testing remained a cornerstone of their strategy, allowing them to handle complexity and team independence without sacrificing stability.

COMMON PITFALLS

Without discipline and isolation, contract testing efforts can introduce new risks. Excessive mocking may detach tests from real-world behavior, creating a false sense of security that crumbles during integration. Contracts neglected over time can drift from actual system behavior, leading to unexpected breakages when teams finally test across boundaries. Rigid contracts that over-specify internal behaviors rather than external agreements can slow down development and discourage innovation. Another common mistake is failing to validate mocks against live services periodically, allowing mock definitions to become stale. True resilience requires actively maintaining alignment with evolving dependencies.

SUCCESS INDICATORS

Systems that apply this principle consistently exhibit faster, more stable test suites. Test failures are rare, but when they occur, they reliably signal defects in the code under test rather than unpredictable external issues. Integration problems are caught early, often during development rather than during cross-team coordination or after release. Teams spend less time firefighting mysterious failures and releasing features. Collaboration improves as service providers and consumers negotiate and evolve contracts deliberately rather than reacting to surprises. Over time, stability, predictability, and delivery velocity all increase as dependency-related uncertainty shrinks.

SUMMARY

The Isolation and Contract Testing principle ensures that software is tested in clean, predictable conditions and integrates safely with its environment. By isolating external dependencies and codifying expectations through contracts, teams build systems that are faster to test, safer to evolve, and more resilient in production. Instead of testing someone else's assumptions, engineers validate their own logic against stable, verifiable agreements. In doing so, they turn integration points into robust collaborations.

REFERENCES

M. Fowler, "Mocks Aren't Stubs," *martinFowler.com* (blog), 2007.

G. Meszaros, *xUnit Test Patterns: Refactoring Test Code*, Addison-Wesley, 2007.

Pact Foundation, "Consumer Driven Contracts," *Pact documentation*, retrieved on August 13, 2025 from https://docs.pact.io/#consumer-driven-contracts.

55 · Chaos Engineering and Mutation Testing

"In war, the first casualty is the plan." — Carl von Clausewitz, On War, Book I

INTRODUCTION

The Chaos Engineering and Mutation Testing principle combines two proactive strategies to validate how systems survive under stress and whether tests truly protect them. Together, these practices build concrete evidence and resilience into the core of both systems and teams.

KEY CONCEPT

Chaos engineering involves controlled failure injection. Teams simulate adverse conditions such as network outages, delayed services, or crashed nodes to observe system behavior. The goal is to uncover system weaknesses and ensure the system degrades gracefully rather than catastrophically. Mutation testing focuses on the integrity of the test suite itself. Instead of trusting that tests are sufficient, mutation testing injects small, deliberate faults into the codebase, such as flipping logical operators or changing conditionals. A strong test suite detects these injected faults immediately. A weak test suite lets them slip through unnoticed.

Both techniques operate on the same principle: resilience is proven by surviving targeted disruption and scrutiny.

WHY IT MATTERS

Building robust systems requires more than green test runs. Real failures rarely resemble the happy path. Chaos experiments expose system weaknesses, such as retry loops misfiring under latency or cascading failures from simple network partitions that conventional functional testing overlooks. Mutation testing exposes gaps that traditional code coverage often overlooks, especially in edge cases. Practicing chaos engineering and mutation testing gives teams visibility and predictability because they understand how the system behaves when something inevitably fails. They accelerate recovery, tighten feedback loops, and reduce the human and financial cost of incidents. Over time, systems that are constantly challenged become stronger because of it.

IN PRACTICE

Chaos engineering starts with a hypothesis. You define what you expect to happen if a service fails or latency spikes. Then you use tools like Chaos Monkey, Gremlin, or Chaos Toolkit to inject those failures in a controlled environment. Your metrics, traces, and logs should make it clear whether the system behaved as expected or revealed new weaknesses. In the beginning, start small and run experiments on isolated components before moving on to more complex scenarios. As you figure things out, scale up the scope and reach of your tests.

Mutation testing pushes your test suite in a different way. You use tools like PIT, MutPy, or Stryker to introduce small faults into the code. These mutations run automatically, and your test suite is re-executed. A strong suit should catch them. When a mutation survives, it's a sign that your tests may not be verifying behavior well enough. Use those signals to guide better test design.

Both chaos engineering and mutation testing rely on automation. Track your mutation scores over time and

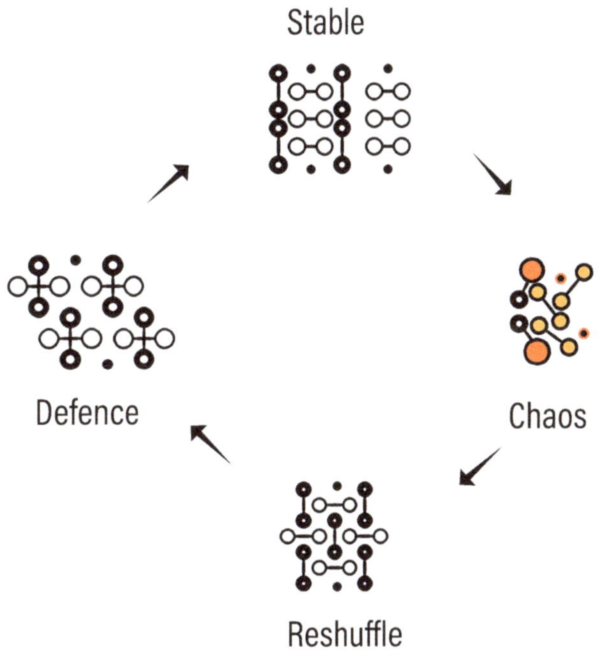

Figure 55 – Chaos Engineering and Mutation Testing

CASE STUDY

When Capital One shifted to a cloud-first architecture, system complexity grew fast. To stay ahead of unexpected failures, they embraced chaos engineering and started injecting controlled faults to test how services behave under stress. The team started by defining what "normal" looks like for an application, then ran experiments to simulate outages, latency spikes, and server crashes. Using tools like Chaos Monkey and AWS-native features, they tested scenarios like crashing containers in their notification service to verify if traffic rerouted smoothly and alerting systems responded correctly.

These experiments uncovered weaknesses early and gave teams practical experience responding to failures. Over time, systems became more resilient, and recovery times improved. Chaos engineering also shifted the team's mindset; developers and site reliability engineers began thinking more critically about failure, building more robust systems from the start. By making chaos testing part of their routine, Capital One improved uptime, built trust in their systems, and made resilience a habit, not a reaction.

treat improvements as real engineering goals. Eventually, you want chaos experiments to run regularly as part of your continuous resilience testing.

COMMON PITFALLS

Chaos engineering fails when teams run experiments without clear hypotheses. Randomly breaking services without defined expectations turns tests into noise, not insight. Mutation testing loses value if surviving mutants are ignored or if mutations are treated as low-priority artifacts instead of test design failures. Poor observabilities impair both practices. Without fine-grained monitoring and tracing, chaos experiments reveal little, and undetected mutations provide no corrective feedback.

Unsafe execution is another risk. Chaos tests without proper containment can cause real outages, while excessive mutation testing can slow pipelines to the point of frustrating developers. Cultural resistance can also be a barrier. Many teams still view induced failures as reckless rather than essential. Without organizational buy-in, chaos and mutation practices are unlikely to move beyond isolated experiments.

SUCCESS INDICATORS

When engineered resilience practices are fully embraced, system behavior under stress becomes predictable rather than surprising. Chaos experiments reveal few new vulnerabilities over time because architecture improves iteratively based on real-world insights. Mutation scores rise steadily, reflecting a test suite that covers code and also guards against regressions meaningfully.

Operational metrics show reduced mean time to recovery, fewer cascading failures, and more graceful degradation under adverse conditions. Development velocity increases because teams trust their safety nets. Incident retrospectives reveal smaller blast radii and faster diagnoses. Instead of fearing failure events, engineers anticipate them and practice recovering from them.

SUMMARY

The Chaos Engineering and Mutation testing principle transforms quality assurance from checking for correctness into actively challenging both systems and tests. Chaos engineering injects failure into distributed architectures to validate resilience. Mutation testing injects faults into codebases to validate test effectiveness. By deliberately introducing controlled disruption, teams build systems that do not simply survive ideal conditions but thrive under pressure.

REFERENCES

D. North, "*Introducing BDD*," Dan North & Associates, Ltd.,2006. https://dannorth.net/blog/introducing-bdd/

J. F. Smart, *BDD in Action: Behavior-Driven Development for the Whole Software Lifecycle*, Manning Publications, 2014.

C. Rosenthal and N. Jones, *Chaos Engineering: System Resiliency in Practice*, O'Reilly Media, 2020.

Y. Jia and M. Harman, "An Analysis and Survey of the Development of Mutation Testing," *IEEE Transactions on Software Engineering*, vol. 37, no. 5, pp. 649–678, 2011.

S. Shunmugasundaram, "Continuous Chaos—Introducing Chaos Engineering into DevOps Practices," *Capital One Tech*, August 10, 2018.

56 • Automated UI Testing

"The interface is the product." — Jef Raskin, creator of the Apple Macintosh project

INTRODUCTION

Manual UI testing can't keep up with the pace of modern feature delivery. The Automated UI Testing principle focuses on embedding automated UI tests into development pipelines and safeguarding the whole user journey by validating interfaces through simulated interactions. This turns quality assurance into a continuous process, ensuring that interfaces behave predictably across devices, browsers, and versions.

KEY CONCEPT

Automated UI testing means reproducing real user behavior to validate critical workflows like authentication, purchasing, and profile management. Effective implementation captures three dimensions: full end-to-end user simulation, visual integrity validation, and consistent cross-browser, cross-mobile performance. These tests must trigger automatically on every code change, offering immediate feedback on regressions. A well-architected test suite mirrors realistic user flows, stabilizes interaction timing to avoid flaky results, and adapts as the product evolves. Rather than simply verifying individual UI components, automated UI tests verify the experience as a whole, making sure that small changes do not disrupt the system's visual and functional consistency.

WHY IT MATTERS

Broken interfaces destroy user trust faster than functional bugs in the backend. A misplaced button, broken navigation, or unexpected layout shift can frustrate users within seconds. Without automated UI testing, visual regressions slip into production unnoticed, costing teams both credibility and time. Automated UI tests protect the user experience by exposing defects early, giving developers a rapid feedback loop that keeps pace with modern continuous deployment practices. Over time, this safety net does more than prevent emergencies; it accelerates delivery and improves design consistency.

IN PRACTICE

You build effective UI automation by starting with the user journeys that matter most. You focus on the actions your users perform frequently or depend on for critical outcomes. Your tests should follow these paths end-to-end, both checking that the interactions succeed and that the right messages, state changes, and visual cues appear. To keep your tests clean and maintainable, use structured patterns like the Page Object Model. As the UI evolves, this structure helps you avoid rewriting tests every time a button or layout shifts. Make sure your tests run across a range of browsers and devices so you can trust the results no matter where users access your product.

While checking for user actions, avoid using fixed timeouts. Instead, configure your scripts to wait for elements to become ready. This reduces flakiness and improves reliability. Also, add visual checks because things like Snapshot comparisons and layout validation can catch rendering issues that functional checks miss.

Integrate your UI tests into your CI pipeline. Treat any broken UI path as a serious issue. A failure here should block the release just like a failing unit test would. As your product evolves, update your test suite based on what you learn in production.

COMMON PITFALLS

Many teams fall into the trap of building tentative, unmaintainable test suites. Over-reliance on hard-coded waits, rigid element selectors, or insufficient scenario coverage causes tests to fail unpredictably, undermining trust in automation itself. Neglecting less common user paths can create dangerous blind spots for regression testing and can cause issues to be missed until the software hits production. Teams sometimes

CASE STUDY

As TransUnion, a major credit bureau in the U.S., moved toward continuous deployment, its manual UI testing process became a constraint. The QA team relied on weekly test cycles using hundreds of hardcoded assertions to validate key user flows across its credit monitoring portal. This approach was too slow and rigid to support faster releases, especially as the site expanded to support features like credit locking, mobile views, and responsive layouts.

To support higher deployment velocity without sacrificing quality, TransUnion adopted automated visual testing using an automated UI testing tool. The new system was layered into the existing Selenium and Python framework and replaced manual checks with full-page visual snapshots. These automated tests ran during every pull request and deployment, detecting UI regressions early in the release cycle. With the automated tests, engineers no longer needed to write or maintain hundreds of individual assertions, because layout differences, cross-browser quirks, and content mismatches were handled visually. This shift was a move from test maintenance to true user experience validation.

The results were clear. Regression testing time dropped from 30 hours per release to about 2 hours. With automated UI checks built into the pipeline, the team moved from weekly releases to near-daily deployments. Visual inconsistencies were caught before code went live, which reduced the number of escaped defects and stabilized build quality. It also cut down duplicate test coverage and enabled a faster rollout across platforms. TransUnion's transition to automated UI testing improved both speed and reliability. Engineers delivered changes with more confidence, and the team had a system that scaled with the product. The effort paid off in more frequent releases, faster feedback, and fewer production issues.

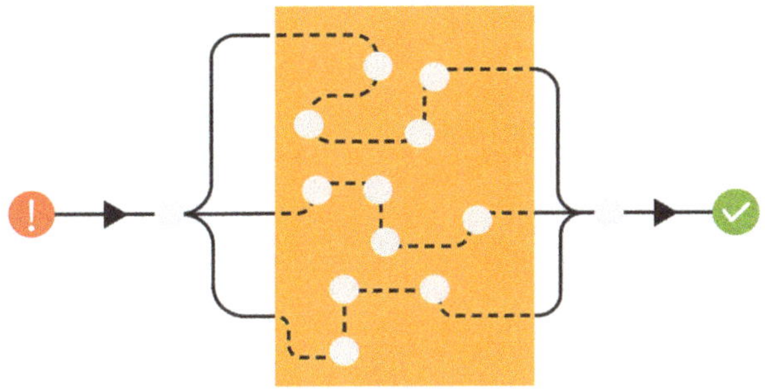

Figure 56 – Automated UI Testing

focus too narrowly on functionality, missing non-functional regressions like slow load times, broken responsiveness, or accessibility violations. Another significant risk is treating UI testing as an isolated activity rather than embedding it directly into the CI/CD feedback cycle, which leads to reactive firefighting instead of proactive prevention.

SUCCESS INDICATORS

When automated UI testing is applied correctly, teams experience fewer last-minute rollbacks and fewer emergency hotfixes for user-facing defects. Release cycles become faster, core user workflows are validated with every commit, and user complaints about broken interfaces decline sharply as defects are caught long before they reach production. Over time, there is a stronger alignment between developers, designers, and product owners. Systems behave consistently across platforms, reinforcing brand reliability and user satisfaction with every release.

SUMMARY

Automated UI testing transforms interface validation from a manual, risky process into an embedded assurance check. By simulating real user journeys, continuously validating visual and functional behavior, and integrating tightly with deployment pipelines, teams ensure that every interaction feels stable and predictable.

REFERENCES

M. Harman, Y. Jia, and Y. Zhang, "Achievements, Open Problems and Challenges for Search-Based Software Testing," *Proceedings of the IEEE International Conference on Software Testing*, Verification and Validation, pp. 1–12, 2015.

G. J. Myers, C. Sandler, and T. Badgett, *The Art of Software Testing*, 3rd ed., Wiley, 2011.

Applitools, "TransUnion Cuts Weekly Testing Time from 30 hours to 2 with Applitools" [case study]; retrieved July 4, 2025, from Applitools website. https://applitools.com/case-studies/transunion/

57 • User Experience and Accessibility Focus

"Good design is good business." — Thomas J. Watson Jr., former IBM CEO

INTRODUCTION

Software quality is not limited to speed, scalability, or security. True quality includes how users experience the product and whether it can be used by everyone, regardless of ability. The User Experience and Accessibility Focus principle ensures that applications are not only functional and reliable but also intuitive and inclusive. By treating usability and accessibility as first-class concerns alongside reliability, teams create products that reach more users and stand out in a crowded market.

KEY CONCEPT

User experience and accessibility work hand-in-hand to define how users interact with technology. Usability focuses on designing intuitive, efficient interfaces that reduce cognitive load and make interactions seamless. Accessibility ensures that those interfaces are usable by people with visual, auditory, motor, or cognitive disabilities. Inclusive design practices push development teams to consider diverse user needs from the outset instead of bolting accessibility onto a finished product. Standards like the Web Content Accessibility Guidelines (WCAG) offer a clear framework for ensuring that interfaces meet a baseline of accessibility. True excellence emerges when teams combine technical compliance with real-world feedback, building products that serve all users naturally and gracefully.

WHY IT MATTERS

Prioritizing user experience and accessibility is a moral imperative and a practical advantage. Products that are easy to navigate and welcoming to diverse users reach broader audiences, gain greater adoption, and create stronger emotional connections. Accessibility compliance also mitigates legal risks, protecting organizations from lawsuits and regulatory penalties. Vitally, accessible design often improves usability for everyone, leading to clearer layouts, simpler workflows, and better user satisfaction. Companies that bake inclusivity into their development process strengthen their brand reputation, customer loyalty, and overall market competitiveness.

IN PRACTICE

Creating software that excels in user experience and accessibility starts early and continues throughout development. It begins with understanding user needs by

CASE STUDY

Microsoft has pioneered a robust, sustainable model for embedding user experience and accessibility into product development. Across platforms like Windows, Office, and Teams, Microsoft applies an inclusive design process that begins with engaging users with disabilities early and often. Design teams incorporate assistive technologies like screen readers, color contrast analyzers, and keyboard-only navigation tools into every sprint. Accessibility validation is part of their CI/CD pipelines, using tools such as Accessibility Insights to detect and address barriers before release. Real-world user research supplements compliance audits, ensuring that experiences are technically accessible and genuinely usable. The results have been transformative. Windows' Ease of Access settings, Office's Accessibility Checker, and Teams' live captions feature demonstrate leadership in making digital experiences truly inclusive. Microsoft's success shows that embedding accessibility and user-centered design leads to broader adoption and to better, more thoughtful technology overall.

engaging diverse user groups during research and prototyping. Testing is an ongoing collaboration between designers, engineers, and real users, including those with disabilities. Teams leverage tools like Figma with accessibility plugins or simulate various impairments to validate interface behavior. They design with clarity and simplicity, avoiding unnecessary complexity that might confuse or exclude users. Accessibility audits are run at every major milestone, guided by WCAG standards, and integrated into CI/CD pipelines to prevent regressions. Documentation is clear, navigation flows are predictable, and feedback mechanisms are built into interfaces to support users who encounter difficulties.

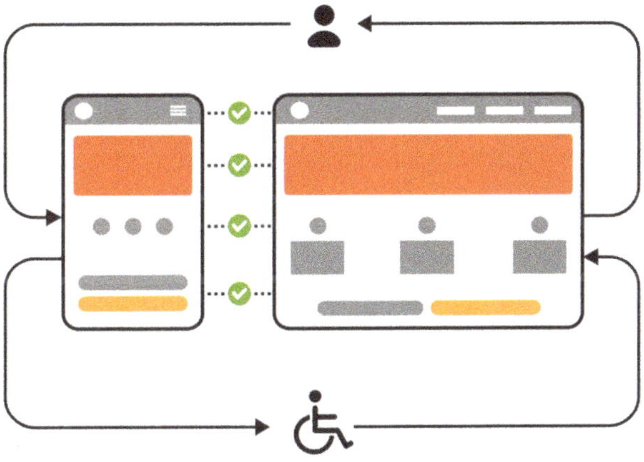

Figure 57 – User Experience and Accessibility Focus

COMMON PITFALLS

Many teams fail by treating accessibility as a checkbox exercise rather than a core quality attribute. Products may technically comply with guidelines but still deliver frustrating experiences if real users are not involved during testing. Some teams overcomplicate interfaces in the pursuit of visual novelty, sacrificing clarity and usability. Others allow accessibility fixes to drift endlessly on the backlog, prioritizing features over inclusivity. Shallow compliance without empathy leads to brittle designs that miss the richness of human diversity. Truly inclusive design requires intentionality, empathy, and a willingness to refactor based on customer feedback.

SUCCESS INDICATORS

When user experience and accessibility are genuinely prioritized, systems feel natural and welcoming to all users. Usability testing shows that tasks are completed efficiently and with minimal friction across a wide range of user profiles. Accessibility audits pass consistently because inclusion was designed from the start. Support ticket volumes related to usability challenges decrease, and customer satisfaction surveys note ease of use. Adoption rates increase across broader demographic groups, including users with varying levels of ability. In the end, users trust the product because it respects their needs and anticipates their challenges without forcing them to struggle or adapt.

SUMMARY

The User Experience and Accessibility Focus principle reminds us that software quality is defined by how well it serves real people in real situations. High-performing systems that fail to be intuitive or inclusive ultimately fall short. By embedding user-centered design and accessibility best practices into every phase of development, teams create products that reach broader audiences, meet critical legal and ethical obligations, and build deeper, more lasting connections with users. True quality means everyone, everywhere, can experience it.

REFERENCES

S. Keates, P. J. Clarkson, and C. Lebbon, "Access for All: Designing Accessible Interfaces for Everyone," *Interacting with Computers*, vol. 19, no. 3, pp. 243–262, 2007.

World Wide Web Consortium (W3C), "Web Content Accessibility Guidelines (WCAG) 2.1," *W3C*, 2024.

Microsoft, "Microsoft Inclusive Design," retrieved on August 14, 2025 from https://www.microsoft.com/design/inclusive.

Microsoft, "How Accessibility Fosters Inclusion: Five Lessons Learned," *Inside Track*, 2022. https://www.microsoft.com/insidetrack/blog/how-accessibility-fosters-inclusion-five-lessons-learned/

58 · Compliance and Regulatory Adherence

"The safety of the people shall be the highest law." — Cicero, De Legibus, Book III

INTRODUCTION

When you think about software quality, you usually picture performance, correctness, and usability. However, in regulated industries, those factors only scratch the surface. Especially if you're building for healthcare, finance, or government, your software also needs to pass legal and ethical scrutiny. That means meeting external mandates and not just internal expectations. The Compliance and Regulatory Adherence principle broadens the definition of quality to include alignment with legal standards, regulatory policies, and ethical obligations.

KEY CONCEPT

You don't get to opt into compliance. It's baked into the domain you're working in. Whether you're subject to HIPAA, GDPR, System and Organization Controls (SOC) 2, International Organization for Standardization (ISO) standards, or industry-specific audits, compliance becomes part of how you define "done." If you build a banking app, the Payment Card Industry Data Security Standard (PCI-DSS) guides how you handle payment data. If your platform touches personal health records, HIPAA mandates encryption, auditing, and access control. These requirements shape how you write code, how you test it, and how you deliver it.

Compliance must be embedded directly into the development lifecycle to build compliant systems. That means regulatory checks aren't saved for post-release cleanups. They're part of every planning session, pull request, and deployment. Static code analysis, policy scanning, audit logging, and vulnerability detection should all live inside your CI/CD workflows. If compliance is bolted on late, you risk nonconformance and reputational harm. If it's integrated early, you stay ahead of audits, avoid retrofits, and deliver trustworthy systems from day one.

WHY IT MATTERS

When compliance is left to the legal team or saved for the final weeks before launch, you create a gap between development and accountability. That gap doesn't just slow you down. It opens you up to lawsuits and lost user trust. Every regulation you fail to follow increases your liability. Every missed audit trail and every last-minute fix costs far more than a design-time decision would have.

By treating compliance as a core part of quality, you bake in trust. You reduce the risk of accidental data exposure and give yourself room to scale. Regulations often become prerequisites when entering new re-gions or markets. If your architecture isn't prepared to show who did what, when, and why, you'll hit walls faster than you can push through them. A system built with the Compliance and Regulatory Adherence principle inspires trust and builds acceptance among users and stakeholders.

IN PRACTICE

You start by identifying which laws, certifications, and internal policies apply to your system. For example, if you're in fintech, you'll need to think about auditability and data retention. If you handle personal data in the EU, GDPR compliance is non-negotiable. Once you've mapped the rules, you trace them to parts of your codebase and assign ownership. For example, this could mean making sure that your authentication flow is secure and compliant with what the regulation demands, or that your logs are helpful and prove that the system behaves as expected under scrutiny.

To implement this principle, you wire compliance checks directly into your development pipeline. Each commit triggers code scanning for known vulnerabilities and license violations. Each merge logs approvals and policy validations. Every build becomes a verifiable record of what changed, why, and whether it passed the required controls. When you release, you have a trail of evidence that shows you're operating responsibly.

Your documentation also evolves alongside the code. You don't wait for an audit to collect it. Incident response plans, test case coverage, access control reviews, and architectural decisions all live where they're easy to review and update. With that in place, developers understand the data rules. QA knows which flows require traceability. Product managers know where features intersect with compliance requirements. Compliance becomes less of a bottleneck and more of a design constraint.

COMMON PITFALLS

When teams treat compliance as someone else's job, it quickly turns into an afterthought. Delaying compliance activities until the end of a project leads to missed requirements and patchwork fixes. You can't

CASE STUDY

At ThoughtSpot, a technology company focused on business intelligence analytics search software, compliance is not treated as a separate audit layer. It's part of how the system is built and released. Serving regulated industries like healthcare and finance, ThoughtSpot mapped requirements like GDPR and SOC 2 directly to development workflows. For data access controls and retention policies, they identified which rules applied and documented how compliance was achieved. This alignment was enforced directly in the CI/CD pipeline. CI/CD tooling enforced checks for encryption, access logging, and license compliance on every merge. Metadata from test runs, deployment logs, and change approvals was captured automatically, providing a continuous audit trail.

When the company expanded into European markets, it didn't have to retrofit GDPR readiness. Their processes had already traced regulatory requirements to code, tests, and operational practices. That groundwork made compliance an easy extension. Instead of slow releases, it gave product, engineering, and legal teams the trust and clarity to move fast.

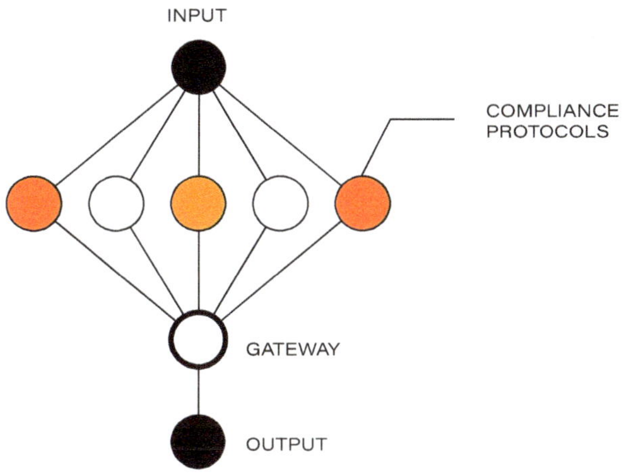

Figure 58 – Compliance and Regulatory Adherence

generate audit logs after the fact. If you wait too long, compliance becomes reactive and expensive. Another common mistake is relying on manual processes to ensure conformance. If your security review depends on someone remembering to run a checklist, it may be skipped when other priorities take precedence. Automation is your friend. You also have to invest in training and awareness. When engineers and product leads don't understand the rules that govern their systems, even the best tools won't save you.

Finally, don't assume compliance is static. Regulations evolve, especially in fast-moving domains like AI and cybersecurity. If your architecture is rigid or your processes can't adapt, yesterday's compliance becomes tomorrow's liability.

SUCCESS INDICATORS

Compliance isn't something you declare. You demonstrate it with hard evidence. A healthy system will feel ready for an audit any day of the week. Your team won't scramble for logs, approval records, or policy documents. They'll already be in place. Release decisions will feel confident, not cautious. When an incident happens, your records show exactly what happened, who was involved, and how recovery followed the procedure.

Even better, you'll see fewer violations over time. Vulnerabilities are caught before they ship. Misconfigured access is flagged during development. Everyone in the delivery pipeline knows which regulations apply and how to uphold them, and when the rules change, your team adapts quickly. The trust you build with users and regulators becomes a lasting advantage.

SUMMARY

The Compliance and Regulatory Adherence principle reminds you that software quality is about working features and proving those features operate safely, ethically, and legally. In regulated domains, a product that fails to comply can't be trusted, no matter how elegant or powerful it is. By embedding compliance into your design, development, and delivery, you build systems that scale and withstand scrutiny. You create reliable and responsible software, and in a world of growing regulation, that's a core part of quality.

REFERENCES

B. Kitchenham, S. L. Pfleeger, and N. Fenton, "How to Improve Software Quality: A Practical Guide," *IEEE Software*, vol. 19, no. 5, pp. 96–102, 2002.

B. Beyer, C. Jones, J. Petoff, and N. Murphy, *Site Reliability Engineering: How Google Runs Production Systems*, O'Reilly Media, 2016.

ThoughtSpot, "ThoughtSpot Trust Center," *ThoughtSpot.com*, retrieved on August 13, 2025 from https://www.thoughtspot.com/legal/trust.

59 • Dark Launch and Shadow Traffic

"Trust, but verify." — Ronald Reagan

INTRODUCTION

The Dark Launch and Shadow Traffic principle offers a way to separate the danger of deployment from the impact on users. This strategy runs code live in production while keeping it hidden or inactive, allowing teams to validate correctness and stability under real-world conditions without exposing users to risk. Dark launching means deploying features in an inactive state controlled by feature flags, while shadow traffic means routing live user requests to the new code paths without affecting the user experience. This principle transforms releases from a leap of faith into a deliberate, measured validation process.

KEY CONCEPT

The dark launch begins by deploying code behind feature flags, ensuring that even though the code is live in production, it does not alter the user experience. The feature might execute silently in the background, or it might be exposed only to internal users or test accounts, but in all cases, its effects are invisible to the broader public. In parallel, shadow traffic techniques duplicate real user requests and send them to the new system or service. The system processes these requests as if they were live, but the outputs are hidden and logged for analysis. Together, these practices validate system behavior and performance in the real world without putting users at risk.

This approach also formalizes the separation between deployment and release. Teams can deploy features continuously and safely, validating everything under production load before deciding to flip the switch and expose the changes to users. Parallel runs through shadow traffic allow engineers to compare outputs from old and new code paths silently, highlighting regressions or inconsistencies early and invisibly.

WHY IT MATTERS

Most real-world software problems, such as scaling issues, regressions, performance degradations, and others, do not appear until the system runs under actual production conditions. Dark launch and shadow traffic provide a safety net by letting you detect these issues without risking user experience. Features get real-world exposure to load, edge cases, and integration complexity before going live. Deployment becomes a safer, continuous process instead of an all-or-nothing gamble. Teams adopting this principle see fewer emergency rollbacks, fewer user-facing incidents, and greater engineering efficiency. By decoupling deployment from exposure, development velocity increases, yet stability improves simultaneously.

Dark launches are especially powerful when launching new interfaces, workflows, or features that involve backend changes. Shadow traffic is critical when migrating databases, rewriting services, or replacing core algorithms. Regardless, the core idea is to trust but verify.

IN PRACTICE

You implement dark launches by using feature flags to keep new functionality off by default. You deploy the feature behind a toggle, then enable it only for internal testers or small user cohorts. This lets you validate the behavior without exposing it to the full user base. For backend changes, you mirror production traffic through shadow routing. Use load balancers, gateways, or custom routing layers to send requests to new code paths without producing live output. This gives you real traffic volume without affecting the user experience.

During this dark phase, instrument everything. Track execution time, error rates, resource usage, and output correctness. For UI features, use visual validation. For backend logic, verify that the data is right. These checks help you catch issues early and build trust in your features. As the feature stabilizes, roll it out gradually. Start with internal users, then move to small public

CASE STUDY

LinkedIn's engineering teams have consistently relied on dark launches and shadow traffic to upgrade their recommendation algorithms without disrupting the user experience. When revamping the feed ranking models, they deployed the new algorithm behind a feature flag, ensuring that the new scoring system ran in production without affecting what users saw. Shadow traffic mechanisms mirrored real user feed requests to the latest ranking engine, allowing engineers to evaluate how the new algorithm performed on live data. They were able to track metrics such as latency, scoring accuracy, and system load in real time.

Throughout this phase, output comparisons between the existing and new algorithms highlighted subtle ranking differences and exposed unexpected scaling challenges that were not detected during pre-production testing. Silent monitoring helped LinkedIn tune model parameters, optimize infrastructure, and fix bugs without impacting users. Only after extensive shadow traffic validation and performance tuning did LinkedIn gradually expose the new feed ranking system to internal users, then to a small public cohort, and finally to the broader user base.

The success of this approach was evident in a significant reduction in feed latency, improved user engagement metrics, and zero major incidents during rollout. By using dark launch and shadow traffic practices, LinkedIn rolled out a major platform update through a smooth release, strengthening both system resilience and user trust.

groups before full release. Keep monitoring closely at each stage. If something breaks, you want to catch it early. Be careful with data. Shadow systems must not write to production databases. Use flags, separate tables, or isolated environments to keep writes safe. Test your feature toggles under load to make sure they work as expected when switching states.

Once the release is done, clean up. Remove unused flags, routing rules, and extra code paths. Leaving them in place creates technical debt. A clean launch process helps you move fast without leaving a mess behind.

COMMON PITFALLS

Teams sometimes leak features unintentionally by exposing links, APIs, or side effects like notification emails, undermining the purpose of a dark launch. Even when invisible, dark-launched features can strain resources, consuming more CPU, memory, or database input/output operations per second (IOPS) than anticipated, leading to degraded system health. Inaccurate shadow traffic configurations may misrepresent real load or omit edge cases, giving teams a false sense of security.

Another common mistake is allowing features to remain dark indefinitely, adding dead code and unnecessary complexity. Some teams also fail to design toggles that can be reliably turned off under load, making rollbacks risky. Misinterpreting shadow metrics can lead to misguided optimization efforts. Finally, prematurely launching a feature to 100% of users without completing phased validation defeats the purpose entirely.

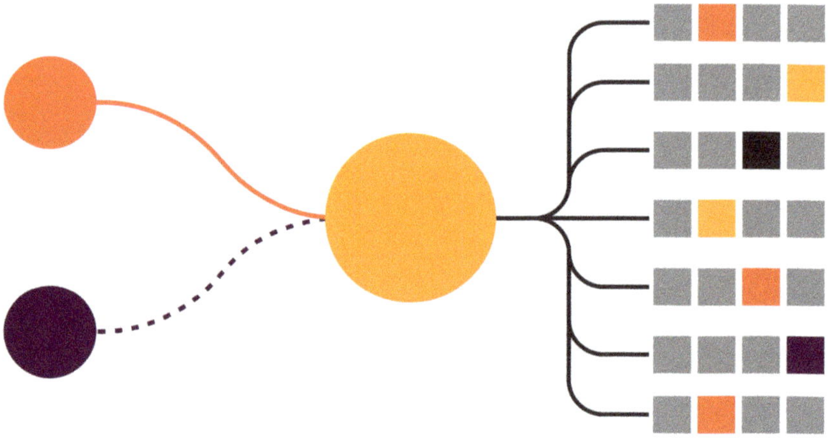

Figure 59 – Dark Launch and Shadow Traffic

SUCCESS INDICATORS

Teams successfully applying the Dark Launch and Shadow Traffic principle experience significantly smoother deployments. New services handle production load silently for days or weeks before user exposure, giving teams high confidence before the public rollout. When incidents occur, feature flags offer instant rollback without requiring full system reversion. Engineering velocity increases as teams ship code frequently and merge incomplete features without fear. Internal metrics confirm stability under shadow load, and validation dashboards show low error rates and healthy performance benchmarks. User-visible incidents during new feature launches decrease over time while internal defect detection improves. The organization begins to embrace controlled, data-driven delivery as the norm.

SUMMARY

The Dark Launch and Shadow Traffic principle redefines how modern teams deploy and release software. By running features and systems silently in production, organizations detect regressions, verify correctness, and confirm scalability long before users ever interact with the changes. This strategy turns release processes from high-stakes gambles into predictable, reliable validations. When used consistently, dark launching and shadow traffic accelerate delivery, improve customer experience, and build better systems over time.

REFERENCES

M. Fowler, "Feature Toggles (aka Feature Flags)," *martinFowler.com* (blog), 2017. https://martinfowler.com/articles/feature-toggles.html

W. Gancarczyk, "Shadow Traffic: A Guide Reduce Risk of a New Service Release," *Doctolib*, 2024. https://medium.com/doctolib/shadow-traffic-a-guide-to-reduce-risk-of-a-service-deployment-c67fd4ca3528

S. Gajera and C. Blinn, "Migrating Functionality Between Large-Scale Production Systems Seamlessly," *Uber Blog*, 2019. https://www.uber.com/blog/migrating-functionality-between-production-systems/

60 • Scalability and Performance Testing

"Measure what is measurable and make measurable what is not so." — Galileo Galilei

INTRODUCTION

The Scalability and Performance Testing principle ensures that software is capable of performing reliably and efficiently under varying loads. It moves beyond functional testing to validate the system's behavior under stress, uncovering bottlenecks before they become outages. This principle advocates embedding performance and scalability testing into everyday development to prevent costly surprises when the system finally hits the production load.

KEY CONCEPT

Performance testing measures how quickly and efficiently a system responds under both normal and peak conditions. Load testing simulates increasing numbers of concurrent users or requests to verify whether the system can sustain expected traffic levels. Stress testing deliberately overwhelms the system to identify breaking points and evaluate how gracefully it fails. Scalability testing assesses how system performance changes as resources are added, ensuring the ability to scale horizontally across machines or vertically with bigger machines. Together, these practices answer the question of whether the system can perform under load and scale reliably.

Effective scalability and performance testing require automated, repeatable tests integrated into CI/CD workflows. They validate system behavior continuously as the codebase evolves. Only when performance data is gathered systematically, under realistic traffic patterns and production-like environments, can teams build systems that stay resilient under pressure.

WHY IT MATTERS

Performance and scalability are not luxuries. They define the real-world user experience. A slow website during peak hours loses users in seconds. An unstable backend during a product launch damages reputation and revenue. Testing for speed and resilience directly protects the customer relationship, ensuring that fast systems retain users and resilient systems avoid costly outages. Without systematic performance testing, teams risk discovering limitations only after they impact users in production. This reactive posture is expensive and stressful. Proactively understanding load limits, resource behavior, and scaling patterns gives teams the concrete evidence to promise reliability and the ability to deliver it.

IN PRACTICE

You start by defining the performance metrics like response time, throughput, error rate, and resource usage. In parallel, you build test scenarios that reflect how the system will be used in the real world. Simulate both steady traffic growth and sharp spikes so you can see how the system responds under pressure. Run your load and stress tests in environments that match production as closely as possible. Avoid using scaled-down setups that hide real bottlenecks. When testing scalability, add instances or increase resources to verify that the system grows cleanly and efficiently.

Include these performance tests in your CI pipeline. Run them regularly so regressions are caught early. Use observability tools to monitor thresholds and trigger failure conditions on purpose. This shows you

CASE STUDY

During the height of the COVID-19 pandemic, the UK Health Security Agency faced a scale challenge that exceeded any prior government IT load. Its systems, originally built to handle around 300,000 daily test results, had to expand to support millions of transactions per day without slowing down or failing. To meet national testing demands, the UKHSA restructured its approach by embedding automated load and scalability testing into its development process. The UKHSA developed a fully automated testing platform using cloud infrastructure. The system simulated real-world usage at scale, running load and stress tests that mirrored millions of concurrent test result submissions and thousands of data queries. Test environments were designed to reflect production architecture, allowing engineers to observe behavior under conditions that closely matched peak demand. These insights fed directly into development teams, accelerating both detection and remediation.

Performance tests were integrated into CI/CD pipelines and executed continuously. Any regression in metrics such as response time, CPU usage, or throughput would block the release. This structure gave developers clear performance feedback early in the lifecycle, avoiding late-stage surprises and delays. Within each team, performance testing became a standard responsibility rather than a specialized or downstream task.

Through iterative load testing and architectural tuning, the UKHSA increased system capacity from 300,000 to 6 million tests per day, a twentyfold increase. The testing cycle, once measured in weeks, was reduced to just two hours per release. Delivery velocity improved by 60 percent as developers could push updates confidently without fearing undetected performance risks. Production incidents related to scalability dropped by nearly 90 percent, and no critical performance defects were observed in live environments.

In an agency not historically known for rapid software delivery, this transformation created a foundation of operational resilience at a national scale. By mid-2021, the UKHSA had proven its systems could absorb even the most extreme pandemic surges without degradation. This case highlights the impact of early, continuous performance testing on large-scale system reliability.

how the system behaves when things go wrong. When you find a bottleneck, whether it's in code, database queries, or third-party services, you optimize it and test again. Track percentile latencies, especially the 95th and 99th. That is where users start to feel the difference. If you want your system to perform under real-world pressure, you need to measure what real users actually experience.

COMMON PITFALLS

Teams often make mistakes by designing load tests that bear little resemblance to real usage patterns, missing the very bottlenecks users are likely to encounter. Test environments that fail to replicate production scale produce misleading results, giving a false sense of readiness. Some teams restrict performance validation to superficial endpoints like login pages while neglecting critical background services or asynchronous workflows, leaving major vulnerabilities untested. Others treat scalability as a theoretical concern, validating performance at small loads but never measuring system behavior at 10X or 100X growth.

Another common mistake is treating performance testing as a one-time event rather than a continuous discipline. Code changes, database tuning, and evolving traffic patterns demand continuous validation. Metrics gathered without clear thresholds lead to noise rather than actionable insights. Finally, focusing on median performance instead of the slowest cases hides real problems, allowing critical user experiences to degrade unnoticed.

SUCCESS INDICATORS

When scalability and performance testing are properly integrated, systems maintain fast response times, predictable throughput, and stable resource usage across a range of traffic levels. Auto-scaling mechanisms trigger at appropriate thresholds without manual intervention, keeping services resilient under spikes. Latency at the 95th and 99th percentiles remains consistent, ensuring a good experience for all users. Production incidents related to load go down dramatically with measured rollouts backed by hard performance evidence. Engineering teams move faster because performance risks are caught in development and are not discovered during midnight fire drills. Business leaders no longer ask whether the system can handle a product launch or marketing campaign because they already know, based on continuous, validated performance metrics.

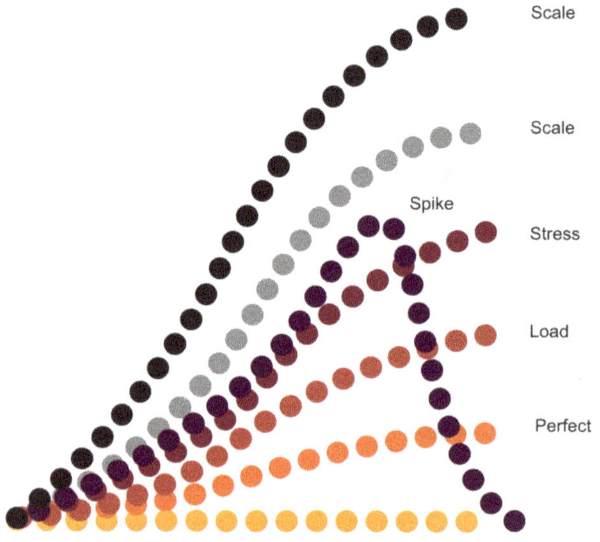

Figure 60 – Scalability and Performance Testing

SUMMARY

By simulating real-world load and pushing systems to their limits in controlled environments, the Scalability and Performance Testing principle finds weaknesses in the system before users do. This proactive testing helps prevent outages and poor user experiences by ensuring that infrastructure can scale without breaking. In a world where traffic surges can make or break a product's success, embedding continuous performance and scalability testing into your development process is essential for meeting system SLAs and achieving resilience at scale.

REFERENCES

R. Jain, *The Art of Computer Systems Performance Analysis: Techniques for Experimental Design, Measurement, Simulation, and Modeling*, Wiley, 1991.

D. A. Menascé, V. A. F. Almeida, and L. W. Dowdy, *Performance by Design: Computer Capacity Planning by Example*, Prentice Hall, 2004.

Team Capacitas, "Case Study: Large Scale Transformation with DevSecOps," *Capacitas*, 2024. https://www.capacitas.co.uk/case-studies/case-study-large-scale-transformation-with-devsecops

61 • Backward Compatibility and Dependency Checks

"A contract is only as good as the willingness to uphold it."— Justice Oliver Wendell Holmes Jr.

INTRODUCTION

Software systems do not exist in isolation. Every application relies on a network of internal and external APIs, libraries, services, and protocols to deliver functionality. As these systems evolve, changes are inevitable. However, unverified changes can disrupt dependent systems and break functionality. The Backward Compatibility and Dependency Checks principle ensures that evolution happens responsibly. It prioritizes preserving expected behavior for existing consumers or, when breaking changes are necessary, communicating and coordinating those changes explicitly. This principle reinforces trust and minimizes disruption.

KEY CONCEPT

Backward compatibility refers to the ability of a system to accept inputs or interact with components designed for earlier versions without failure. Dependency checks ensure that changes made to a system or service do not silently break the systems that rely on it. These two ideas are inseparable. Maintaining backward compatibility means validating assumptions against internal systems and against all consumers, many of whom may not upgrade immediately. Where backward compatibility cannot be preserved, clear communication through versioning, deprecation notices, and structured release notes is mandatory. Thoughtful compatibility management prevents cascading failures across tightly coupled services and allows software ecosystems to evolve safely.

WHY IT MATTERS

In distributed systems, mobile apps, SaaS platforms, and APIs, even small internal changes can have unpredictable effects across a network of dependencies. When these effects are unanticipated, they result in broken features, degraded performance, and increased support costs. Research consistently shows that software maintenance, particularly in relation to dependency management and API evolution, consumes a significant portion of long-term development effort. A disciplined approach to backward compatibility reduces this burden, allowing systems to evolve without destabilizing their clients. It also creates space for innovation because teams are confident that updates will not break current functionality. By embedding compatibility and dependency validation into the development lifecycle, organizations protect both their product stability and their reputation.

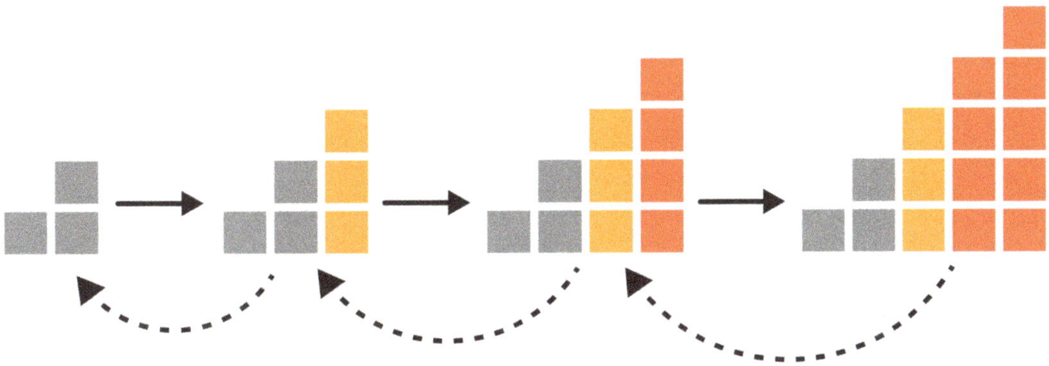

Figure 61 – Backward Compatibility and Dependency Checks

IN PRACTICE

You apply backward compatibility and dependency checking with both technical discipline and cultural commitment. Before changing any interface, validate how it affects downstream consumers. Use contract testing, integration snapshots, and semantic versioning to enforce that discipline. If a breaking change is necessary, announce it clearly. Provide migration guides and transitional support so others can adapt without disruption.

Automate your dependency checks through static analysis tools and automated scans to catch contract violations early, before they reach production. Watch your critical dependencies over time. When you upgrade libraries, change database versions, or shift protocols, confirm that existing behavior still holds. Treat your APIs and service interfaces as first-class elements in the system. Evolve them deliberately and assume that backward compatibility is your default. When you do this well, you avoid surprise breakages and earn trust with your customers and stakeholders.

CASE STUDY

In 2020, Google Chrome introduced stricter cookie handling rules by enforcing SameSite=None; Secure for cross-site cookies. This change risked breaking authentication flows and embedded services across millions of websites. To maintain backward compatibility, Chrome's team staged the rollout behind feature flags, allowed enterprise opt-outs, and launched an extensive developer education campaign. Real-world monitoring helped identify issues early, and gradual enforcement gave developers time to adapt. By carefully checking dependencies and communicating proactively, Chrome upgraded security without widespread disruption, proving that backward compatibility is just as much about community support as it is about technical precision.

COMMON PITFALLS

Despite its importance, backward compatibility often receives inadequate attention during development. One common failure is silent-breaking changes. Silent modifications to APIs, response formats, or database schemas can introduce regressions for unsuspecting clients. Another pitfall is ambiguous versioning, where semantic versioning principles are violated, and consumers cannot predict the impact of an update. Overconfidence in unit testing also creates blind spots, as tests that validate internal behavior may miss real-world contract violations. Even when deprecations are announced, poor communication channels or vague migration instructions can leave consumers struggling to adapt, increasing friction and technical debt. In dependency management, failure to perform regular vulnerability and compatibility scans exposes systems to unexpected failures when third-party libraries change or become obsolete. Ultimately, most pitfalls trace back to a lack of discipline in treating external-facing interfaces as stable contracts deserving explicit, continuous care.

SUCCESS INDICATORS

Successful application of this principle is visible across multiple dimensions of software delivery and maintenance. System upgrades happen predictably without triggering widespread regression or urgent hotfixes. New features ship alongside clear deprecation paths that users understand and can adopt at their own pace. Dependency updates are smooth because compatibility issues are detected early and addressed systematically. Release notes consistently include compatibility impact assessments, building transparency between engineering teams and users. Over time, systems that practice rigorous compatibility management experience lower support burdens, faster adoption of new versions, and stronger user trust. Engineers gain confidence in evolving systems without fearing unintentional breakage, and the organization builds a reputation for reliability in the eyes of both internal stakeholders and external consumers.

SUMMARY

Backward compatibility and dependency checks are foundational to sustainable software evolution. They ensure that systems grow without breaking the trust of their users and dependents. Teams build resilient, adaptable products by embedding compatibility validation into development workflows, practicing transparent communication about breaking changes, and managing dependencies proactively. This principle is essential in modern software ecosystems where integrations are deep and frequent. Upholding it transforms software changes from risky disruptions into continuous, stable improvement opportunities.

REFERENCES

T. Mens, "Introduction and Roadmap: History and Challenges of Software Evolution," in Software Evolution, T. Mens and S. Demeyer, eds., 2008 ed., Springer, 2008.

D. Dig and R. Johnson, "How Do APIs Evolve? A Story of Refactoring," Journal of Software Maintenance and Evolution: Research and Practice, vol. 18, no. 2, pp. 83–107, 2006.

B. Palser, "Get Ready for New SameSite=None; Secure Cookie Settings," Google Search Central Blog, January 14, 2020.

A FINAL THOUGHT

All books are inherently biased and incomplete. They show one-sided views and limitations of the author. This book is no different. It reflects what I've seen and what I believe is worth sharing. It does not claim to be complete. It cannot be.

For example, this book does not cover how to discover the principles themselves. It does not offer a framework for identifying future patterns. It looks back, not forward. Even in that, the view is partial. Others would tell a different story. There are also entire areas this book sets aside. It does not go deep into what happens after software is released. It does not explore the long arc of maintenance, monitoring, support, and the quiet work of keeping things alive. Those parts are essential. Most engineers spend more time fixing and extending than they do building. That story deserves its own attention, and I plan to return to it separately.

A parting thought: principles alone do not give us progress; judgment does. As you know, science and systems do not care about how we feel about our work. They will continue to solve some of our problems, and in the process, they will create newer and more deeply human problems. Your job (privilege) is to continue that journey, because progress is not guaranteed. We rise not because we are born wiser, but because we are born into a richer inheritance. We stand on the accumulated work of those who came before; what they learned, preserved, and left behind. If we lose the thread, we fall back. If we carry it, we move forward.

If there is anything worth taking from this book, let it be this: progress is possible. You do not have to be right all the time. You only have to decide what you stand for and practice it often enough that others feel it too.

That will be enough.

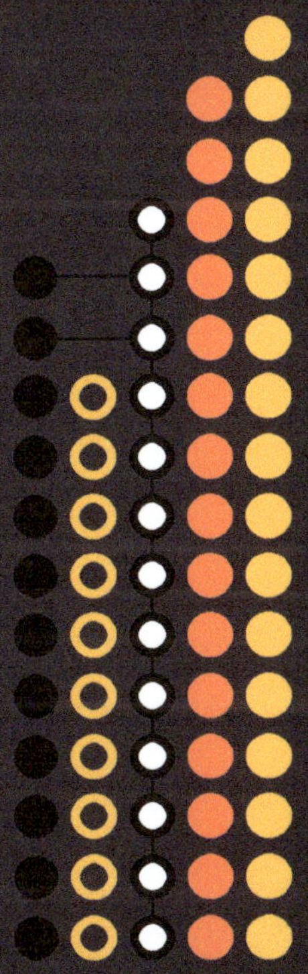

Acknowledgments

I want to thank the many contributors whose works are featured and ask that readers review the Credits section to learn more about these very talented individuals, their bodies of work, and the companies they work with. Thank you to my colleagues at Amazon and elsewhere I've worked for, spending countless hours reviewing, teaching, and learning lessons together. A special thanks to the research team (Khyati Morparia), design team (Molly Seabrook, Rudy P Angel, Thabo Mofokeng), and editorial team (Liz Wheeler).

About the Author

Dhaval Parmar is a Director at Amazon, where he leads global product and engineering teams for Prime, working on the systems, experiments, and AI that shape how more than 200 million paid Prime members worldwide experience membership, pricing, and major shopping events such as Prime Day. Over the past decade, he has launched zero-to-one products that serve millions of customers and have driven billions in sales. He has grown product and engineering hubs across continents, and he obsesses over making sure products and systems are ready to serve and delight customers around the world.

Before Amazon, Dhaval worked in finance and healthcare, building actuarial and cloud platforms where getting the numbers wrong was not an option. That mix of high-stakes domains shaped how he thinks about reliability, data, and real-world constraints. His path has not been a straight line. He has renovated older homes, built mobile apps, and even worked as a kite runner, literally chasing down escaped kites across fields and rooftops.

When he is not thinking about systems, you will find him on a volleyball court, flying something, or doing improv, which he swears is the best training for demo disasters and high-stakes reviews. He likes simple tools, clear thinking, and building things that work long after the hype cycle has moved on.

Say Hello!

I do not run a newsletter or Substack (at least not yet), but I would still like to hear from you. You can reach me in a few places. I am more "antisocial" than social when it comes to social media, but I do show up. The easiest way to reach me is on LinkedIn, and you can always send me an email as well.

I read my own messages and reply personally, which may be a feature or a bug, depending on how you look at it. Either way, I would be glad to hear from you.

https://dparmar.com/connect

PLEASE REVIEW THIS BOOK!

If you enjoyed this book, please take a minute to leave a review on Amazon. Reviews help other readers decide what to pick up next, and they tell the great recommendation machine that this book is worth showing to more people. Your review also gives me a way to improve. Think of it as leaving a helpful note in the margins. Even a short comment is greatly appreciated.

I appreciate your support.

https://dparmar.com/review

Appendices

GLOSSARY

acceptance criteria	Clear, testable conditions that a feature must meet to be considered complete.
access control	A mechanism that defines who can access or modify resources in a system.
access modifiers	Keywords in code that define the visibility of classes, methods, or variables.
actor model	A concurrency model where components (actors) communicate only by message passing.
aggregation	A composition pattern where a container object holds references to other objects.
alert fatigue	Reduced responsiveness to alerts due to excessive or low-priority notifications.
anomaly detection	Identifying unusual patterns or behaviors that deviate from expected norms.
apache cassandra	A distributed NoSQL database optimized for availability and horizontal scalability.
apache kafka	A high-throughput event streaming platform used for real-time data pipelines.
API	A defined interface that enables communication between different software systems.
api contract	A formal agreement detailing how an API behaves, including inputs and outputs.
api gateway	A central entry point that routes and manages external requests to backend services.
application layer	The system layer where user-facing logic and application protocols reside.
asynchronous	A programming approach where tasks run independently of the main process.
at-least-once delivery	A message delivery guarantee ensuring each message is delivered at least once.
atomic operation	An operation that runs completely or not at all, with no intermediate state.

audit logging	The recording of events or actions for security, compliance, or analysis.
audit trail	A time-stamped record of actions or events used for tracking and verification.
automated ui testing	Programmatic tests that verify the functionality and layout of user interfaces.
backpressure	A system response to overload by slowing or rejecting incoming requests.
backward compatibility	The ability of a system to support older interfaces or behavior after changes.
barrier	A synchronization method where threads wait until all participants reach a point.
baseline	A reference point used to compare future performance or behavior.
batch job	A background task that processes data in large groups without user interaction.
BDD	Behavior-Driven Development, where tests are written in business-readable language.
bootstrapping	The process of starting a system using a minimal initial setup.
bottleneck	A limiting point in a system that reduces overall performance.
boundary value analysis	A testing method focused on edge cases at input limits.
bounded context	A clearly defined domain area where terms and logic remain consistent.
breaking change	A modification that disrupts existing system behavior or contracts.
broker	A component that mediates communication between producers and consumers.
build pipeline	An automated process that compiles, tests, and prepares code for deployment.
camelcase	A naming style where each word starts with a capital letter and no spaces.
canonical source	The single, trusted source of truth for a system or data model.
cap theorem	A theory stating that distributed systems can only satisfy two of consistency, availability, and partition tolerance at once.
CD	Continuous Delivery, the practice of automating software release to production.

centralized state management	Storing and managing application state in one place for predictability.
chaos engineering	Intentional fault injection to test system resilience under stress.
chaos monkey	A tool that randomly disables services to test system fault tolerance.
chaos testing	Simulating failures to evaluate system behavior and recovery.
checkpointing	Saving the current state of a process so it can resume from that point if interrupted.
checksum	A value used to detect errors in data by comparing expected and actual values.
choreography	A decentralized coordination pattern where services react to events independently.
CI	Continuous Integration, the practice of merging code changes frequently with automated testing.
ci/cd	A set of practices combining Continuous Integration and Continuous Delivery or Deployment.
circuit breaker	A design pattern that prevents repeated failures by stopping calls to unstable services.
code churn	Frequent changes to code that may signal instability or unclear requirements.
code review	The process of systematically examining code to catch issues and improve quality.
cognitive load	The mental effort required to understand or work with a system.
cohesion	The degree to which elements in a module belong together functionally.
commit log	A sequential record of transactions or changes made in a system.
commit message	A short description explaining what a code change includes and why it was made.
compensating transaction	A reversal operation used to undo partial effects of a failed transaction.
component	A modular, reusable unit of software that encapsulates specific functionality.
compute isolation	Separating workloads so they don't interfere with each other's performance.

concurrency	The ability to handle multiple tasks at once through interleaving or parallelism.
configuration drift	When system configuration diverges from its intended or documented state.
configuration management	Tools and practices for maintaining system consistency through versioned configurations.
conflict resolution	A strategy for reconciling changes when multiple sources modify the same data.
consumer-driven contract	A test pattern where consumers define expectations that providers must meet.
contention	A condition where multiple operations compete for the same resource.
contract testing	A test that verifies the interaction between services against a shared agreement.
control plane	The part of a system that manages configuration, state, and policies.
controlled disruption	Planned failure injection used to test system reliability and response.
coupling	The degree of dependency between modules; lower coupling is preferred for flexibility.
cpu	Central Processing Unit, the hardware that executes program instructions.
CQRS	Command Query Responsibility Segregation, a pattern that separates read and write logic.
cqs	Command Query Separation, where a method either changes state or returns data, but not both.
CRUD	Create, Read, Update, Delete—the basic operations for persistent storage.
CSV	Comma-Separated Values, a simple text format for tabular data.
data contract	A defined schema that specifies how data should be structured and exchanged.
data locality	Placing computation near the data it processes to reduce latency.
data masking	The process of hiding sensitive data by replacing it with fake but realistic values.
data residency	The legal or policy requirement that data be stored in a specific location.

data virtualization	Accessing data without knowing its physical location or structure.
database per service	A microservice pattern where each service has its own private database.
deadlock	A state where two or more processes wait indefinitely for each other to release resources.
declarative format	A style where you specify what you want, not how to do it.
deduplication	The process of eliminating duplicate data to save space and avoid redundancy.
denormalization	A database optimization that adds redundancy to improve read performance.
dependency	A relationship where one component relies on another to function.
dependency graph	A visual or logical representation of relationships between dependent components.
dependency injection	A design pattern where dependencies are provided to a component rather than hardcoded.
design patterns	Reusable solutions to common problems in software design.
directory-based sharding	Partitioning data using directory metadata that maps to storage locations.
disaster recovery	Strategies to restore operations after a catastrophic system failure.
distributed lock	A mechanism to prevent concurrent access to shared resources in distributed systems.
distributed system	A system where components run on multiple machines but act as one.
dns routing	Using DNS to direct requests to appropriate servers or regions.
domain events	Notifications triggered by changes in a business process or entity.
DRY	Don't Repeat Yourself—a principle encouraging code reuse and elimination of duplication.
edge caching	Storing content closer to users geographically to reduce latency.
egress	Outbound data leaving a network or system.
elasticity	The ability of a system to scale resources up or down based on demand.

entropy	A measure of disorder or randomness, often indicating system complexity.
equivalence partitioning	A test technique that divides input data into equivalent groups to reduce test cases.
event sourcing	A design where state changes are logged as a sequence of events.
event store	A database or log that stores events instead of current state.
eventually consistent	A consistency model where all updates will propagate, but not instantly.
exception handling	Code that detects and manages errors during execution.
exploratory testing	An unscripted approach to testing that relies on curiosity and learning.
fail fast	A principle where systems stop early and visibly when something goes wrong.
failure isolation	Designing systems so that faults in one part don't impact the rest.
fallback path	An alternative path or behavior when the primary one fails.
fan-out	A pattern where one request leads to multiple parallel downstream calls.
fault injection	Introducing failures intentionally to test how the system reacts under stress.
fault isolation	Limiting the scope of a failure so that it doesn't affect unrelated components.
fault tolerance	The ability of a system to continue operating despite failures.
feature branch	A separate branch in version control used to develop and test a new feature.
feature flag	A toggle that enables or disables specific functionality at runtime.
flapping	Rapidly changing state between up and down, often causing instability.
garbage collection	Automatic memory management that reclaims unused resources.
GDPR	General Data Protection Regulation, a European privacy and data protection law.
geo-based sharding	Partitioning data based on geographical regions to improve latency and compliance.
geographical redundancy	Deploying systems across multiple locations to ensure availability during outages.

git	A distributed version control system used for tracking code changes.
given-when-then	A format for BDD tests that describes context, action, and expected outcome.
golden master	A testing technique that compares current output with a known good version.
graceful degradation	Reducing system functionality smoothly under load rather than failing completely.
graph database	A type of database that uses graph structures to represent relationships.
guardrail	A rule or constraint that helps prevent mistakes or dangerous system behavior.
hadoop	An open-source framework for distributed storage and processing of large data sets.
happy path	The default, successful execution path through a system.
hash-based sharding	Partitioning data using a hash function to determine shard placement.
health check	A check used to determine if a system or service is running correctly.
HIPAA	A U.S. law governing healthcare data privacy and security.
horizontal scaling	Adding more machines to handle increased load.
hot path	A frequently executed code path that is critical to performance.
hotfix	A quick fix for a critical bug, often deployed outside regular cycles.
http	The foundational protocol used for communication over the web.
http 429	An HTTP response code indicating too many requests in a short time.
IAM	Identity and Access Management, controlling user permissions and authentication.
ID	A unique identifier used to reference an object or record.
idempotent operation	An operation that has the same effect no matter how many times it's performed.
ieee	Institute of Electrical and Electronics Engineers, a standards organization.

immutable	Data or objects that cannot be changed after creation.
immutable infrastructure	A model where infrastructure is replaced rather than modified.
incident response	The process of managing and resolving unexpected system issues or outages.
inclusive design	Designing systems to be usable by people with diverse abilities.
input domain	The complete set of valid inputs for a system or function.
interface segregation	A principle that encourages splitting large interfaces into smaller, more specific ones.
interface stability	The ability of an interface to avoid breaking changes over time.
invariants	Conditions that are always expected to be true during program execution.
ISO	International Organization for Standardization, which develops global standards.
iterative development	An approach where software is built incrementally through repeated cycles.
jitter	Randomized delay added to avoid simultaneous retries or collisions.
job scheduling	Coordinating the timing and order of background tasks or batch jobs.
JSON	JavaScript Object Notation, a lightweight format for data exchange.
JVM	Java Virtual Machine, the runtime environment for executing Java bytecode.
keyboard-only navigation	The ability to use a system fully via keyboard, supporting accessibility.
KPI	Key Performance Indicator, a measurable value that tracks progress or performance.
latency	The time delay between a request and its corresponding response.
law of demeter	A design principle that limits how much a unit knows about others in the system.
layered architecture	A design model that separates system concerns into horizontal layers.
legacy system	An older system still in use, often difficult to modify or scale.

living documentation	Up-to-date documentation that evolves with the system and its tests.
load balancer	A tool that distributes incoming traffic across multiple servers.
load test	A test that evaluates how a system performs under expected load conditions.
load testing	Assessing system behavior under typical or peak user activity levels.
logical isolation	Keeping components separate at the software level for modularity and safety.
loose coupling	Designing components to be independent and minimally dependent on each other.
magic numbers	Hardcoded values with no explanation, making code harder to understand.
mapreduce	A data processing model for distributed computing using map and reduce functions.
mental model	How a person understands how a system works based on experience.
message broker	A component that mediates and routes messages between services.
message ordering	Ensuring messages are processed in the sequence they were sent.
message passing	Communication between components using messages instead of shared state.
metadata	Data that describes other data, such as schema, structure, or tags.
metaprogramming	Writing code that manipulates or generates other code at runtime.
metric	A quantifiable measure used to evaluate system performance or behavior.
microservice	A small, independent service that performs a specific function within a system.
mock	A simulated object used in testing to replace real components.
modularity	Dividing a system into independent, interchangeable components.
monolith	A system where all features and services are built into a single application.
mutex	A synchronization primitive that ensures only one thread accesses a resource at a time.
named constants	Descriptive names used for fixed values instead of hardcoding them.

network partition	A network failure that splits systems into disconnected groups.
normalization	Organizing data to reduce redundancy and improve consistency.
observability	The ability to understand internal system state through outputs like logs and metrics.
onboarding	Introducing new users or developers to a system or team.
operational resilience	The ability to continue operations during disruptions or failures.
ownership model	Defines who is responsible for managing and maintaining parts of the system.
parallelism	Executing multiple tasks at the same time on separate processors or threads.
partitioning	Splitting data or workloads into distinct segments to improve performance or scalability.
payload	The actual data carried in a message or request, excluding headers.
PCI-DSS	Payment Card Industry Data Security Standard for protecting cardholder data.
PII	Personally Identifiable Information, any data that can identify an individual.
playbook	A documented procedure for handling specific tasks or incidents.
polyglot persistence	Using multiple database types within the same system.
profiling	Measuring how code uses resources like memory or CPU.
pure function	A function that always produces the same output for the same input and has no side effects.
query routing	The process of directing database queries to the appropriate server or shard based on rules or context.
race condition	A bug that occurs when the outcome of operations depends on their timing or order in concurrent execution.
range-based sharding	A method of partitioning data based on ranges of a shard key, such as dates or numeric IDs.

rate limiter	A control mechanism that limits the number of requests or actions allowed in a given time window.
rate limiting	The technique of restricting the rate of requests to a system to prevent overload or abuse.
read replica	A copy of a primary database used for read operations to reduce load and improve scalability.
readme	A file that provides an overview of a software project, including setup instructions and usage guidance.
redundancy	The duplication of components or data to ensure reliability and fault tolerance in case of failure.
referential integrity	A database constraint that ensures foreign keys correctly reference primary keys in related tables.
regression testing	Testing existing features to confirm that new changes haven't introduced unexpected bugs.
replication	The act of copying and maintaining the same data across multiple systems or databases.
representative value	A data value that typifies a class or condition, used in sampling and testing scenarios.
reprocessing	Running data or tasks again, often to correct errors or apply updated logic.
resilience testing	Evaluating a system's ability to recover from failures or continue functioning under stress.
resource management	The practice of allocating and optimizing computing resources like CPU, memory, and bandwidth.
retry loop	A logic construct that repeatedly attempts a failed operation until it succeeds or a limit is reached.
retry storm	A system failure pattern caused by many components retrying failed requests at once, overwhelming resources.
revert	Undoing a change in code or configuration to return a system to its previous state.
risk map	A visual representation of risks plotted by likelihood and impact to guide decision-making.

risk-based testing	A testing strategy that prioritizes tests based on the probability and impact of failure.
rollback	The act of restoring a system to a previous stable version after a failed change.
rollback plan	A predefined set of actions to reverse a deployment or system change safely.
rollback strategy	An approach for undoing updates in a controlled way, typically to mitigate incidents.
root cause	The fundamental reason behind a problem or system failure.
routing layer	A software layer responsible for directing requests to the correct service or component.
RPO	Recovery Point Objective; the maximum acceptable amount of data loss measured in time during an outage.
RTO	Recovery Time Objective; the target duration within which a system must be restored after a disruption.
runtime	The period when a program is executing, including access to memory, environment, and system resources.
runtime coupling	A dependency between systems or services that must be available at the same time to work correctly.
sandbox	An isolated environment used for testing or running untrusted code without affecting production systems.
sanity testing	A quick check to confirm that basic functionality works after a change or build.
scaffolding	Temporary code or structure used to support development, especially in early stages of building an application.
self-documenting code	Code that is clear and readable enough to explain its purpose without additional comments.
semantic versioning	A versioning system using MAJOR.MINOR.PATCH to indicate backward compatibility and the type of changes made.
semaphore	A concurrency control mechanism that manages access to shared resources using counters.

separation of concerns	A design principle that organizes code so that each part handles a distinct responsibility.
service boundary	The defined limits of a service's responsibility, interface, and data ownership.
service degradation	A system's intentional reduction in functionality to preserve core services during failure or overload.
service mesh	An infrastructure layer that manages service-to-service communication, often handling retries, security, and observability.
shadow traffic	A practice of duplicating production traffic to a test system to validate changes without affecting users.
shard	A horizontal partition of data used to improve scalability by distributing load across databases or servers.
sharding key	The field used to determine how data is divided among shards in a distributed system.
shared nothing architecture	A design where each component operates independently without shared memory or disk to avoid bottlenecks.
shared schema	A database structure used by multiple services or tenants, which can introduce tight coupling.
shared state	Data or configuration that is accessible across multiple parts of a system, often increasing complexity.
side effect	A change in system state or interaction with the outside world that occurs during function execution.
SLA	Service Level Agreement; a formal commitment on service reliability, availability, or performance between provider and user.
smoke testing	A basic set of tests that verify the core features of an application work before deeper testing.
smoke tests	Initial tests to catch major failures early in the development or deployment process.
snake_case	A naming convention where words are joined by underscores, often used in variables or filenames.

snapshot	A read-only copy of data captured at a specific point in time, used for backup or rollback.
snapshotting	The process of creating snapshots to preserve system state or data versions.
SOC 2	A compliance framework for managing customer data based on five trust service principles: security, availability, processing integrity, confidentiality, and privacy.
solid	A set of five object-oriented design principles that promote maintainable and scalable software.
spring boot	A Java-based framework that simplifies building and deploying standalone, production-grade applications.
SRE	Site Reliability Engineering: a discipline that applies software engineering to infrastructure and operations for reliable systems.
ssot	Single Source of Truth; the authoritative place where data is maintained to avoid duplication and inconsistency.
stale data	Information that is outdated or no longer reflects the current state of the system.
staleness	The degree to which data is out of sync with its source or the real world.
state tracking	Monitoring and recording changes in a system's state over time for consistency and debugging.
static analysis	The examination of code without running it to detect bugs, style issues, or vulnerabilities.
static code analysis	Same as static analysis; focuses on evaluating code structure, logic, and patterns before execution.
strangler fig pattern	A technique for modernizing legacy systems by gradually replacing parts with new components.
stress testing	A performance test that applies extreme load to evaluate how a system behaves under pressure.
strong consistency	A data guarantee that ensures all reads return the most recent write for a given item.

structured logging	Logging where messages follow a predictable format, making them easier to search and analyze.
support ticket	A formal request logged by a user or system to report issues or request help.
synchronization	Coordinating access to shared resources to ensure correct behavior in concurrent systems.
systems thinking	An approach that views systems holistically, considering interactions and feedback loops between components.
task scheduling	The process of assigning and running tasks at specific times or intervals in a system.
TDD	Test-Driven Development; a practice where tests are written before code to guide design and correctness.
technical debt	The accumulated cost of quick fixes or shortcuts that compromise long-term code quality.
telemetry	The automated collection of system data (e.g., metrics, logs) used for monitoring and analysis.
template repository	A reusable codebase that provides a base structure or boilerplate for new projects.
tenant	An isolated user group or customer within a multi-tenant system, each with its own data and configuration.
test coverage	A metric that measures how much of the codebase is executed by automated tests.
test gaps	Portions of code or functionality that are not covered by tests, often increasing risk.
test pyramid	A testing strategy that favors many unit tests, fewer integration tests, and even fewer end-to-end tests.
test suite	A collection of test cases that verify the behavior of software components or features.
thread	A lightweight process that enables concurrent execution within a program.
throttle	A control mechanism to intentionally limit system usage or traffic volume.
throttling	The act of slowing down or limiting requests to prevent system overload or abuse.

throughput	The amount of work or requests a system can handle in a given time period.
tight coupling	A design flaw where components are highly dependent on each other, reducing flexibility and reusability.
timeout	A defined period after which an operation is aborted if no response is received.
token bucket	An algorithm used to control data transmission rates while allowing bursts within a limit.
tracing	Following a request's journey through a system to help diagnose performance or reliability issues.
trade-off	A conscious decision to accept one benefit at the cost of another in system design.
traffic shaping	Regulating network or request traffic to improve performance or enforce policies.
transactional messaging	A messaging approach that ensures messages are sent and processed exactly once, often tied to database transactions.
transpiler	A tool that converts code from one programming language or version to another.
triage	The act of prioritizing issues or bugs based on impact and urgency.
trunk	The main development branch in version control, typically where the most recent stable code lives.
UI	User Interface; the part of a system users interact with, such as buttons, forms, and displays.
unit test	A small, fast test that checks the behavior of a single function or component in isolation.
user engagement metrics	Measurements that reflect how users interact with a product, like click-through or session time.
UX	User Experience; the overall feeling and usability of a system from the end user's perspective.
vanity metrics	Numbers that look impressive but don't directly reflect product success or actionable insights.
WCAG	Web Content Accessibility Guidelines; standards for making web content accessible to users with disabilities.

CREDITS

Term	Definition
Code Should Be Familiar	R. C. Martin, *Clean Code: A Handbook of Agile Software Craftsmanship*, Prentice Hall, 2009. R. P. Buse and W. Weimer, "Learning a Metric for Code Readability," *IEEE Transactions on Software Engineering*, vol. 36, no. 4, pp. 546–558, 2010. Google Engineering Practices, "Google Engineering Practices Documentation," retrieved July 6, 2025, from https://google.github.io/eng-practices. google.github.io+6google.github.io . T. Winters, T. Manshreck, & H. Wright. *Software Engineering at Google: Lessons Learned from Programming Over Time* (Kindle ed.). O'Reilly Media, 2020.
Explicit over Implicit	R. C. Martin, *Clean Code: A Handbook of Agile Software Craftsmanship*, Prentice Hall, 2009. J. Hughes, "Why Functional Programming Matters," *The Computer Journal*, vol. 32, no. 2, pp 98–107, 1989. J. Fried, "Launch: Basecamp 3," *Signal v. Noise*, November 3, 2015.
Fail Safe, Fail Fast, Fail Loud	M. Nygard, *Release It! Design and Deploy Production-Ready Software*, Pragmatic Bookshelf, 2007. D. Patterson, et al. "Recovery Oriented Computing (ROC): Motivation, Definition, Techniques, and Case Studies." University of California, Berkeley, 2002.
The Boy Scout Rule	M. Feathers, *Working Effectively with Legacy Code*, Prentice Hall, 2004. R. C. Martin, *Clean Code: A Handbook of Agile Software Craftsmanship*, Prentice Hall, 2008. J. DeWyze. "The 25 Percent Rule for Tackling Technical Debt." *Shopify Engineering Blog*, February 16. 2023. https://shopify.engineering/technical-debt-25-percent-rule A Chang. "Refactoring Legacy Code with the Strangler Fig Pattern." *Shopify Engineering Blog*, March 11, 2020. https://shopify.engineering/refactoring-legacy-code-strangler-fig-pattern

Commit Meaningful Changes	Torvalds, L. (2005). Git: A version control system for the Linux kernel. *Git SCM*. https://git-scm.com/book/en/v2/Getting-Started-A-Short-History-of-Git Atlassian Community. (2021, March 9). *Git best practices*. Atlassian. https://community.atlassian.com/forums/Bitbucket-articles/Git-Best-Practices/ba-p/1628803
Avoid Premature Optimization	D. E. Knuth, "Structured Programming with Go to Statements," *ACM Computing Surveys*, vol. 6, no. 4, pp. 261–301, 1974. M. Fowler, "Yet Another Optimization Article," *IEEE Software*, 2002. https://www.martinfowler.com/ieeeSoftware/yetOptimization.pdf X. Qi, "HipHop for PHP: More Optimizations for Efficient Servers," *Engineering at Meta*, 2011. https://engineering.fb.com/2011/03/30/web/hiphop-for-php-more-optimizations-for-efficient-servers/
Orthogonality	A. Hunt and D. Thomas, *The Pragmatic Programmer: Your Journey to Mastery*, 2nd ed., Addison-Wesley Professional, 2019. E. Gamma, R. Helm, R. Johnson, and J. Vlissides, *Design Patterns: Elements of Reusable Object-Oriented Software*, Addison-Wesley Professional, 1994. S. Mazzone, "Observability in Event-Driven Architectures," *Datadog Architecture Center*, November 20, 2024.
Don't Repeat Yourself (DRY)	A. Hunt and D. Thomas, *The Pragmatic Programmer*, Addison-Wesley Professional, 1999. M. Fowler, "Technical Debt Quadrant," *martinFowler.com* (blog), 2009. GitHub, "GitHub's Engineering System Success Playbook," *GitHub Resources*, 2025. https://resources.github.com/engineering-system-success-playbook/
Separation of Concerns	L. Constantine and E. Yourdon, *Structured Design: Fundamentals of a Discipline of Computer Program and Systems Design*, Prentice Hall, 1979. M. Richards and N. Ford, *Fundamentals of Software Architecture: An Engineering Approach*, O'Reilly Media, 2020. F. Buschmann, R. Meunier, H. Rohnert, P. Sommerlad, and M. Stal, *Pattern-Oriented Software Architecture: A System of Patterns*, Wiley, 1996. S. Liu, "Airbnb at Scale: From Monolith to Microservices" [Video]. InfoQ/QCon Plus 2022, YouTube, posted 2023. https://www.youtube.com/watch?v=PIw1WF1UXNc

Command–Query Separation	B. Meyer, *Object-Oriented Software Construction*, 2nd ed., Prentice Hall, 2000 E. Yemelyanau and J. Grice, "Netflix Tudum Architecture: From CQRS with Kafka to CQRS with RAW Hollow," *Netflix TechBlog*, 2025. https://netflixtechblog.com/netflix-tudum-architecture-from-cqrs-with-kafka-to-cqrs-with-raw-hollow-86d141b72e52
High Cohesion and Low Coupling	L. Constantine and E. Yourdon, *Structured Design: Fundamentals of a Discipline of Computer Program and Systems Design*, Prentice Hall, 1979. K. J. Lieberherr, I. Holland, and A. J. Riel, "Object-oriented Programming: An Objective Sense of Style," *ACM SIGPLAN Notices*, vol. 23, no. 11, pp. 323–334, 1988. S. Panichella, M. I. Rahman, and D. Taibi, "Structural Coupling for Microservices," *arXiv*, 2021. https://doi.org/10.48550/arXiv.2103.04674 E. Stiller, "Real-Time Messaging Architecture at Slack," *InfoQ*, 2023. https://www.infoq.com/news/2023/04/real-time-messaging-slack/
SOLID Design	R. C. Martin, *Agile Software Development: Principles, Patterns, and Practices*, Prentice Hall, 2002. M. Richards and N. Ford, *Fundamentals of Software Architecture*, O'Reilly Media, 2020. B. Smith, "Introducing Stripe Workflows: Tailoring Payments to Your Business Needs," *Stripe Dev Blog*, May 7, 2025.
Write Code That Writes Code	E. Murphy-Hill, C. Parnin, and A.P. Black, "How We Refactor, and How We Know It," *IEEE Transactions on Software Engineering*, vol. 38, no. 1, pp. 5–18, 2012. K. Hotta, Y. Sasaki, Y. Sano, Y. Higo, and S. Kusumoto, "An Empirical Study on the Impact of Duplicate Code," *Advances in Software Engineering*, pp 1–22, 2012. GitHub, "Creating a Template Repository," GitHub Docs, retrieved July 25, 2025, from https://docs.github.com/en/repositories/creating-and-managing-repositories/creating-a-template-repository
Don't Reinvent the Wheel	P. Mohagheghi and R. Conradi, "An Empirical Software Reuse Benefits in a Large Telecom Project," *ACM Transactions on Software Engineering and Methodology*, 17(3), 1–31, 2008. https://doi.org/10.1145/1375642.1375644 E. Gamma, R. Helm, R. Johnson, and J. Vlissides, *Design Patterns: Elements of Reusable Object-Oriented Software*. Addison-Wesley Professional, 1994. N. Hunt, "Netflix Case Study: Netflix Innovation with AWS," Amazon Web Services, 2016. https://aws.amazon.com/solutions/case-studies/netflix-case-study/

Concurrency vs. Parallelism	C. Hewitt, "Actor Model of Computation: Scalable Robust Information Systems," *arXiv*, 2010 (last revised 2015). https://doi.org/10.48550/arXiv.1008.1459 Scrums.com Editorial Team, "Parallelism and Concurrency in Engineering," *Scrums.com*, 2024. https://www.scrums.com/software-engineering/parallelism-and-concurrency-in-engineering S. Kumari, "How Twitter Leverages Scala Programming for its Massive Platform!" *LinkedIn*, 2024. https://www.linkedin.com/pulse/how-twitter-leverages-scala-programming-its-massive-platform-kumari-wkmxc
Encapsulate with Abstractions	E. Gamma, R. Helm, R. Johnson, and J. Vlissides, *Design Patterns: Elements of Reusable Object-Oriented Software*, Addison-Wesley Professional, 1994. R. C. Martin, *Clean Code: A Handbook of Agile Software Craftsmanship*, Prentice Hall, 2008. W. Shih, "Increasing the Level of Abstraction as a Strategy for Accelerating the Adoption of Complex Technologies," *Strategy Science* 6(1), 2020. https://doi.org/10.1287/stsc.2020.0116
The Law of Demeter	L. D. Erman, F. Hayes-Roth, V. R. Lesser, and D. R. Reddy, "The Hearsay-II Speech-Understanding System: Integrating Knowledge to Resolve Uncertainty," *ACM Computing Surveys*, vol. 12, no. 2, pp. 213–253, 1980. E. Gamma, R. Helm, R. Johnson, and J. Vlissides, *Design Patterns: Elements of Reusable Object-Oriented Software*, Addison-Wesley Professional, 1994.
Composition over Inheritance	E. Gamma, R. Helm, R. Johnson, and J. Vlissides, *Design Patterns: Elements of Reusable Object-Oriented Software*, Addison-Wesley, 1994. K. Fedoseev, N. Askarbekuly, E. Uzbekova, and M. Mazzara, "A Case Study on Object-Oriented and Data Oriented Design Paradigms in Game Development," *preprint*, 2020. DOI:10.13140/RG.2.2.16657.66405 Unity Technologies, "Introduction to Components," *Unity Documentation*, retrieved May 3, 2025, from https://docs.unity3d.com/Manual/Components.html
Dependency Injection	M. Seemann and S. Deursen, *Dependency Injection Principles, Practices, and Patterns*, Manning Publications, 2019. P. Sun and D.-K. Kim, "Analyzing Impact of Dependency Injection on Software Maintainability," *arXiv*, ˆ2022. https://doi.org/10.48550/arXiv.2205.06381 A. Kolawole, "Taming the Dependencies: Mastering Dependency Injection in Go with UberFx," *Medium*, 2024.

Service Decomposition	E. Evans, *Domain-Driven Design: Tackling Complexity in the Heart of Software*, Addison-Wesley Professional, 2003. D. Eldenk and H. A. Çetin, "Incidents During Microservice Decomposition: A Case Study," *arXiv*, arXiv:2505.09813, May 2025. Golden Owl Solutions, "Microservices for eCommerce: A Smarter Choice than Monolith? (2024)", *Golden Owl Blog*, 2025.
API Gateway Pattern	C. Richardson, *Microservices Patterns: With Examples in Java*, Manning Publications, 2018. T. Nguyen and T. T. Nguyen, "API Gateway in Microservices Architecture: A Systematic Review," *Journal of Information Systems and Technology Management*, vol. 16, no. 3, pp. 1–18, 2019. N. Silnitsky, "How Wix Accelerated Open Platform Dev with Standardized APIs & Schemas," *Wix Engineering*, March 11, 2023.
Shared Nothing Architecture	P. J. Denning, "The Locality Principle," *Communications of the ACM*, vol. 48, no. 7, pp. 19–24, 2005. J. L. Hennessy and D. A. Patterson, *Computer Architecture: A Quantitative Approach*, 5th ed., Elsevier, 2011. S. S, Krishnaswamy, M. Matthew, and S. Goyal, "Evolution of Data Lifecycle Management at Uber," *Uber Blog*, August 17, 2023.
Spread Your Infrastructure	E. Chisom, et al., "Disaster Recovery in Cloud Computing: Site Reliability Engineering Strategies for Resilience and Business Continuity," *International Journal of Management and Organizational Research*, 3(1), 36–48, 2025. A. Ajibola, "Cloud-Native Reliability Engineering: A Comprehensive Guide to Failure Resilience Patterns in Distributed Systems," *SSRN*, 2025. http://dx.doi.org/10.2139/ssrn.5260195 S. Kabbour, "How Duolingo Reduces AWS Compute Costs by 60%," *Renova Cloud*, retrieved on July 31, 2025 from https://renovacloud.com/en/how-duolingo-reduces-aws-compute-costs-by-60/ .
Batch Processing	G. Simuni, "Batch Processing with Apache Hadoop MapReduce: A Performance and Scalability Study," *SSRN*, 2024. https://ssrn.com/abstract=4991394 or http://dx.doi.org/10.2139/ssrn.4991394 K. Shvachko, K. Hairong, S. Radia, and R. Chansler, "The Hadoop Distributed File System," *Proceedings of the 2010 IEEE Symposium on Mass Storage Systems and Technologies*, 2010. N. Marz and J. Warren, *Big Data: Principles and Best Practices of Scalable Realtime Data Systems*, Manning Publications, 2015.

Saga Pattern	H. Garcia-Molina and K. Salem, "Sagas," *ACM SIGMOD Record*, vol. 16, no. 3, pp. 249–259, 1987. S. Newman, *Building Microservices: Designing Fine-Grained Systems*, O'Reilly Media, 2015. J. Bonér, "The Reactive Principles," white paper, 2022, available at https://www.reactiveprinciples.org.
The CAP Theorem	S. Gilbert and N. Lynch, "Brewer's Conjecture and the Feasibility of Consistent, Available, Partition-Tolerant Web Services," *ACM SIGACT News*, vol. 33, no. 2, pp. 51–59, 2002. E. Brewer, "CAP Twelve Years Later: How the "Rules" Have Changed," *Computer* 45(2), 2012. A. Lakshman and P. Malik, "Cassandra: A Decentralized Structured Storage System," *ACM SIGOPS Operating Systems Review*, vol. 44, no. 2, pp. 35–40, 2010.
Eventual Consistency	W. Vogels, "Eventually Consistent," *Communications of the ACM*, vol. 52, no. 1, pp. 40–44, 2009. G. DeCandia et al., "Dynamo: Amazon's Highly Available Key-Value Store," *ACM SIGOPS Operating Systems Review*, pp. 205–220, 2007. S. Schirmer, "API First Transformation at Etsy—Concurrency," *Etsy Code as Craft*, 2016. https://www.etsy.com/codeascraft/api-first-transformation-at-etsy-concurrency
Single Source of Truth	M. Fowler, *Patterns of Enterprise Application Architecture*, Addison-Wesley Professional, 2003. M-A. Sicilia, ed., *Handbook of Metadata, Semantics and Ontologies*, World Scientific Publishing Company, 2012. B. Reselman, "Implementing a Single Source of Truth in an Enterprise Architecture," *Red Hat Blog*, 2021. https://www.redhat.com/en/blog/single-source-truth-architecture S. Butterworth, "Introducing Entitlements: GitHub's Open Source Identity and Access Management Solution," *GitHub Blog*, 2022. https://github.blog/news-insights/product-news/introducing-entitlements-githubs-open-source-identity-and-access-management-solution/
Message Ordering and Exactly Once Processing	M. Kleppmann, *Designing Data-Intensive Applications: The Big Ideas Behind Reliable, Scalable, and Maintainable Systems*, O'Reilly Media, 2017. Apache Software Foundation. (n.d.). *Apache Kafka documentation: Introduction to the platform*. https://kafka.apache.org/documentation/#intro_platform M. Koppa, (2023, September 7). "Scaling Kafka to Support Paypal's Data Growth", *The PayPal Technology Blog*, 2023

Auto-Scaling	C. Pahl and P. Jamshidi, "Microservices: A Systematic Mapping Study," *Proceedings of the 6th International Conference on Cloud Computing and Services Science*, vols. 1 and 2, pp. 137–146, 2016. S. Newman, *Building Microservices: Designing Fine-Grained Systems*, O'Reilly Media, 2015. D. Morrison and E. Sheng, "Dynamic Kubernetes Cluster Scaling at Airbnb," *The Airbnb Tech Blog*, 2022.
Multi-Tenancy	S. Newman, *Building Microservices: Designing Fine-Grained Systems*, O'Reilly Media, 2015 I. Ejeh, "What Is Multi-Tenancy and Why It Matters for B2B SaaS," *Clerk Blog*, 2025. https://clerk.com/blog/what-is-multi-tenancy-and-why-it-matters-for-B2B-SaaS F. Weingarten, "Scaling Shopify's Multi-Tenant Architecture across Multiple Datacenters," *Proceedings of SREcon16 Europe (USENIX Association)*, 2016.
The Hollywood and Tell, Don't Ask	E. Gamma, R. Helm, R. Johnson, and J. Vlissides, *Design Patterns: Elements of Reusable Object-Oriented Software*, Addison-Wesley Professional, 199. L. Bass, P. Clements, and R. Kazman, *Software Architecture in Practice* (3rd ed.), Addison-Wesley Professional, 2012. B. Nguyen, "Using Server Sent Events to Simplify Real-time Streaming at Scale," *Shopify Engineering Blog*, 2022. https://shopify.engineering/server-sent-events-data-streaming
The Principle of Least Astonishment (POLA)	J. Nielsen, "10 Usability Heuristics for User Interface Design," *NN/g*, 1994, updated 2004. S. Krug, *Don't Make Me Think: A Common-Sense Approach to Web Usability*, 2nd ed., New Riders, 2005. GitHub, "Design Principles," *GitHub Well-Architected*, retrieved on August 8, 2025 from https://wellarchitected.github.com/library/productivity/design-principles/ . Apple, "Human Interface Guidelines," *Apple Developer*, retrieved on August 8, 2025 from https://developer.apple.com/design/human-interface-guidelines/.
Exponential Backoff	M. Brooker, "Timeouts, Retries, and Backoff with Jitter," The Amazon Builders' Library, 2019. https://aws.amazon.com/builders-library/timeouts-retries-and-backoff-with-jitter/ P. Murugan, "Exponential Backoff with Jitter: A Powerful Tool for Resilient Systems," Presidio, 2023. https://www.presidio.com/technical-blog/exponential-backoff-with-jitter-a-powerful-tool-for-resilient-systems/ Google Cloud, "Retry Requests," *Google Cloud Pub/Sub Documentation*, retrieved on August 8, 2025 from https://cloud.google.com/pubsub/docs/retry-requests.

Adaptive Load Protection	M. T. Nygard, *Release It!: Design and Deploy Production-Ready Software*, Pragmatic Bookshelf, 2007. L. A. Barroso, J. Clidaras, and U. Hölzle, *The Datacenter as a Computer: An Introduction to the Design of Warehouse-Scale Machines* (2nd ed.), Morgan & Claypool, 2013. J. Tiesinga, "How Agoda Handles Load Shedding in Private Cloud," *Agoda Engineering*, 2024. https://medium.com/agoda-engineering/load-shedding-private-cloud-first-81ddd5ab53ac
Data Locality and Stack Flattening	S. Usman, R. Mehmood, I. Katib, and A. Albeshri, "Data Locality in High-Performance Computing, Big Data, and Converged Systems: An Analysis of the Cutting Edge and a Future System Architecture," *Electronics*, vol. 12, no. 1, pp. 53–72, 2023. P. J. Denning, "The Locality Principle," *Communications of the ACM*, vol. 48, no. 7, pp. 19–24, 2005. L. Neiman and J. Fan, "How DoorDash Standardized and Improved Microservices Caching," *DoorDash Blog*, 2023. https://careersatdoordash.com/blog/how-doordash-standardized-and-improved-microservices-caching/
Schema Evolution	P. Sadalage and S. Ambler, *Refactoring Databases: Evolutionary Database Design*, Addison-Wesley Professional, 2006. H. Hagen, "Version Control Your Database on AWS Using Flyway," *AWS Blog*, 2023. https://www.tecracer.com/blog/2023/03/version-control-your-database-on-aws-using-flyway.html S. Belefqih, Z. Ahmed, and M. Berquedich, "Schema Extraction in NoSQL Systems: A Systematic Literature Review," *Recent Advances in Computer Science and Communications*, 17(8), 2023. M. Kleppmann, *Designing Data-Intensive Applications: The Big Ideas Behind Reliable, Scalable, and Maintainable Systems*, O'Reilly Media, 2017.
Sharding	A. Lakshman and P. Malik, "Cassandra: A Decentralized Structured Storage System," *ACM SIGOPS Operating Systems Review*, vol. 44, no. 2, pp. 35–40, 2010. A. Payong, "Database Sharding: Strategies for Seamless Scaling and Performance Optimization," *Redgate, Simple Talk*, 2024. S. Steele, "How Figma's Databases Team Lived to Tell the Scale," *Shortcut*, Figma's editorial newsletter, March 14, 2024.

Decentralized and Polyglot Persistence	E. Evans, *Domain-Driven Design: Tackling Complexity in the Heart of Software.* Addison-Wesley Professional, 2003. S. Newman, *Building Microservices: Designing Fine-Grained Systems*, O'Reilly Media, 2015. T. Garrett, "Polyglot Persistence Architectures: When to Use Multiple Database Types," *Dev3lop*, April 25, 2025. J. Kazanavičius, D. Mažeika, and D. Kalibatienė, "An Approach to Migrate a Monolith Database into Multi-Model Polyglot Persistence Based on Microservice Architecture: A Case Study for Mainframe Database," *Applied Sciences*, vol. 12, no. 12, p. 6189, June 2022, doi: 10.3390/app12126189.
Event Sourcing and Snapshots	M. Fowler, "Event Sourcing," *martinFowler.com* (blog), 2005. https://martinfowler.com/eaaDev/EventSourcing.html V. Vernon, *Implementing Domain-Driven Design*, Addison-Wesley Professional, 2013. P. Helland, "Immutability Changes Everything," *Communications of the ACM*, 59(1), 64–70, 2015, https://doi.org/10.1145/2844112.
Read-Heavy vs. Write-Heavy Optimization	M. Kleppmann, *Designing Data-Intensive Applications: The Big Ideas Behind Reliable, Scalable, and Maintainable Systems*, O'Reilly Media, 2017. B. Schwartz, P. Zaitsev, and V. Tkachenko, *High-Performance MySQL: Optimization, Backups, and Replication*, 3rd ed., O'Reilly Media, 2012. H. Tadiparthi, H. Patel, and R. Ponugumati, "Scale Read and Write Workloads with Amazon Redshift," *AWS Blogs*, 2022. https://aws.amazon.com/blogs/big-data/scale-read-and-write-workloads-with-amazon-redshift/ Twitter Engineering, "Manhattan, Our Real-time, Multi-tenant Distributed Database for Twitter Scale," *X Engineering* (blog), 2014.
Data Backup and Migration Strategy	M. Swanson, P. Bowen, A. W. Phillips, D. Gallup, and D. Lynes, Contingency Planning Guide for Federal Information Systems, National Institute of Standards and Technology (NIST), *NIST Special Publication* 800-34 Rev. 1, 2010. M. Fischer et al., "AWS Well-Architected Framework: Reliability Pillar," *Amazon Web Services*, 2024. Amazon Web Services, Inc., "Migrating Critical ERP Workloads to AWS Using SAP on AWS with 3M Company" [case study], retrieved July 4, 2025, from the AWS website. https://aws.amazon.com/solutions/case-studies/3m-migrating-critical-erp-workloads/

Shift-Left and Test Pyramid	M. Fowler, "The Practical Test Pyramid," *martinFowler.com* (blog), 2018. https://martinfowler.com/articles/practical-test-pyramid.html M. Kleppmann, *Designing Data-Intensive Applications: The Big Ideas Behind Reliable, Scalable, and Maintainable Systems*, O'Reilly Media, 2017. P. Gupta, M. Ivey, and J. Penix, "Testing at the Speed and Scale of Google," *Google Testing Blog*, 2011. https://testing.googleblog.com/2011/06/testing-at-speed-and-scale-of-google.html P. Norman, "Sensenmann: Code Deletion at Scale," *Google Testing Blog*, April 28, 2023. https://testing.googleblog.com/2023/04/sensenmann-code-deletion-at-scale.html.
Unified and Layered Testing Strategy	J. Humble and D. Farley, *Continuous Delivery: Reliable Software Releases Through Build, Test, and Deployment Automation*, Addison-Wesley Professional, 2010. G. Kim, J. Humble, P. Debois, and J. Willis, *The DevOps Handbook: How to Create World-Class Agility, Reliability, and Security in Technology Organizations*, IT Revolution Press, 2016. A. Hristov, "How Automated Testing Enables DevOps," Atlassian, retrieved on August 13, 2025 from https://www.atlassian.com/devops/devops-tools/test-automation.
Defensive Testing	B. Beyer, C. Jones, J. Petoff, and N. Murphy, *Site Reliability Engineering: How Google Runs Production Systems*, O'Reilly Media, 2016. "Principles of Chaos Engineering," 2017, last updated 2019, principlesofchaos.org. https://principlesofchaos.org/ Ali Basiri, Niosha Behnam, Ruud de Rooij, Lorin Hochstein, Luke Kosewski, Justin Reynolds, Casey Rosenthal, "Chaos Engineering", *IEEE Software*, vol.33, no. 3, pp. 3541, MayJune 2016, DOI: 10.1109/MS.2016.60 B. Violino, "Main Line Health Deploys Chaos Engineering to Bolster Healthcare Resilience," *CSO*, 2024. https://www.csoonline.com/article/3490060/main-line-health-deploys-chaos-engineering-to-bolster-healthcare-resilience.html
Behavior-Driven Development (BDD)	D. North, "Introducing BDD," Dan North & Associates, Ltd.,2006. https://dannorth.net/blog/introducing-bdd/ J. F. Smart, *BDD in Action: Behavior-Driven Development for the Whole Software Lifecycle*, Manning Publications, 2014. Planview, "Nationwide Building Society Taps Planview Solution to Underpin Agile Transformation Initiative," *Planview*, retrieved on August 10, 2025 from https://www.planview.com/resources/case-study/nationwide-building-society-planview-transformation/.

Efficient Test Design	G. J. Myers, C. Sandler, and T. Badgett, *The Art of Software Testing*, 3rd ed., Wiley, 2011. C. Kaner, J. Bach, and B. Pettichord, *Lessons Learned in Software Testing: A Context-Driven Approach*, Wiley, 2001. P. A. D. A. Santi, R. Afwani, M.A. Albar, S.E. Anjarwani, and A.Z. Mardiansyah, "Black Box Testing with Equivalence Partitioning and Boundary Value Analysis Methods (Study Case: Academic Information System of Mataram University)" [conference paper]. *In Proceedings of the First Mandalika International Multi-Conference on Science and Engineering 2022 (MIMSE 2022)*, pp. 207–219, Atlantis Press, 2002.
Risk-Based Testing	P. Ammann and J. Offutt, *Introduction to Software Testing*, Cambridge University Press, 2008. M. Pezzè and M. Young, *Software Testing and Analysis: Process, Principles, and Techniques*, Wiley, 2007. ING Tech Blog, "Risk-Driven Testing at Scale," G. Kim, J. Humble, P. Debois, and J. Willis, *The DevOps Handbook: How to Create World-Class Agility, Reliability, and Security in Technology Organizations*, IT Revolution Press, 2016. J. Bach, "How to Investigate Intermittent Problems," *Satisfice*, 2005. https://www.satisfice.com/blog/archives/34
Defect Clustering	T. J. Ostrand, E.J. Weyuker, and R.M. Bell, "Predicting the Location and Number of Faults in Large Software Systems," *IEEE Transactions on Software Engineering*, 31(4), 340–355, 2005. N. Nagappan and T. Ball, "Use of Relative Code Churn Measures to Predict System Defect Density," in *Proceedings of the 27th International Conference on Software Engineering* (pp. 284–292), 2005. M. Pezzè and M. Young, *Software Testing and Analysis: Process, Principles, and Techniques*, Wiley, 2007. P. Rooney, "Microsoft's CEO: 80-20 Rule Applies to Bugs, Not Just Features," *CRN*; retrieved July 5, 2025, from CRN website. https://www.crn.com/news/security/18821726/microsofts-ceo-80-20-rule-applies-to-bugs-not-just-features

Code Coverage Is Not Quality	M. Seemann, "Code Coverage Is a Useless Target Measure," *ploeh blog*, 2015. https://blog.ploeh.dk/2015/11/16/code-coverage-is-a-useless-target-measure/ M. Hilton, J. Bell, and D. Marinov, "A Large-scale Study of Test Coverage Evolution," in *Proceedings of the 2018 33rd ACM/IEEE International Conference on Automated Software Engineering*, pp. 53–63, 2018. https://doi.org/10.1145/3238147.3238183 S. Pittet, "What Is Code Coverage?" Atlassian, retrieved on August 10, 2025 from https://www.atlassian.com/continuous-delivery/software-testing/code-coverage.
Test Data Management	Gopinath, R., Alipour, M. A., Ahmed, I., Jensen, C., & Groce, A. (April 2014). *An empirical comparison of mutant selection approaches* (Technical Report, School of Engineering and Computer Science, Oregon State University). J. Humble and D. Farley, *Continuous Delivery: Reliable Software Releases Through Build, Test, and Deployment Automation*, Addison-Wesley Professional, 2010. Perforce Software. (n.d.). Mizuho Securities: Managing risk with a secure, centralized development platform. https://www.perforce.com/customers/case-studies/pdx/mizuho-securities
State and Data Integrity Testing	T. Y. Chen and S. C. Mak, "A Survey on State-Based Testing: Techniques and Issues," *IEEE Transactions on Software Engineering*, vol. 23, no. 8, pp. 512–525, 1997. C. Batini and M. Scannapieco, *Data Quality: Concepts, Methodologies and Techniques*, Springer, 2006. IEEE, "IEEE Standard for Software and System Test Documentation," in *IEEE Std 829-2008*, 2008. https://standards.ieee.org/standard/829-2008.html
Golden Master Testing	G. Meszaros, *xUnit Test Patterns: Refactoring Test code*, Addison-Wesley, 2007. S. Davies, "How to Test Legacy Software (That Was Not Designed to Be Tested) When Modernising," *Codurance*, 2022. https://codurance.com/publications/how-to-test-legacy-software-when-modernising M. Pearl, "Setting Up the Golden Master Using ApprovalTests.Net," *Mark Pearl on Software*, 2015. https://blog.markpearl.co.za/Setting-Up-The-Golden-Master M. Feathers, *Working Effectively with Legacy Code*, Prentice Hall, 2004.

Isolation and Contract Testing	M. Fowler, "Mocks Aren't Stubs," *martinFowler.com* (blog), 2007. G. Meszaros, xUnit Test Patterns: Refactoring Test Code, Addison-Wesley, 2007. Pact Foundation, "Consumer Driven Contracts," Pact documentation, retrieved on August 13, 2025 from https://docs.pact.io/#consumer-driven-contracts.
Chaos Engineering and Mutation Testing	D. North, "Introducing BDD," Dan North & Associates, Ltd.,2006. https://dannorth.net/blog/introducing-bdd/ J. F. Smart, *BDD in Action: Behavior-Driven Development for the Whole Software Lifecycle*, Manning Publications, 2014. C. Rosenthal and N. Jones, *Chaos Engineering: System Resiliency in Practice*, O'Reilly Media, 2020. Y. Jia and M. Harman, "An Analysis and Survey of the Development of Mutation Testing," *IEEE Transactions on Software Engineering*, vol. 37, no. 5, pp. 649–678, 2011. S. Shunmugasundaram, "Continuous Chaos—Introducing Chaos Engineering into DevOps Practices," Capital One Tech, August 10, 2018.
Automated UI Testing	M. Harman, Y. Jia, and Y. Zhang, "Achievements, Open Problems and Challenges for Search-Based Software Testing," *Proceedings of the IEEE International Conference on Software Testing, Verification and Validation*, pp. 1–12, 2015. G. J. Myers, C. Sandler, and T. Badgett, *The Art of Software Testing*, 3rd ed., Wiley, 2011. Applitools, "TransUnion Cuts Weekly Testing Time from 30 hours to 2 with Applitools" [case study]; retrieved July 4, 2025, from Applitools website. https://applitools.com/case-studies/transunion/
User Experience and Accessibility Focus	S. Keates, P. J. Clarkson, and C. Lebbon, "Access for All: Designing Accessible Interfaces for Everyone," *Interacting with Computers*, vol. 19, no. 3, pp. 243–262, 2007. World Wide Web Consortium (W3C), "Web Content Accessibility Guidelines (WCAG) 2.1," *W3C*, 2024. Microsoft, "Microsoft Inclusive Design," retrieved on August 14, 2025 from https://www.microsoft.com/design/inclusive. Microsoft, "How Accessibility Fosters Inclusion: Five Lessons Learned," *Inside Track*, 2022. https://www.microsoft.com/insidetrack/blog/how-accessibility-fosters-inclusion-five-lessons-learned/

Compliance and Regulatory Adherence	B. Kitchenham, S. L. Pfleeger, and N. Fenton, "How to Improve Software Quality: A Practical Guide," *IEEE Software*, vol. 19, no. 5, pp. 96–102, 2002. B. Beyer, C. Jones, J. Petoff, and N. Murphy, *Site Reliability Engineering: How Google Runs Production Systems*, O'Reilly Media, 2016. ThoughtSpot, "ThoughtSpot Trust Center," ThoughtSpot.com, retrieved on August 13, 2025 from https://www.thoughtspot.com/legal/trust.
Dark Launch and Shadow Traffic	M. Fowler, "Feature Toggles (aka Feature Flags)," *martinFowler.com* (blog), 2017. https://martinfowler.com/articles/feature-toggles.html W. Gancarczyk, "Shadow Traffic: A Guide Reduce Risk of a New Service Release," *Doctolib*, 2024. https://medium.com/doctolib/shadow-traffic-a-guide-to-reduce-risk-of-a-service-deployment-c67fd4ca3528 S. Gajera and C. Blinn, "Migrating Functionality Between Large-Scale Production Systems Seamlessly," *Uber Blog*, 2019. https://www.uber.com/blog/migrating-functionality-between-production-systems/
Scalability and Performance Testing	R. Jain, *The Art of Computer Systems Performance Analysis: Techniques for Experimental Design, Measurement, Simulation, and Modeling*, Wiley, 1991. D. A. Menascé, V. A. F. Almeida, and L. W. Dowdy, *Performance by Design: Computer Capacity Planning by Example*, Prentice Hall, 2004. Team Capacitas, "Case Study: Large Scale Transformation with DevSecOps," *Capacitas*, 2024. https://www.capacitas.co.uk/case-studies/case-study-large-scale-transformation-with-devsecops
Backward Compatibility and Dependency Checks	T. Mens, "Introduction and Roadmap: History and Challenges of Software Evolution," in *Software Evolution*, T. Mens and S. Demeyer, eds., 2008 ed., Springer, 2008. D. Dig and R. Johnson, "How Do APIs Evolve? A Story of Refactoring," *Journal of Software Maintenance and Evolution: Research and Practice*, vol. 18, no. 2, pp. 83–107, 2006. B. Palser, "Get Ready for New SameSite=None; Secure Cookie Settings," *Google Search Central Blog*, January 14, 2020.

INDEX

A–C

D–F

G–L

M–R

S–Z

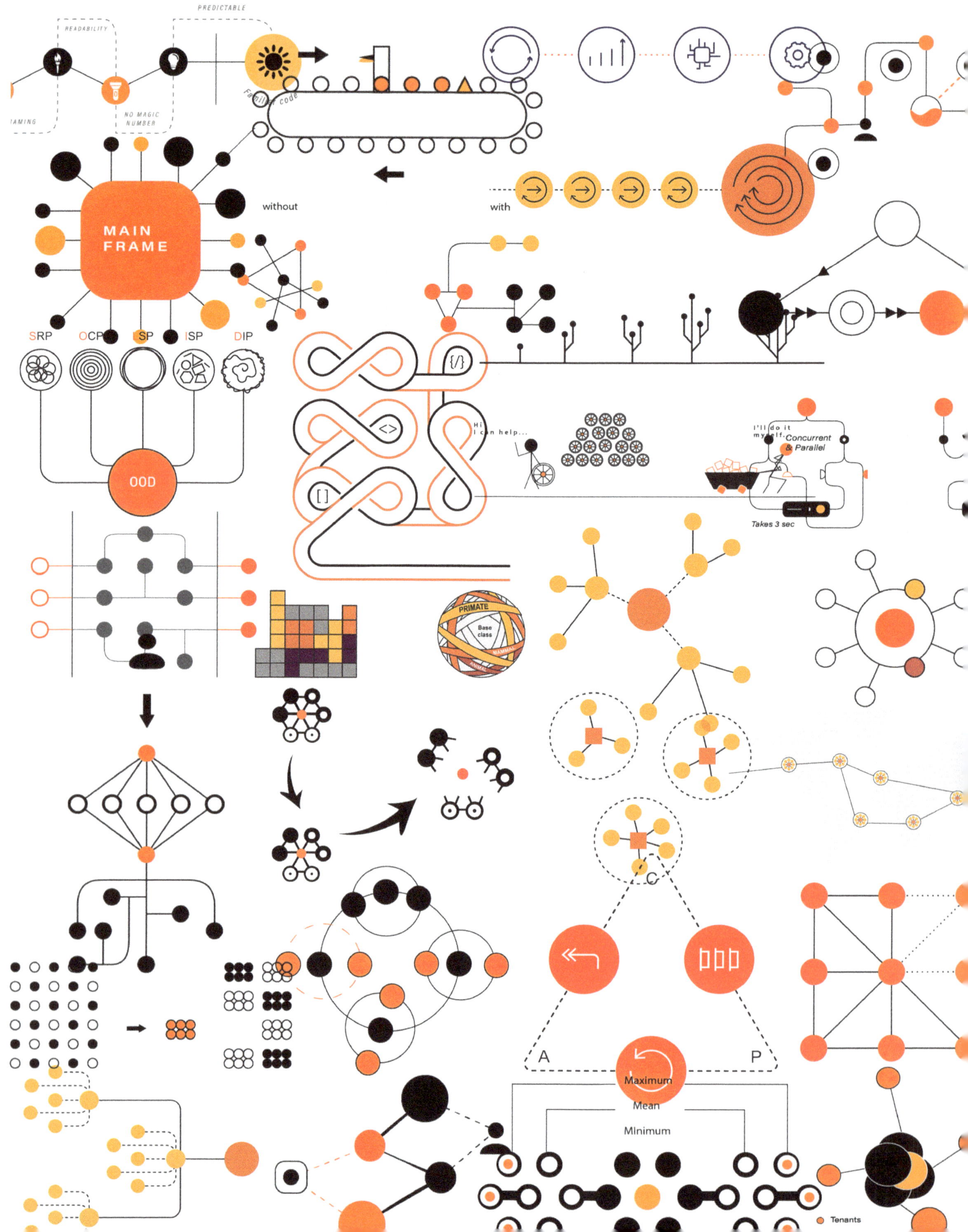
PREDICTABLE
READABILITY
NO MAGIC NUMBER
Familiar code
MAIN FRAME
without
with
SRP
OCP
LSP
ISP
DIP
OOD
Concurrent & Parallel
Takes 3 sec
PRIMATE
Base class
C
A
P
Maximum
Mean
Minimum
Tenants

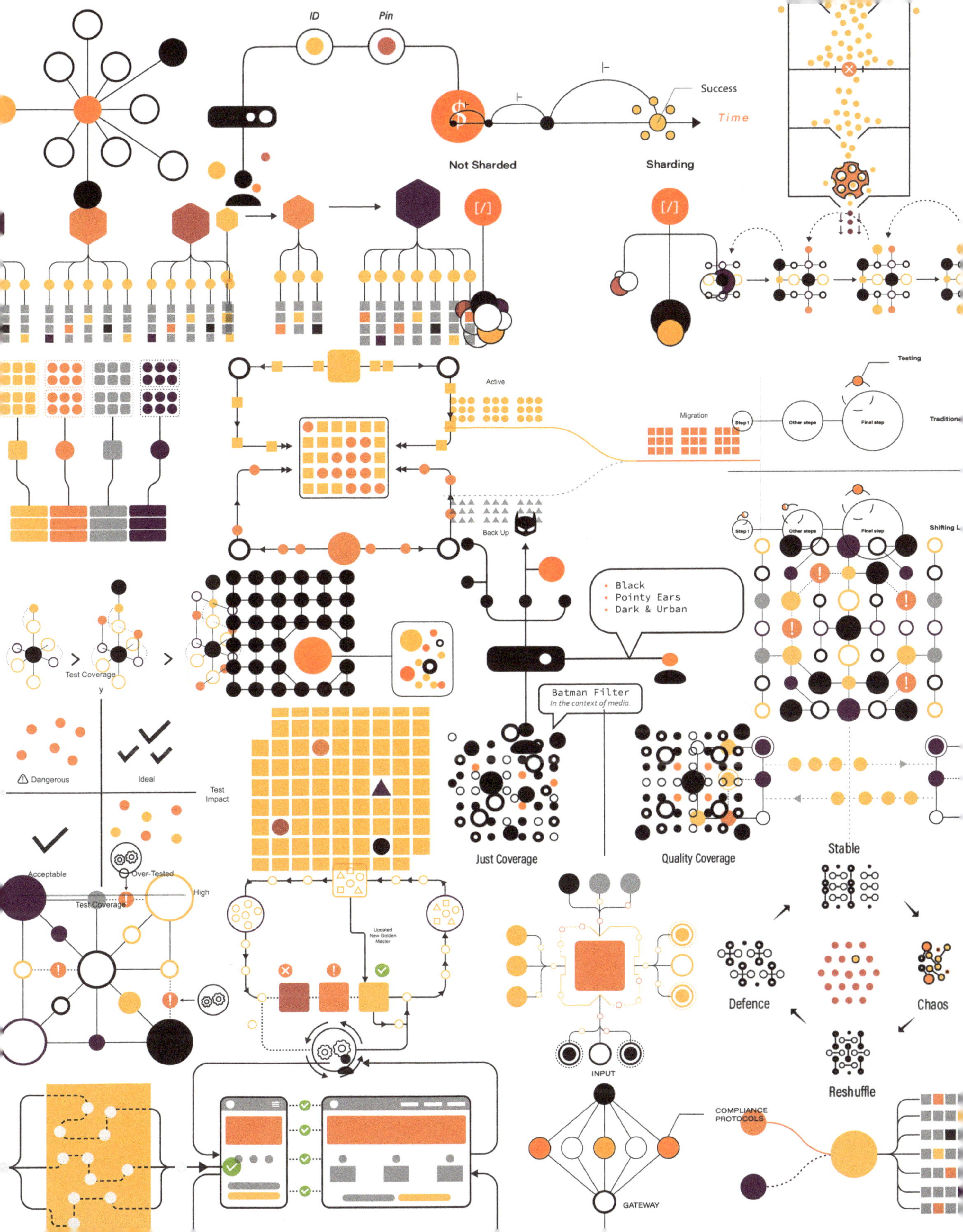
ID
Pin
Success
Time
Not Sharded
Sharding
Active
Migration
Testing
Step 1
Other steps
Final step
Back Up
Black
Pointy Ears
Dark & Urban
Batman Filter
In the context of media.
Test Coverage
y
Dangerous
Ideal
Test Impact
Acceptable
Over-Tested
High
Test Coverage
Updated New Golden Master
Just Coverage
Quality Coverage
Stable
Defence
Chaos
Reshuffle
INPUT
GATEWAY
COMPLIANCE PROTOCOLS

www.ingramcontent.com/pod-product-compliance
Ingram Content Group UK Ltd.
Pitfield, Milton Keynes, MK11 3LW, UK
UKHW060220061026
15625UKWH00007B/424

9 781970 973068